THE NEW YORK FESTIVALS

THE
NEW YORK
FESTIVALS
The World's Best Work

ANNUAL EIGHT

INTERNATIONAL
ADVERTISING
AWARDS

For additional information,
or to learn how your work may be submitted to
THE NEW YORK FESTIVALS
INTERNATIONAL ADVERTISING AWARDS
for possible inclusion in subsequent Annuals,
please address inquiries to:

THE NEW YORK FESTIVALS
780 King Street
Chappaqua, NY 10514 USA
Phone: 914-238-4481
Fax: 914-238-5040

Visit us on the World Wide Web at
http://www.nyfests.com

ISBN 0-9655403-4-0

DISTRIBUTED TO THE TRADE IN NORTH AMERICA BY
Watson-Guptill Publications
1515 Broadway
New York, NY 10036

DISTRIBUTED THROUGHOUT THE REST OF THE WORLD BY
Harper Collins International
10 East 53rd Street
New York, NY 10022-5299

THIS YEAR'S JACKET

CREATIVE TEAM
Terri Barrett-Vaden, Barrett Design, Richmond, VA
Bruce Goldman, Picture Radio, Richmond, VA

STOCK PHOTOGRAPH (ATLAS STATUE)
Tony Stone Images

ORIGINAL PHOTOGRAPH (WORLDMEDAL) AND RETOUCHING
The Bowyer Studio, Richmond, VA

BOOK DESIGN AND PRODUCTION
James Wasserman, Studio 31, P.O. Box 293116, Davie, FL 33329-3116

Produced by Phoenix Offset
Printed in China

CONTENTS

OFFICIAL REPRESENTATIVES OF THE NEW YORK FESTIVALS

ARGENTINA & URUGUAY
Eduardo Flehner
Exhibition International Co.-
Atomic Films
Castillo 1366
Buenos Aires 1414
Phone 541-14-771-0400
Fax 541-14-771-6003

**AUSTRALIA &
NEW ZEALAND**
Jenny Bates
Bates & Partners
Level 1, 121 Alexander Street
Crows Nest NSW 2065
Phone 612-9966-9599
Fax 612-9966-9626

BRAZIL
Armando Ferrentini
Editora Referencia Ltda.
Rua Francois Coty, 228 Cambuci
Cep No 10524-030
Sao Paulo SP
Phone 5511-274-0766/6914-5186
Fax 5511-272-8445

**CHILE, COLOMBIA,
ECUADOR & PARAGUAY**
Edgardo Mermet Ovalle
Val Morgan FilmSuez
Napoleon 3037-Of. 73
Las Condes, Santiago de Chile
Phone 56-2-233-8223
Fax 56-2-233-8216

CHINA
Gao Jun
Shangai Meikao Creative &
Consulting Co., Ltd.
Fl. 25 Shanghai Kerry Center
1515 Nanjing West Road
Shanghai 200040
Phone 86-21-5298-6622
Fax 86-21-3222-0220

CHINESE TAIPEI
Tomming Lai
United Advertising Company
10/F No. 83, Sec. 1,
Chungking S. Road
Taipei
Phone 886-2-2314-3366
Fax 886-2-2314-3314

FRANCE
Dominique Boischot
Les Films de la Perrine
6, Cite Paradis
Paris 75010
Phone 33-1-56-0390-30
Fax 33-1-56-0390-20

**GERMANY, AUSTRIA &
SWITZERLAND**
Peter Strahlendorf
Kattjahren 8
Hamburg D-22359
Phone 49-40-609-00910
Fax 49-40-609-00915

**GREECE, CYPRUS &
MIDDLE EAST**
Stacy Solomonides
Thorn Tree Advertising, Ltd.
PO Box 20925
Nicosia
Phone 357-2-492-777
Fax 357-2-493-431

HONG KONG & MACAU
Jimmy Lam
Longyin Review
Shun Feng International Centre,
Rm. 1205
182 Queen's Road East
Wanchai
Phone 85-2-2824-9999
Fax 85-2-2824-9998

ISRAEL
Billi Laniado
Laniado Marketing
    Communications Ltd.
29 Hamered St.
Tel Aviv 68125
Phone 972-3-517-7977
Fax 972-3-517-0258

ITALY
Gruppo Pubblicita Italia
Via Stradella 3
Milano 20129
Phone 39-02-29-400-554
Fax 39-02-29-520-533/401-816

JAPAN
Soji George Tanaka
TanakaPlus
1-7, Mure 3-Chome, Mitaka-shi
Tokyo 181
Phone 81-422-45-1774
Fax 81-422-44-5634

MEXICO
Clemente Camara Rojas
Clemente Camara Y Asociados
Felix Parra 187
Col. San Jose Insurgentes
Mexico D. F. 03900
Phone 525-660-9887
Fax 525-680-5911

**THE NETHERLANDS &
BELGIUM**
Peter Kanters
PKPR
Honingstraat 14b
Hilversum 1211 AW
Phone 31-35-62381-85
Fax 31-35-62382-08

PERU
Teresa Barrenechea Q.
Asociacion Peruana de Agencias
de Publicidad
Avenida 2 de Mayo
655 Miraflores
Lima 18
Phone/Fax 51-1445-4903

SCANDINAVIA
Lars Grunberger
Avisator & Attract AB
Biblioteksgatan 29
Box 5019
Stockholm S-102 41
Phone 468-555-400-13
Fax 468-555-400-55

**SINGAPORE, MALAYSIA,
INDONESIA, PHILIPPINES &
THAILAND**
Jenny Wee
Block 110, Lorong 1
Toa Payoh, #03-336
Singapore 310110
Phone 65-9764-2457
Fax 65-352-2389

SOUTH AFRICA
Arlene Donenberg
The Creative Directors' Forum
PO Box 4651
Rivonia 2128
Phone 27-11-803-9324
Fax 27-11-233-8840

SPAIN & PORTUGAL
Pedro Solana
Rambla de Catalunya 49, 4o3a
Barcelona 08007
Phone 34-93-487-8766
Fax 34-93-488-3554

TURKEY
G.A. Ogud, Jr.
AVC Marketing Services Group
Eski Buyukdere Cad. Ozcan Sok
No. 18
IV Levent
Istanbul 80650
Phone 90-212-280-9112
Fax 90-212-270-9155/282-6927

UNITED KINGDOM
Charles Sciberras
International Agency
Facilities Ltd.
The Long Barn - Funges Farm
Bassetsbury Lane -
High Wycombe
Bucks HP11 1QZ
Phone 44-1494-452-018
Fax 44-1494-550-332

VENEZUELA
Thais Hernandez
A.N.D.A
Urb. Santa Eduvigis, 1ra.
Av. de Santa Eduvigis
Residencias Primavera P.B.
Oficina B. Apdo 61762
Caracas
Phone 582-284-1163/285-6841
Fax 582-283-6553

THE GRAND AWARD

HISTORY OF
THE NEW YORK FESTIVALS

For forty-two years, THE NEW YORK FESTIVALS has honored excellence in communications media which touch the hearts and mind of readers, listeners and viewers worldwide. Founded in 1957 as an international awards competition designed primarily to reward outstanding achievements in non-broadcast media, the Festival achieved pre-eminence in the industrial/educational area in the course of its first twenty years.

During the 1970's, two other international competitions were added which would experience unrivaled growth in prestige and importance — TV and cinema advertising and TV programming and promotion. Competitions for international radio advertising, programming and promotion were launched in 1982, and for print advertising, collateral materials, design, photography and illustration in 1984. In keeping pace with the changing trends and technologies, an international interactive multimedia competition was added in 1992; and in 1994, The Globals, an awards competition for international healthcare communications. In 1995, the AME International Awards were launched as the first global forum for the recognition of the effectiveness as well as the creativity of advertising/marketing campaigns.

The New York Festivals experienced exponential expansion, from 1,000 entries in 1979, to more than 16,000 entries in all media in 1999. Industry acceptance and participation are symbolized by the Festival's prestigious Board of Distinguished Judges and Advisors, comprising a veritable "Who's Who" of the world leaders in communications. In 1999, more than 12,000 print, radio and TV advertising from sixty-four countries competed for honors.

A SALUTE TO
THE WORLD'S BEST WORK

This book is dedicated proudly and respectfully, to the creative men and women everywhere in the world who produced the great work in these pages. THE NEW YORK FESTIVALS is pleased to showcase the winners of its 1999 international print & design competition. The Grand Award winners, WorldMedalists and Finalists featured in these pages rose to the top in the most multinational of all awards competitions.

The best was chosen by the best. Entries were evaluated by panels of judges comprised of hundreds of agency creatives and production professionals convened in New York and in major advertising centers throughout the world. This comprehensive process determined the Finalists — the highest scoring of which went on to achieve Gold, Silver and Bronze WorldMedals in their respective categories. Members of the Festivals' International Board of Distinguished Judges & Advisors chose the Grand Award Trophy winners.

The New York Festivals, America's international awards show is one of only three such events with truly global coverage. The 1999 awards, which marked our 42nd anniversary, attracted more than 12,000 advertising entries from sixty-four countries. Submissions from outside the USA exceeded sixty percent of the total. Global, as well, is our continuing relationship with the United Nations, whose Department of Public Information sponsors our prestigious awards for public service advertising which best exemplifies the ideals and goals of the UN.

Not to be forgotten — our judges — the world's most creative and experienced advertising professionals. We are grateful for their commitment and discernment. Special thanks to the worldwide chair of The New York Festivals Board of Distinguished Judges & Advisors, John Nieman of D'Arcy and welcome to Phil Dusenberry of BBDO who succeeds John in 2000.

Can your work survive in a tough global market? This eighth edition of The World's Best Work provides copious answers.

Gerald M. Goldberg, President
THE NEW YORK FESTIVALS

BOARD OF DISTINQUISHED JUDGES & ADVISORS

BOARD OF DISTINQUISHED JUDGES & ADVISORS

1999 ADVERTISING JUDGES

1999 PRINT & RADIO ADVERTISING JUDGES

Mike Abadi
NEW YORK, NY

Manuel Ruiz Acsina
LOWE - MEXICO
MEXICO

Adam Albercht
CRAMER KRASSELT
MILWAUKEE, WI

Josef Astor
JOSEF ASTOR STUDIO
NEW YORK, NY

Jaime Atria
LEO BURNETT
SANTIAGO, CHILE

Kevin Barclay
YOUNG & RUBICAM
VANCOUVER, CANADA

Howard Beauchamp
BENSIMON BYRNE/DMB&B
TORONTO, CANADA

Juan Carlos Bertovelli
J.WALTER THOMPSON
CARACAS, VENEZUELA

Stephanie Blackman
STEPHANIE BLACKMAN DESIGN
NEW YORK, NY

Ferran Blanch
TIEMPO BBDO S.A. DE PUBLICIDAD
BARCELONA, SPAIN

Christian Bock
BOZELL WORLDWIDE
NEW YORK, NY

Diego Borbolan
EURO RSCG BARCELONA
BARCELONA, SPAIN

Eduardo Bottder
AL PUNTO ADVERTISING
SANTA ANA, CA

Mark Brady
JUST PARTNERS
RICHMOND, VA

Kevin Brown
SPRECHER BRETALOT & CO
MILWAUKEE, WI

Chris Brown
BOZELL
COSTA MESA, CA

Chris Buhrman
BVK/MCDONALD
MILWAUKEE, WI

Julie Byrne
MILLER HUBER
SAN FRANCISCO, CA

Ricardo Calliet-Bois
CALLIET-BOIS AD & DESIGN
CULVER CITY, CA

Luis Camano
BALD & BEAUTIFUL
VENICE, CA

Salvador Capiello
ROBERTO ELIASCHEV/APL
CARACAS, VENEZUELA

R. Cavalcanti
BBDO MEXICO
MEXICO

Andrea Cedillo
OGILVY & MATHER
MEXICO

Eugene Cheong
OGILVY & MATHER
SINGAPORE

Sandy Choi
SANDY CHOI ASSOCIATES LIMITED
HONG KONG

Norman Christianson
CUATRO Y MEDIO
MEXICO

Bettina Cirone
SPOTLIGHT MEDIA
NEW YORK, NY

Helen Clarkson
HORIZON COMMUNICATIONS
EAST HANOVER, NJ

Joel Cleveland
CLEVELAND CREATIVE INC.
LARCHMONT, NY

Mariano Favetto
CONILL ADVERTISING
NEW YORK, NY

Craig Cooper
BBDO CANADA
TORONTO, CANADA

Craig Cooper
BBDO CANADA
TORONTO, CANADA

Michael Cornell
GINGER MOON DESIGN
NEW YORK, NY

Louis Couco
LMC COMMUNICATIONS INC.
NEW YORK, NY

Ernie Cox
BIGGS/GILMORE
KALAMAZOO, MI

Tom Crimp
AUXILIARY RESOURCES
GRAND RAPIDS, MI

David Derex
DEREX PHOTOGRAPHY
WESTWOOD, NJ

Bic Dirks
LAWRENCE & MAYO ADVERTISING
NEWPORT BEACH, CA

Jody Dole
JODY DOLE STUDIO
NEW YORK, NY

Douglas Donelan
JEFF ST. ONGE & FRIENDS
NEW YORK, NY

Scott Dresden
BRAINBOW, INC.
WHITE PLAINS, NY

Steven Drifka
BENDER, BROWNING, DOLBY &
SANDERSON
MILWAUKEE, WI

Carolyn Durkalski
SAN FRANCISCO, CA

Kathleen Eams
NEW YORK, NY

John Edmonds
COSSETTE COMMUNICATIONS
VANCOUVER, CANADA

Agustin Elbaile
MCCANN ERICKSON
BARCELONA, SPAIN

Steve Elrick
BARTLE BOGLE HEGARTY LTD.
SINGAPORE

Jeff Ericksen
BVK/MCDONALD
MILWAUKEE, WI

Nicolette Eus
VANCOUVER, CANADA

Mark Fairbanks
KOHNKE HANNEKEN
MILWAUKEE, WI

Hector Fernandez
BBDO MEXICO
MEXICO

Juan Finger
VINIZIUS YOUNG & RUBICAM
BARCELONA, SPAIN

Brad Fleming
BIGGS/GILMORE
KALAMAZOO, MI

Mark Fong
DENTSU YOUNG & RUBICAM SINGAPORE
SINGAPORE

Mike Fromowitz
TBWA SINGAPORE
SINGAPORE

Paul Garner
COHN & WELLS
SAN FRANCISCO, CA

Alfred Gescheidt
PHOTOGRAPHY & DESIGN CONCEPTS
NEW YORK, NY

Peter Goddard
TORONTO STAR
TORONTO, CANADA

Bruce Goldman
PICTURE RADIO
RICHMOND, VA

Chris Gonzalez
Z GROUP
NEW YORK, NY

Andy Gould
BIGGS/GILMORE
KALAMAZOO, MI

Richard Griffin
FERREL COLVILLO
NEW YORK, NY

Flick Hatcher
YOUNG & RUBICAM VANCOUVER
VANCOUVER, CANADA

Jason Headley
COHN & WELLS
SAN FRANCISCO, CA

Edgar Hernandez
CLEMENTE CAMARA Y ASSOCIATES
MEXICO CITY,. MEXICO

Alberto Hernandez
CONCEPT/LOWE VENEZUELA
CARACAS, VENEZUELA

Danny Higgins
BBDO
SINGAPORE

Jose A. Hinojosa
IMAX PRODUCCIONES S.A.
MEXICO

Brian Howlett
AXMITH MCINTYRE WICHT
TORONTO, CANADA

Gary Humenik
COHN & WELLS
SAN FRANCISCO, CA

Soiel Husbands
SFINTERACTIVE INC.
SAN FRANCISCO, CA

Alberto Israel R.
IDB/FCB CHILE
SANTIAGO, CHILE

John Jaeckel
SEFTON ASSOCIATES
GRAND RAPIDS, MI

Carl Jones
BBDO MEXICO
MEXICO CITY,. MEXICO

Marla Katz
REAL NETWORKS
SEATTLE, WA

Graham Kelly
LEO BURNETT
SINGAPORE

Rick Kemp
J WALTER THOMPSON
TORONTO, CANADA

1999 ADVERTISING JUDGES

Tham Khai Meng
BATEY ADS
SINGAPORE

Dan Koel
CRAMER KRASSELT
MILWAUKEE, WI

Regan LaMothe
LAMOTH, NOWICKI & KNEPS
BATTLE CREEK, MI

Shelley Lanman
DRAFT WORLDWIDE
NEW YORK, NY

Lucero Lara
LEO BURNETT
MEXICO

Freeman Lau
KAN & LAU DESIGN CONSULTANT
HONG KONG

Martin Lek
MARTIN SALEMAN & ASSOCIATES
SINGAPORE

Liz Lesnick
RANDOM HOUSE
NEW YORK, NY

Doug Levy
IMC2
DALLAS, TX

Scott Lietzke
ISL CONSULTING
SAN FRANCISCO, CA

Justin Lim
TBWA SINGAPORE
SINGAPORE

Wally Littman
W/LITTMAN DESIGN
TEANECK, NJ

Linda Locke
LEO BURNETT
SINGAPORE

Mark Loete
MARK LOETE PHOTOGRAPHY
NEW YORK, NY

Kelly Lucas
LYONS LAVEY NICKEL SWIFT
NEW YORK, NY

David Lyon
NICE LTD
NEW YORK, NY

Katherine MacDonald
WASSERMAN & PARTNERS
VANCOUVER, CANADA

Sharoz Makarechi
FERRELL COLVILLO
NEW YORK, NY

Len May
PRICEWATERHOUSE COOPERS
PHILADELPHIA, PA

Martin Mayo
WOODBRIDGE, NJ

Thom McElvoy
MCELVOY COMMUNICATIONS
NEWPORT BEACH, CA

Jack McGoldrick
GREY
NEW YORK, NY

Bruce McKay
SAATCHI & SAATCHI
TORONTO, CANADA

Salvador Mejia O
CLEMENTE CAMARA Y ASSOC
MEXICO

Victor Melillo
CONCEPT LOWE
CARACAS, VENEZUELA

Edgardo Mermet
VAL MORGAN FILM SUEZ
SANTIAGO, CHILE

Dennis Milbauer
PHOTOGRAPHER
NEW YORK, NY

Greg Miller
MAXWELL & MILLER
KALAMAZOO, MI

Eileen Miller
EILEEN MILLER PHOTOGRAPHY
NEW YORK, NY

Diane Mitchell
D.MITCHELL STUDIOS
NEW YORK, NY

Mark Mizgala
PALMER JARVIS DDB
VANCOUVER, CANADA

Tomaz Mok
MCCANN-ERICKSON GUNAMING
HONG KONG, HONG KONG

Ruben Montoya
J.WALTER THOMPSON
CARACAS, VENEZUELA

Arcadi Moradell
INSTITUTO INTERNACIONAL DISENO
IMAGEN
BELLA TERRA, SPAIN

Ernst Moradell
BELLA TERRA, SPAIN

Stephen Morgan
TCO INC. ADVERTISING
TORONTO, CANADA

Erendiro Ramirez Mota
HERNANDEZ NAFARRATE & ASSOC.
MEXICO

Sean Mullen
NELSON & SCHMIDT
MILWAUKEE, WI

Steven Mulliken
COHN & WELLS
SAN FRANCISCO, CA

Rodrigo Munizara
LOWE & PARTNERS
MEXICO

Carlos Musquez
ALCONE MARKETING
IRVINE, CA

Joe Nagy
THE MARTIN AGENCY
RICHMOND, VA

Chew Ping Nan
BBDO SINGAPORE
SINGAPORE

Peter Newman
DIGITAL ILLUSTRATION
NEW YORK, NY

Frieda Ng
FCB
WANCHAI, HONG KONG

Simon Nickson
COHN & WELLS
SAN FRANCISCO, CA

Davide Nicosia
NICE-NICOSIA CREATIVE EXPRESSO LTD.
NEW YORK, NY

Chris Non
SIDDAL, MATUS & COUGHTER
RICHMOND, VA

Dan Oftelie
LAGUNA BEACH, CA

Hector Orellana G.
LEO BURNETT
SANTIAGO, CHILE

Claudio Osorio Pacheco
IDB/FCB
SANTIAGO, CHILE

Carmen Padron
J.WALTER THOMPSON
CARACAS, VENEZUELA

Roy N. Pari
AL PUNTO ADVERTISING
SANTA ANA, CA

Educrdo Perez
CLEMENTE CAMARA Y ASSOC.
MEXICO

Craig Piseris-Henderson
INTERNET SERVICES INTERNATIONAL
FORT MEYERS, FL

Lou Pollack
LM POLLACK STUDIO
BROOKLYN, NY

Stan Poulos
GREY DIRECT
NEW YORK, NY

Jason Price
FOOTE, CONE & BELDING
NEW YORK, NY

Dale Roberts
TAXI ADVERTISING & DESIGN
TORONTO, CANADA

Florencia Ros
J.WALTER THOMPSON
CARACAS, VENEZUELA

Mitchell Rosenbaum
MITCHELL ROSENBAUM CO.
NEW YORK, NY

1999 ADVERTISING JUDGES

Jason Ross
M&C SAATCHI
SINGAPORE

Colin Ruffell
AMMIRATI PURIS LINTAS
QUARRY BAY, HONG KONG

Clint Runger
ARCHRIVAL
LINCOLN, NE

Manuel Salcedo
PHINEAS TAYLOR BARNUM
BARCELONA SPAIN

Cesar Sanchez
CASANUDA PENDRILL PUBLICIDAD
IRVINE, CA

Dan Scherk
BFS
VANCOUVER, CANADA

Franci Shafer
FRANCI GRAPHIC DESIGN
WEEHAWKEN, NJ

Jeff Shattuck
MCCANN ERICKSON
SAN FRANCISCO, CA

Edward Shen
DDB
HONG KONG

Harry Shilling
NEW YORK, NY

Larry Sivitz
IDEA BANK INTERACTIVE
BAINBRIDGE ISLAND, WA

Ryan Smith
CRAMER-KRASSELT
MILWAUKEE, WI

Peter Soh
SINGAPORE DRESS HOLDINGS
SINGAPORE

Wick St. Offarra
CITY SMART GLOBAL SERVICES LLC
MILL VALLEY, CA

Chris Stavenjad
COMMUNIQUE
TORONTO, CANADA

Bob Tacy
C-E COMMUNICATIONS
WARREN, MI

Francis Tan
DDB SINGAPORE
SINGAPORE

Victor Tanaka
IRVINGTON, NY

Joel Tarman
TOWNSEND & O'LEARY
IRVINE, CA

Dayanica Ortega Telesio
CLEMENTE CAMARA Y ASSOC
MEXICO

Ron Thompson
COSSETTE COMMUNICATIONS
TORONTO, CANADA

Fred Tong
EURO RSCG PARTNERSHIP
HONG KONG

Mary Torres
JMC Y & R
CARACAS, VENEZUELA

Patrick Tow
DENTSU YOUNG & RUBICAM
SINGAPORE

Margaret Tsui
HONG KONG

Carol Turturro
YOUNG & RUBICAM
NEW YORK, NY

Amy Walberg
BVK/MCDONALD
MILWAUKEE, WI

David Walker
GREY VANCOUVER
VANCOUVER, CANADA

Sn Walsh
CADMUS COM
RICHMOND, VA

Gary Watson
AMBROSE CARR LINTON CARROLL
TORONTO, CANADA

Stefan Wegner
TBWA CHIAT/DAY
TORONTO, CANADA

Bob Weirup
TAYLOR WAIRUP ADVERTISING
RICHMOND, VA

Joe Wittkop
JOE WITTKOP STUDIOS
NEW YORK, NY

Henry Wong
SAATCHI & SAATCHI
TORONTO, CANADA

Stanley Wong
TBWA HONG KONG
HONG KONG

EJ Wood
HORIZON COMMUNICATIONS INC
EAST HANOVER, NJ

Rob Worling
CUNDARI
TORONTO, CANADA

Shari Worthington
CIRRUS TECHNOLOGY
WORCESTER, MA

Gregory Yeo
TBWA SINGAPORE
SINGAPORE

Cameron Young
ALCONE MARKETING GROUP
IRVINE, CA

Juan Zavsicky
LOWE & PARTNERS
MEXICO

Lou Ann Zeller
ZGRAPHICS, LTD.
EAST DUNDEE, IL

1998 UNITED NATIONS DEPARTMENT OF PUBLIC INFORMATION AWARDS

The United Nations Awards were established in 1990 and are presented annually to honor public service advertising that best exemplifies the ideals and goals of the United Nations. Public Service entries which achieve Finalist status in all three of The New York Festivals international print, radio and television advertising competitions are automatically eligible for these prestigious awards.

The 1998 Gold, Silver and Bronze United Nations Awards were selected by a blue ribbon panel of judges (see below) convened by the United Nations and The New York Festivals on December 14, 1998 in New York. The awards were presented by Mr. Samir Sanbar, Assistant Secretary General of the United Nations Department of Public Information, at The New York Festivals gala Television Advertising Awards Show on January 25, 1999 held at The Marriott Marquis. The winning ads reflect issues of concern to the United Nations such as health, human rights (exploitation of children, racial discrimination), women's issues, literacy, the fight against poverty, sustainable development and the environment.

1998 JUDGES

Juliette Foster
BROADCAST/JOURNALIST
BLOOMBERG

Graciela Hall
INFORMATION OFFICER, SPECIAL PROGRAMMES
UNITED NATIONS

Joanna Piucci
INFORMATION OFFICER
UNITED NATIONS

Jan Ralph
PRODUCER
RALPH & SARDA DESIGN ASSOCIATES

Joyce Rosenblum
PHOTO LIBRARIAN
UNITED NATIONS

Danny Schechter
EXECUTIVE PRODUCER
GLOBALVISION

Richard Sydehham
EXECUTIVE PRODUCER
UNITED NATIONS

Alex Taukatch
CHIEF
UNITED NATIONS

Carolyn Uluc
CHIEF RADIO PRODUCER
UNITED NATIONS

Jin Zhou
CHIEF RADIO PRODUCER
UNITED NATIONS

1998 UNITED NATIONS AWARD WINNERS

FRANCE

UNITED NATIONS GOLD

THIS TV COMMERCIAL ALSO WON A IN FINALIST
CERTIFICATE IN THE NEW YORK FESTIVALS
TV ADVERTISING COMPETITION

OGILVY & MATHER
PARIS

CLIENT Amnesty International
CREATIVE DIRECTOR Bernard Bureau
COPYWRITER Steve Jeffery
ART DIRECTOR Steve Jeffery
AGENCY PRODUCER Laure Bayle
PRODUCTION CO. Wanda Prod
DIRECTOR Rojo

MEDIUM: TELEVISION

1998 UNITED NATIONS AWARD WINNERS

  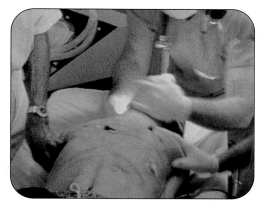

USA

UNITED NATIONS SILVER

THIS TV COMMERCIAL ALSO WON
A FINALIST CERTIFICATE IN THE
NEW YORK FESTIVALS TV ADVERTISING COMPETITION

NKH&W INC.
KANSAS CITY, MO

CLIENT Anti-Methamphetamine
CREATIVE DIRECTOR John Harrington
COPYWRITER Trent Patterson
ART DIRECTOR John Stewart
AGENCY PRODUCER David Palmer
PRODUCTION CO. Earthquake Production/LA
DIRECTOR Jeff Richter
EDITOR Earthquake Edit/LA

MEDIUM: TELEVISION

1998 UNITED NATIONS AWARD WINNERS

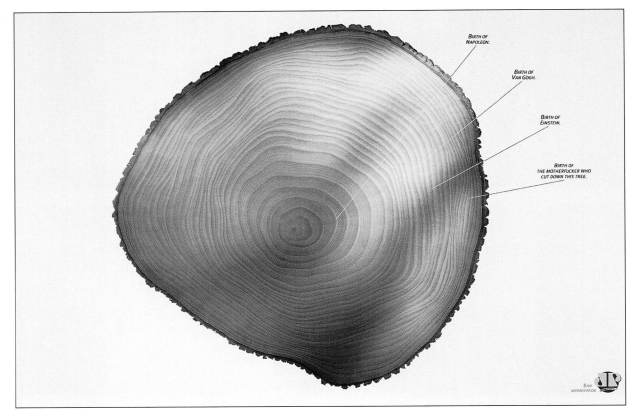

BRAZIL

UNITED NATIONS BRONZE

THIS PRINT AD ALSO WON A
GOLD WORLDMEDAL IN
THE NEW YORK FESTIVALS PRINT
ADVERTISING COMPETITION

ALMAP/BBDO
SAO PAULO

CLIENT Jovem Pan
CREATIVE DIRECTOR
Marcello Serpa
COPYWRITER Cassio Zanatta
ART DIRECTOR
Valdir Bianchi

MEDIUM: PRINT

FINALISTS

POLAND

UNDPI FINALIST
AMMIRATI PURIS LINTAS
WARSAW

MEDIUM Print
CLIENT Blue Line Domestic Violence
Helpline

USA

UNDPI FINALIST
ASHER & PARTNERS
LOS ANGELES, CA

MEDIUM Television
CLIENT California Department of
Health Services

BRAZIL

UNDPI FINALIST
CHROMA FILMS
SAO PAULO

MEDIUM Television
CLIENT Abriog Para Idosos Bezerra De
Menezes

USA

UNDPI FINALIST
DDB NEEDHAM
DALLAS, TX

MEDIUM Print
CLIENT Step Foundation

MALAYSIA

UNDPI FINALIST
DENTSU YOUNG & RUBICAM
KUALA LUMPUR

MEDIUM Radio
CLIENT MIX FM/MIX Environment
Community Service

FRANCE

UNDPI FINALIST
THE GANG FILM
SAINT CLOUD

MEDIUM Television
CLIENT Mentor Foundation Against Drugs

SOUTH AFRICA

UNDPI FINALIST
THE JUPITER DRAWING ROOM
CAPE TOWN

MEDIUM Radio
CLIENT KFM

The New York Festivals
The World's Best Work

MAGAZINE, POSTER, OUTDOOR, TRANSIT

MAGAZINE

GRAND AWARD

BEST MAGAZINE ADVERTISEMENT

CHILE

GRAND AWARD,
BEST MAGAZINE ADVERTISEMENT
BBDO CHILE
SANTIAGO

CLIENT Swatch
CREATIVE DIRECTOR Sebastian Lia/
Hernan Antillo
COPYWRITER Rodrigo Duarte
ART DIRECTOR Carolina Sanchez
PHOTOGRAPHER Eduardo Nunez/Santiago
ILLUSTRATOR Claudio Ubilla/Santiago

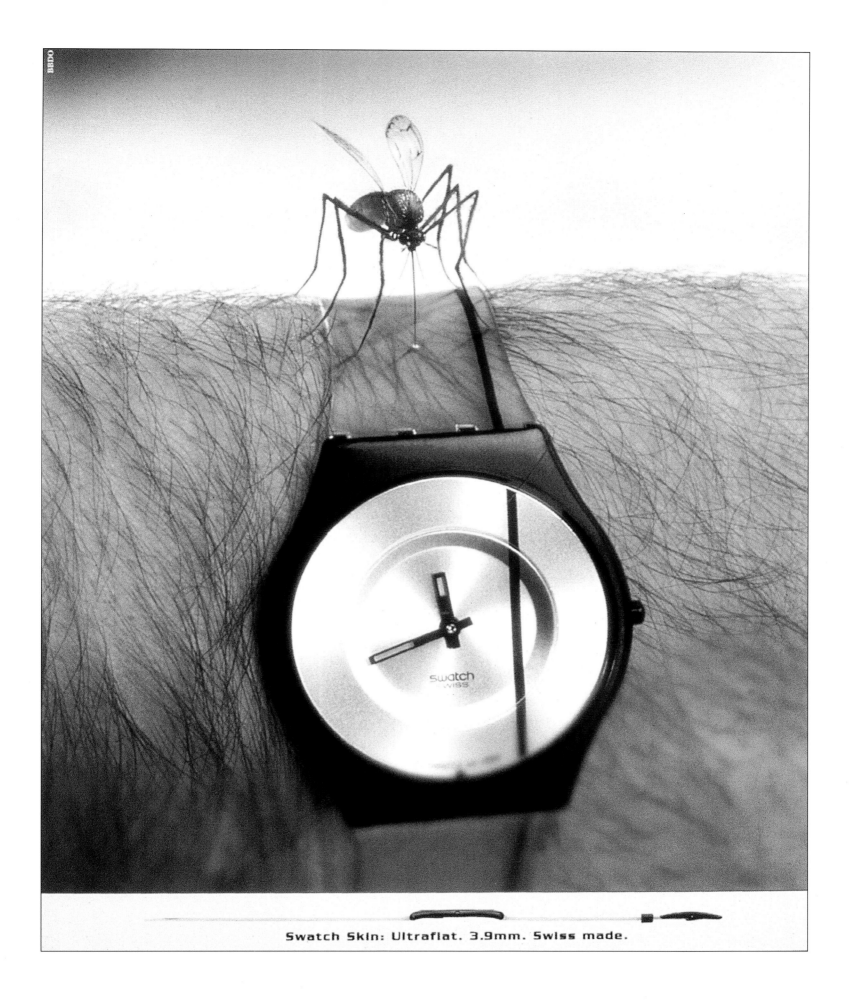

Swatch Skin: Ultraflat. 3.9mm. Swiss made.

ALCOHOLIC BEVERAGES

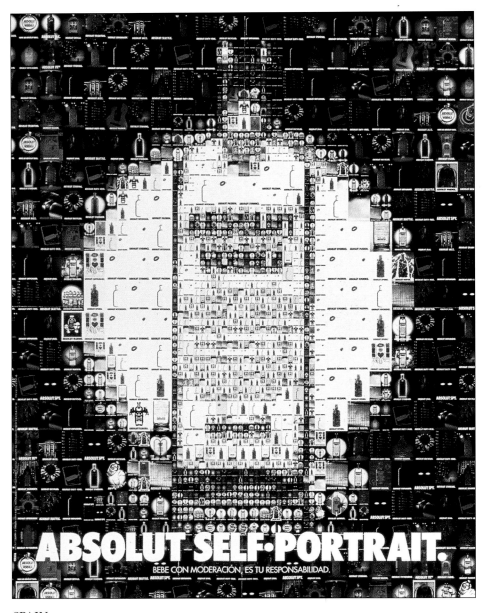

AUSTRALIA

FINALIST, SINGLE
J. WALTER THOMSON
SYDNEY

CLIENT McWilliams's Wines
CREATIVE DIRECTOR Jeff Clulow
COPYWRITER Danny Moth
ART DIRECTOR Ken Buchan
PHOTOGRAPHER Ian Butterworth/Sydney

SPAIN

SILVER WORLDMEDAL, SINGLE
T.B.W.A MADRID
MADRID

CLIENT Absolut Seagram
CREATIVE DIRECTOR Angel Iglesias/Guillermo Gines
COPYWRITER Guillermo Gines
ART DIRECTOR Angel Iglesias

AUSTRALIA

FINALIST, SINGLE
KILLEY WITHY PUNSHON ADVERTISING
ADELAIDE

CLIENT Coopers Beer
CREATIVE DIRECTOR Peter Withy
COPYWRITER Peter Withy
ART DIRECTOR Greg Knagge/Jane Keen
PHOTOGRAPHER Van Elsen/Adelaide

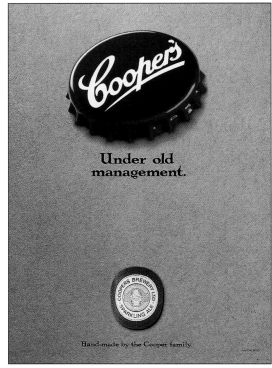

SINGAPORE

BRONZE WORLDMEDAL, SINGLE
TBWA SINGAPORE
SINGAPORE

CLIENT Grand Ridge Brewing Company
CREATIVE DIRECTOR Michael Fromowitz
COPYWRITER Carey Grahame
ART DIRECTOR Koh Hwee Peng
PHOTOGRAPHER Poon Kin Thong/Ric Tang
ILLUSTRATOR Felix Wang

PANAMA

FINALIST, SINGLE
LORENA MORENO
PANAMA

CLIENT Malibu Coconut Rum
CREATIVE DIRECTOR Lorena Moreno
ART DIRECTOR Lorena Moreno/Julian Perez
PHOTOGRAPHER Fernando Bocanegra
ILLUSTRATOR Julian Perez

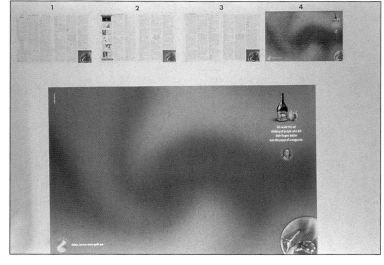

BRAZIL

FINALIST, SINGLE
LOWE LODUCCA
SAO PAULO

CLIENT Baileys
CREATIVE DIRECTOR Celso Loducca/Cristiane Maradei
COPYWRITER Sergio Franco
ART DIRECTOR Sergio Rausch
PHOTOGRAPHER Ricardo Vic/Klaus Mitteldorf/Milenium

AUSTRALIA

FINALIST, SINGLE

YOUNG & RUBICAM ADELAIDE

ADELAIDE

CLIENT Wild Turkey
CREATIVE DIRECTOR Danny Searle
COPYWRITER Jessica Wynne
ART DIRECTOR Dale McGuinness
OTHER Buspack/Melbourne (Production Company)

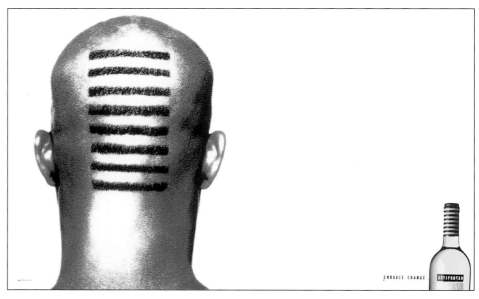

AUSTRALIA

FINALIST, CAMPAIGN

KILLEY WITHY PUNSHON ADVERTISING

ADELAIDE

CLIENT Antipodean Wine Co.
CREATIVE DIRECTOR Peter Withy/Greg Knagge
COPYWRITER Jane Goldney
ART DIRECTOR Geoff Robertson
PHOTOGRAPHER Mike Annese/Adelaide

CANADIAN CALENDAR

APRIL 8 1535. Explorer Jacques Cartier names Canada Canada. What else would you call it? CHEERS.

i am.

CANADIAN CALENDAR

APRIL 9 1926. Hugh Hefner's birthday. Bet that's a party. CHEERS.

i am.

CANADIAN CALENDAR

APRIL 10 1919. Citizens of Quebec overwhelmingly vote to allow the sale of beer and wine. Pretzel and cheese sales soar. CHEERS.

i am.

CANADIAN CALENDAR

APRIL 11 1921. Let's get ready to RUMMMBLE! A boxing match becomes the first live broadcast of a sporting event on radio. CHEERS.

i am.

CANADIAN CALENDAR

MAY 1 1912. Canada's first $5 note issued. Big bucks, considering everything cost a nickel. CHEERS.

i am.

CANADIAN CALENDAR

MAY 2 1844. "The Real McCoy" born in Colchester, Ont. inventor Elijah McCoy, responsible for the ironing board, the lawn sprinkler and the coolest nickname ever. CHEERS.

i am.

CANADIAN CALENDAR

MAY 3 1915. Canadian soldier John McCrae writes poem "In Flander's Field" during a break in battle. CHEERS.

i am.

CANADIAN CALENDAR

MAY 4 1886. The first phonograph is patented. How long until a frat house somewhere receives the first noise complaint? CHEERS.

i am.

CANADIAN CALENDAR

OCTOBER 25 1951. Montreal became the first Canadian city to reach a population of more than one million. No wonder, you can buy cold beer in every corner store. CHEERS.

i am.

CANADIAN CALENDAR

OCTOBER 26 1774. The American Congress invited Canada and Nova Scotia to join the 13 Colonies. Even then, they obviously saw a need for a few ringers on their hockey team. CHEERS.

i am.

CANADIAN CALENDAR

OCTOBER 27 1982. "Dominion Day" (July 1) was renamed "Canada Day." After all, when travelling Europe, who ever says: "Hi, I'm from Dominion." CHEERS.

i am.

CANADIAN CALENDAR

OCTOBER 28 1995. Canadian wire-walks 636m across Yangtze River, China. When asked why, he responds, "Well, I've always wanted to be in a beer ad." CHEERS.

i am.

CANADA

FINALIST, CAMPAIGN

MACLAREN McCANN

TORONTO, ONTARIO

CLIENT Molson Canadian Beer
CREATIVE DIRECTOR Rick Davis/
Mark Fitzgerald/Kerry Reynolds
COPYWRITER Mark Fitzgerald
ART DIRECTOR Kerry Reynolds
PHOTOGRAPHER Kerry Reynolds
OTHER Barbara MacPherson (Producer)

USA

FINALIST, CAMPAIGN

RDW GROUP INC.

PROVIDENCE, RI

CREATIVE DIRECTOR Dan Madole
COPYWRITER C.Meehan/J.Atlas/
D.Madole/J.Manheimer
ART DIRECTOR Dan Madole
PHOTOGRAPHER James Schwartz/
St. Louis, MO

ALCOHOLIC BEVERAGES 7

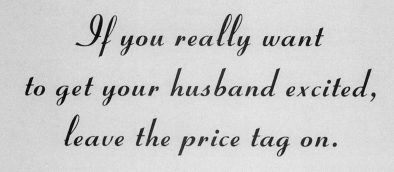

*If you really want
to get your husband excited,
leave the price tag on.*

The styles you want, up to 70% off.

UnderWearhouse

Next to nothings for next to nothing.

USA

GOLD WORLDMEDAL, SINGLE
HMS PARTNERS
COLUMBUS, OH

CLIENT UnderwearHouse
CREATIVE DIRECTOR Stephen Fechtor
COPYWRITER Mark Borcherding
ART DIRECTOR Rocco Volpe
PHOTOGRAPHER Will Shivley
OTHER Dan Miceli (Production Manager)

GERMANY

FINALIST, SINGLE
SPRINGER & JACOBY WERBUNG GMBH
HAMBURG

CLIENT Gortz
CREATIVE DIRECTOR Olaf Oldigs/Thomas Walmrath
COPYWRITER Peter Joob/Amir Kassaei
ART DIRECTOR Wolfgang von Geramb
PHOTOGRAPHER Uwe Bohm

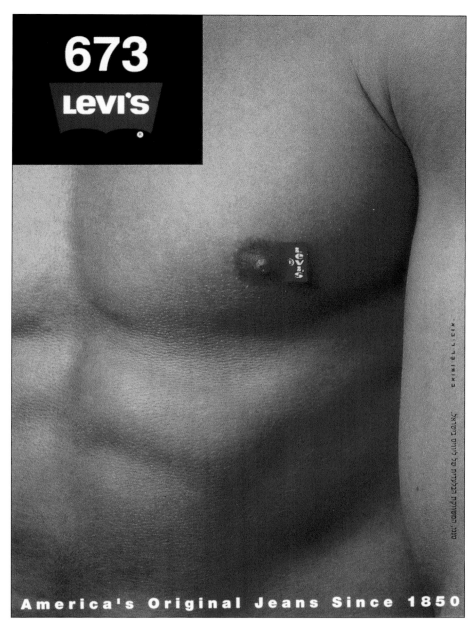

Kein Anzug fragt, ob man Mohamme daner, Christ oder Jude ist. Menschen können von Anzügen lernen.

strellson menswear

GERMANY

BRONZE WORLDMEDAL, CAMPAIGN

RG WIESMEIER WERBEAGENTUR GMBH
MUNICH

CLIENT Strellson Menswwear
CREATIVE DIRECTOR Claudia Jah/
Carlos Obers
COPYWRITER Carlos Obers
ART DIRECTOR Claudia Jah
PHOTOGRAPHER Matthias Ziegler
GRAPHICS COMPANY Manfred Siegler

Hier sehen Sie einen Havanna raucher in Havanna. Und den Sieg der Klasse über die Klassen.

strellson menswear

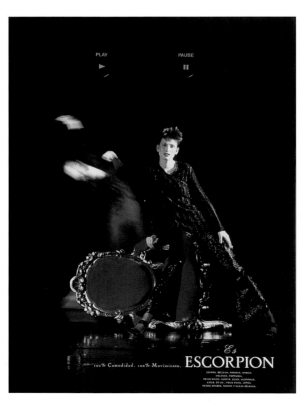

Es
ESCORPION

100% Comodidad. 100% Movimiento.

SPAIN

FINALIST, CAMPAIGN

ABM SERVEIS DE COMUNICACIO
BARCELONA

CLIENT Escorpion
CREATIVE DIRECTOR Jaume Anglada
ART DIRECTOR Maurici Palouzie
PHOTOGRAPHER Josep Bou/
Jaume Diana/Barcelona
OTHER Quim Boix
(Digital Retouching)

THE 18TH HOLE

Three golfers — Dave and a young couple he's been paired up with — are in the middle of a round when the other man's cellular phone rings. The man takes the call and announces that he has to leave. Dave and the woman continue to play, each enjoying the game and the other's company immensely. When they reach the 18th green they find Dave's ball is about 5 feet from the hole and his attractive partner's is well over 30 feet away. Dave says, "I'll tell you what. If I sink this putt, I'm going to buy you a bottle of the finest Champagne back at the clubhouse." He takes his shot and sinks it. His partner then steps up to her enormous putt and says, "I'll tell you what. If I   sink this shot, I'm going to take you back to my house and   make wild, passionate love to you all afternoon."   Dave quickly walks over to her ball and says, "I do   believe, that's a gimme."

PIVOT RULES

WE PLAY GOLF. WHEN IT RAINS WE MAKE CLOTHES.

USA

FINALIST, CAMPAIGN

CMG COMMUNICATIONS
NEW YORK, NY

CLIENT Pivot Rules
CREATIVE DIRECTOR Dave Berger/
Mark D'Arcy
COPYWRITER Mark D'Arcy
ART DIRECTOR Dave Berger

CASUAL / FITNESS / SPORTSWEAR

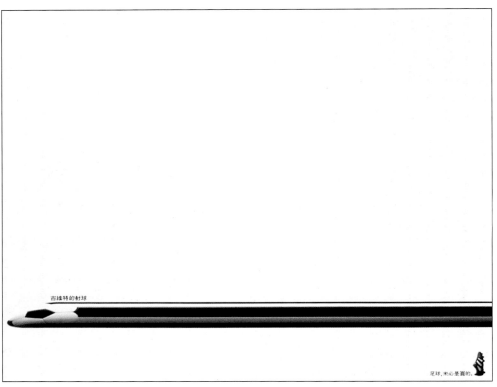

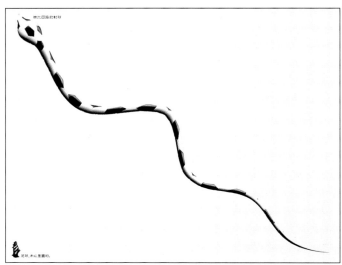

HONG KONG
SILVER WORLDMEDAL, CAMPAIGN
BBDO HONG KONG LIMITED
QUARRY BAY, HONG KONG

CLIENT Adidas
CREATIVE DIRECTOR K.C. Tsang/Paul Chan
COPYWRITER Keenan Ton
ART DIRECTOR Danny Ma/Billy Hau
PHOTOGRAPHER Cotton Shoot/Hong Kong

[O Brasil reinventou um futebol que usa latinhas de cerveja como traves e laranjas como bola.]

BRAZIL
BRONZE WORLDMEDAL, SINGLE
YOUNG & RUBICAM BRASIL
SAO PAULO

CLIENT Umbro Spin - R G Soccer Shoes
CREATIVE DIRECTOR Atila Francucci
COPYWRITER Atila Francucci/Marcos Dyonisio
ART DIRECTOR Sidney Araujo
PHOTOGRAPHER Mario Fontes/Pulsar/Sao Paulo
(Image Bank)

O FOOTBALL E O FUTEBOL.
Todo mundo sabe que o futebol foi inventado pelos ingleses, mas foram os brasileiros que o levaram à categoria de arte.

IF YOUR SON DRIVES LIKE AN ANIMAL, PUT HIM IN THIS CAGE.

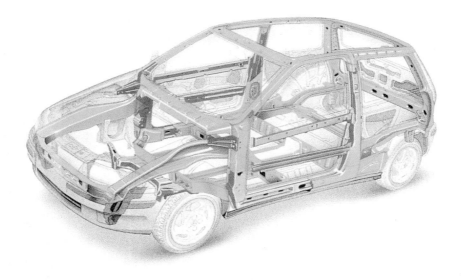

Well, also if he doesn't. Because nobody knows with what kind of animal he can run into the streets. That's why we built the Punto, the safest car in its category.

• Programmed deformation body with undeformable survival cell.
• Protection reinforcement in spars, floors, sider and doors.
• Energy Absorbing Steering-Wheel.

• Anti-sliding special system for front seats, in case of collision.
• Named the safest in its category by "The Independent Consumer Guide" (U.K.) and "Auto Motor & Sport" (Germany).

FIAT Punto

CHILE

GOLD WORLDMEDAL, SINGLE
LEO BURNETT CHILE
SANTIAGO

CLIENT Fiat Punto
CREATIVE DIRECTOR Jaime Atria/Jaime Gonzalez
COPYWRITER Sergio Chauriye
ART DIRECTOR Jaime Gonzalez

USA
FINALIST, SINGLE
ARNOLD COMMUNICATIONS INC.
BOSTON, MA

CLIENT Volkswagen of America, Inc.
CREATIVE DIRECTOR Ron Lawner/
Alan Pafenbach/Lance Jensen
COPYWRITER Lance Jensen

NORWAY

SILVER WORLDMEDAL, SINGLE

BATES NORWAY
OSLO

CLIENT Audi
CREATIVE DIRECTOR
Aris Theophilakis
COPYWRITER
Aris Theophilakis
ART DIRECTOR
Thorbjorn Naug

GERMANY

BRONZE WORLDMEDAL, SINGLE

JVM WERBEAGENTUR GMBH
HAMBURG

CLIENT Audi Quattro
CREATIVE DIRECTOR Stefan Zschaler
COPYWRITER Alexander Jaggy
ART DIRECTOR Pius Wlaker/Ralf Nolting
ILLUSTRATOR Dirk Westphal

The New Renault Twingo Automatic. Left foot optional.

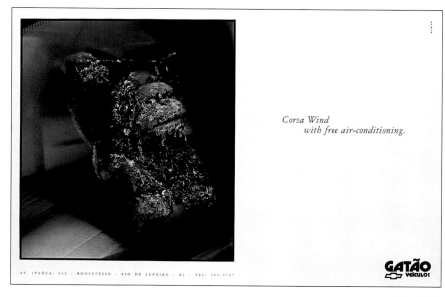

Corsa Wind
with free air-conditioning.

GATÃO
Veículos

BRAZIL

FINALIST, SINGLE
ARTPLAN COMUNICACAO
RIO DE JANEIRO

CLIENT Corsa Wind
CREATIVE DIRECTOR Marcos Apostolo/Chico Abreia
COPYWRITER Marcus Meirelles
ART DIRECTOR Fabio Onofre
PHOTOGRAPHER Jaime Acioli

ARGENTINA

FINALIST, SINGLE
AGULLA Y BACCETTI
BUENOS AIRES

CLIENT Twingo Easy
CREATIVE DIRECTOR R.Agulla/C.Baccetti/
S.Wilhelm/ M.Anselmo/L.Raposo
COPYWRITER Maximiliano Itzkoff
ART DIRECTOR Nicolas Kasakoff

USA

FINALIST, SINGLE
**ARNOLD
COMMUNICATIONS INC.**
BOSTON, MA
CLIENT Beetle/Volkswagen
CREATIVE DIRECTOR
Ron Lawner/
Alan Pafenbach/
Lance Jensen
COPYWRITER Shane Hutton

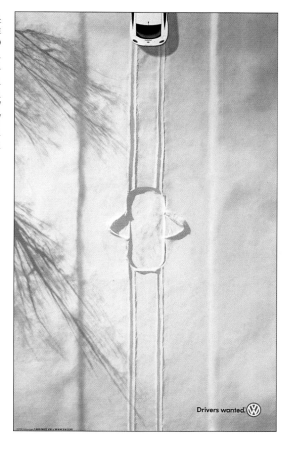

Drivers wanted. VW

0-60 mph: 5.4 sec.   JAGUAR XKR

SPAIN

FINALIST, SINGLE
BASSAT, OGILVY & MATHER
MADRID

CLIENT Jaguar XKR
CREATIVE DIRECTOR
Angel Gonzalez/
Jose Maria Lapena
COPYWRITER Angel Gonzales/
Pedro Moazas
ART DIRECTOR Diego Guirao

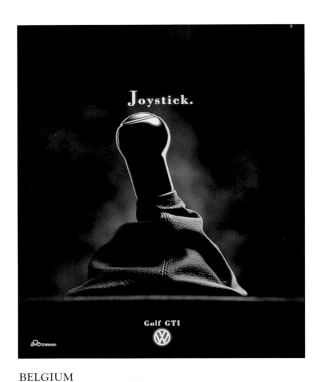

GERMANY
FINALIST, SINGLE
JVM WERBEAGENTUR GMBH
HAMBURG
CLIENT Audi TT
CREATIVE DIRECTOR Hermann Waterkamp
COPYWRITER Doerte Spengler
ART DIRECTOR Holger Bultmann
PHOTOGRAPHER Blinkk

SPAIN
FINALIST, SINGLE
GREY TRACE
BARCELONA

CREATIVE DIRECTOR
Agustin Vaquero/Manuel Twalde/J.Basora
COPYWRITER Manuel Twalde/Quim Crespo
ART DIRECTOR J.Basora/J.Guinart
PHOTOGRAPHER Josep Maria Roca

GERMANY
FINALIST, SINGLE
JVM WERBEAGENTUR GMBH
HAMBURG
CLIENT Audi TT
CREATIVE DIRECTOR Hermann Waterkamp
COPYWRITER Doerte Spengler
ART DIRECTOR Holger Bultmann
PHOTOGRAPHER Blinkk

CHILE
FINALIST, SINGLE
LOWE PORTA
SANTIAGO

CLIENT Toyota Corolla
CREATIVE DIRECTOR Kiko Carcavilla/
Alejandro Armstrong
COPYWRITER Kiko Carcavilla
ART DIRECTOR Jose Pizarro
PHOTOGRAPHER Factory/Santiago
ILLUSTRATOR Jose Pizarro/Santiago

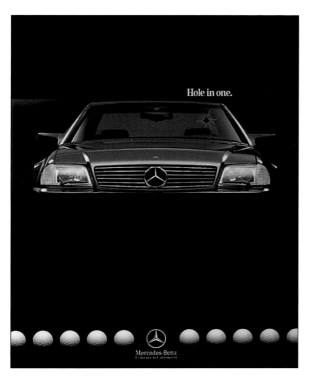

Hole in one.

MEXICO

FINALIST, SINGLE
LOWE & PARTNERS
MEXICO
CLIENT Mercedes Benz
CREATIVE DIRECTOR Manuel Ruiz/Rodrigo Munizaga
COPYWRITER Manuel Ruiz
ART DIRECTOR Flavio Salmon
PHOTOGRAPHER Giancarlo Fiorenza

Ziehen Sie aufs Land.

Dann haben Sie es weiter in die Stadt.   Audi TT. Driven by instinct.

GERMANY

FINALIST, SINGLE
JVM WERBEAGENTUR GMBH
HAMBURG
CLIENT Audi TT
CREATIVE DIRECTOR Hermann Waterkamp
COPYWRITER Doerte Sepengler
ART DIRECTOR Holger Bultmann
PHOTOGRAPHER Blinkk

quattro... are we clear?..

back-wheel drive...

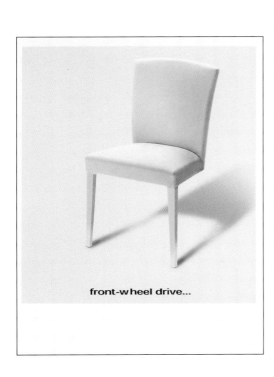

front-wheel drive...

TURKEY

FINALIST, SINGLE
M.A.R.K.A. ILETISIM HIZMETLERI
MASLAK
CLIENT Dogusmotor Servis Ve Ticaret A.S.
CREATIVE DIRECTOR Hulusi Derici
COPYWRITER Ruhi Topcuoglu
ART DIRECTOR Alper Tunga Sen
OTHER Selma Bilgic (Account Director)/
Ilkay Unlu (Account Executive)

"Daddy, are we nearly th

New Opel Sintra 2.2 DTI 16V with direct injection.

OPEL

Polo VW

When your family gets out, it's no longer a family car.

Polo Classic

SPAIN

McCANN-ERICKSON
MADRID

CLIENT Opel
CREATIVE DIRECTOR N. Hollander/J. Baglivo/G. Hernandez
ART DIRECTOR Laura Gutierrez

ARGENTINA

RATTO/BBDO S.A.
BUENOS AIRES

CLIENT Volkwsagen Polo
CREATIVE DIRECTOR Juan Manuel Ricciarelli/
Joaquin Molla
COPYWRITER Joaquin Molla
ART DIRECTOR Juan Manuel Ricciarelli
PHOTOGRAPHER Carlos Mainardi

ARGENTINA

RATTO/BBDO S.A.
BUENOS AIRES

CLIENT Volkswagen Polo
CREATIVE DIRECTOR
Juan Manuel Ricciarelli/Joaquin Molla
COPYWRITER Joaquin Molla
ART DIRECTOR Juan Manuel Ricciarelli
PHOTOGRAPHER Carlos Mainardi

SEE PAGE 25

Coming in November.

New Gol 1.9 Turbo Diesel. VW

USA

PUBLICIS
DALLAS, TX

CLIENT BMW Of North America
CREATIVE DIRECTOR Marshall Lestz/John Tsao
COPYWRITER Steve Grimes
ART DIRECTOR Pete Voehringer

ARGENTINA

RATTO/BBDO S.A.
BUENOS AIRES

CLIENT New Gol 1.9 Turbo Diesel
CREATIVE DIRECTOR Juan Manuel Ricciarelli/Joaquin Molla
COPYWRITER Marcos Calandrelli
ART DIRECTOR Hernan Curioni
PHOTOGRAPHER Sergio Assabi

AUSTRALIA

FINALIST, SINGLE
SAATCHI & SAATCHI
SYDNEY

CLIENT Toyota Hiace
CREATIVE DIRECTOR Michael Newman
COPYWRITER Scot Waterhouse
ART DIRECTOR Steve Carlin
PHOTOGRAPHER Jon Higgs
OTHER Michelle Greenhalgh (Account Supervisor)

GERMANY

FINALIST, SINGLE
SPRINGER & JACOBY WERBUNG GMBH
HAMBURG

CLIENT Mercedes-Benz Deutschland/CLK
CREATIVE DIRECTOR Alexander Schill/
A. Thomsen
ART DIRECTOR D. Hausermann/C. Everke
PHOTOGRAPHER I. Hansen

ENGLAND

FINALIST, SINGLE
WALLIS TOMLINSON
BIRMINGHAM

CLIENT Subaru Forester Turbo
CREATIVE DIRECTOR Geoff Tomlinson
COPYWRITER Richard Elwell
ART DIRECTOR Jon Harrison
PHOTOGRAPHER Pete Davies

THE NETHERLANDS

FINALIST, SINGLE
TBWA/CAMPAIGN COMPANY
AMSTERDAM

CLIENT Nissan Europe
COPYWRITER Massimo van der Plas
ART DIRECTOR Matthijs van Wensveen
PHOTOGRAPHER Matthijs van Roon

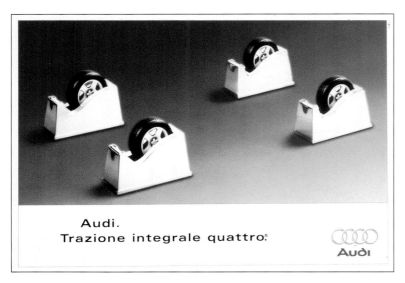

Audi.
Trazione integrale quattro.

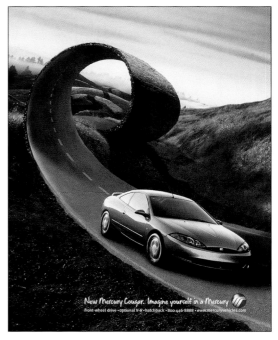

New Mercury Cougar. Imagine yourself in a Mercury
front-wheel drive · optional V-6 · hatchback · 800-446-8888 · www.mercuryvehicles.com

ITALY

FINALIST, SINGLE
VERBA SRL.
MILAN

CLIENT Autogerma
CREATIVE DIRECTOR Stefano Longoni
COPYWRITER Enrico Bonomini
ART DIRECTOR Stefano Longoni

USA

FINALIST, SINGLE
YOUNG & RUBICAM
SAN FRANCISCO, CA

CLIENT Mercury Cougar
CREATIVE DIRECTOR
Michael Belitsos
COPYWRITER
Jim Plegue
ART DIRECTOR
Steve Goldsworthy/
Doug Wood
PHOTOGRAPHER
Graham Westmorland

F-250. THE BIGGEST AND MOST POWERFUL PICK-UP TRUCK IN BRAZIL.

BRAZIL

FINALIST, SINGLE
YOUNG & RUBICAM BRASIL
SAO PAULO

CLIENT Ford F-250
CREATIVE DIRECTOR Alexandre Gama/
Atila Francucci
COPYWRITER Atila Francucci
ART DIRECTOR Alexandre Soares
PHOTOGRAPHER Fernando Zuffo/
Sao Paulo

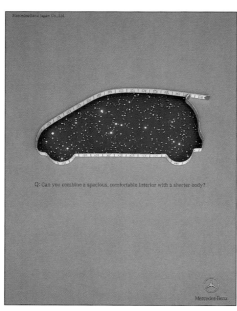

Q: Can you combine a spacious, comfortable interior with a shorter body?

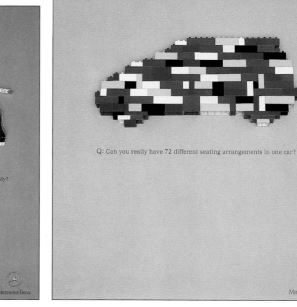

Q: Can you really have 72 different seating arrangements in one car?

JAPAN

FINALIST, CAMPAIGN
DENTSU, INC.
TOKYO

CLIENT Mercedes-Benz Japan Co., Ltd.
CREATIVE DIRECTOR Mitsuhiro Wada
COPYWRITER M.Tsunoda/S.Nishihashi/
K.Murata/K.Toda
ART DIRECTOR J.Nakamura/J.Okamoto
PHOTOGRAPHER Kazuyasu Hagane

The new Land Rover now gets continuous weather reports. From its wheels.

Introducing the most technologically advanced Land Rover ever.

Whether you're expecting rain, snow, or even sunshine, there's one thing the forecast always calls for.

The new Land Rover Discovery Series II.

What's new about it? Practically everything. It's been totally reengineered from top to bottom, inside and out. And with some 13,500 new parts, it offers a range of technological innovations unavailable in any other SUV.

It comes with electronic brake force distribution. A feature that is designed to balance front and rear braking for increased driver control. Even in a torrential "Uh-oh, we didn't leave the windows open, did we?" rainstorm.

Not only that, it's the first four-wheel-drive vehicle with available Active Cornering Enhancement. An ingenious new feature that uses computers and an advanced hydraulic system to help reduce body lean, when the road throws you a curve.

Moreover, with its four-wheel electronic traction control and permanent four-wheel drive, it makes the whole idea of canceling school because of the weather seem totally unnecessary.

Admittedly, a point of view the kids may not share.

And to accommodate all of you, we've made it bigger. We've also added more cargo space. Not to mention three-point safety belts for everyone, including those in the now-available forward-facing rear seats.

Happily, some things haven't changed. The Discovery still comes with a rugged 14-gauge steel chassis, side impact beams, and a steel inner body cage.

And beyond its technological advances, it has another remarkable feature. A starting MSRP of $34,775* So call 1-800-FINE-4WD and see it for yourself. Because there's no better way so ride out a storm.

DISCOVERY SERIES II $34,775*

USA

GOLD WORLDMEDAL, CAMPAIGN
GRACE & ROTHSCHILD
NEW YORK, NY

CLIENT Land Rover North America - Discovery
CREATIVE DIRECTOR Roy Grace
COPYWRITER Rob Strasberg/Rich Bloom
ART DIRECTOR Kim Cable/Don Miller
PHOTOGRAPHER Carl Furuta/Vic Huber/
Los Angeles, CA

Where you'll feel the new Land Rover's technological innovations.

Open lane.

Advancement through Technology

SINGAPORE

FINALIST, CAMPAIGN
AMMIRATI PURIS LINTAS
SINGAPORE
SINGAPORE

CLIENT Audi Website
CREATIVE DIRECTOR Nick Fairhead
COPYWRITER Justin Pereira
ART DIRECTOR Vancelee Teng
PHOTOGRAPHER Mun's Studio/Singapore

Park here.

Advancement through Technology

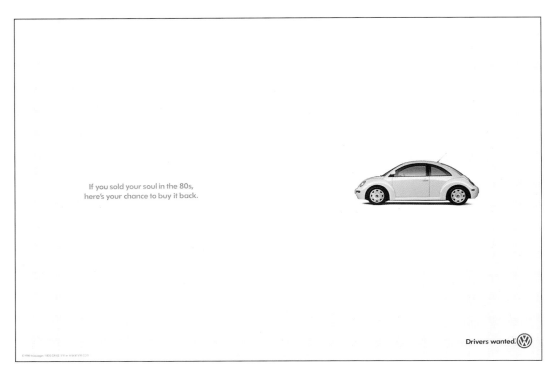

If you sold your soul in the 80s,
here's your chance to buy it back.

Drivers wanted.

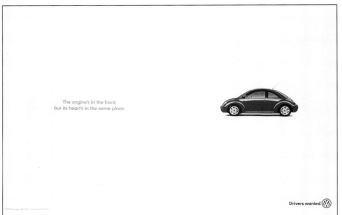

The engine's in the front,
but its heart's in the same place.

Drivers wanted.

USA
SILVER WORLDMEDAL, CAMPAIGN
ARNOLD COMMUNICATIONS INC.
BOSTON, MA

CLIENT Volkswagen
CREATIVE DIRECTOR Ron Lawner/Lance Jensen/
Alan Pafenbach
COPYWRITER Lance Jensen

Digitally remastered.

Drivers wanted.

USA
FINALIST, CAMPAIGN
ARNOLD COMMUNICATIONS, INC.
BOSTON, MA

CLIENT Volkswagen
CREATIVE DIRECTOR Ron Lawner/Lance Jansen
COPYWRITER David Weist

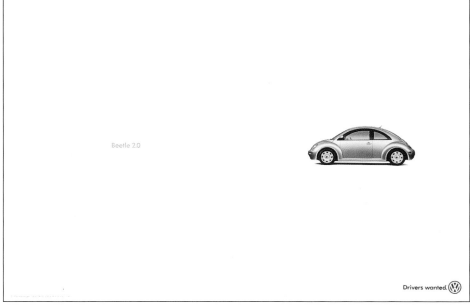

Beetle 2.0

Drivers wanted.

Get away from family life with your family.

There's something worse than your son asking for the car. Not asking for it.

ARGENTINA

BRONZE WORLDMEDAL, CAMPAIGN

RATTO/BBDO S.A.
BUENOS AIRES

CLIENT Volkswagen Polo
CREATIVE DIRECTOR Juan Manuel Ricciarelli/
Joaquin Molla
COPYWRITER Joaquin Molla
ART DIRECTOR Juan Manuel Ricciarelli
PHOTOGRAPHER Carlos Mainardi

Direct
Response.

Freude am Fahren

Form
Follows
Fun.

Freude am Fahren

GERMANY

FINALIST, CAMPAIGN

BBDO DUSSELDORF GMBH
DUSSELDORF

CLIENT BMW Automotive
CREATIVE DIRECTOR Michael Osche
COPYWRITER Arno Haus
ART DIRECTOR Morris Aberham

SPAIN
DE FEDERICO, VALMORISCO Y OCHOA
MADRID

CLIENT Subaru
CREATIVE DIRECTOR Goyo Valmorisco
COPYWRITER Alfredo Negri
ART DIRECTOR Sebastian De La Serna
PHOTOGRAPHER Angel Alvarez

GERMANY
JVM WERBEAGENTUR GMBH
HAMBURG

CLIENT Audi TT
CREATIVE DIRECTOR Hermann Waterkamp
COPYWRITER Doerte Spengler
ART DIRECTOR Hoger Bultmann
ILLUSTRATOR Blinkk

Jaune citron. Beaucoup de jus.

Êtes-vous fait pour Volkswagen?

CANADA

FINALIST, CAMPAIGN

PALM PUBLICITE MARKETING
MONTREAL

CLIENT   Volkswagen-New Beetle
CREATIVE DIRECTOR   Paulette Arsenault
COPYWRITER   Normand Boisvert/M. Andre Rivard
ART DIRECTOR   Yvon Paquette/J. Luc Bouvy
PHOTOGRAPHER   Ron Strong
ILLUSTRATOR   Mettle
OTHER   Trans-Optique/HSP Graphics (Printer)

Vert nature. Coureur des bois.

Êtes-vous fait pour Volkswagen?

THIS SIDE UP

What you need is the Transporter with four link suspension with independent struts.

ARGENTINA

FINALIST, CAMPAIGN
RATTO/BBDO S.A.
BUENOS AIRES

CLIENT   Transporter
CREATIVE DIRECTOR   Juan Manuel Ricciarelli/
Joaquin Molla
COPYWRITER   Esteban Garcia/Joaquin Molla
ART DIRECTOR   Hernan Curioni/
Juan Manuel Ricciarelli
PHOTOGRAPHER   Carlos Mainardi

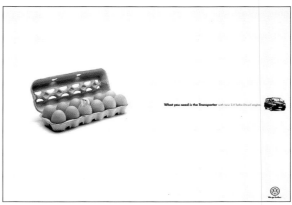

What you need is the Transporter with new 2.4 turbo Diesel engine.

AUTOMOTIVE PRODUCTS

Original parts?

WHEN YOU NEED A MITSUSISHI PART AND YOU DON'T USE A MITSUSISHI PART, YOUR MITSUSISHI STOPS BEING A MITSUSISHI. IT START BEING A MATSUPUISHI WHICH'S NOT THE SAME THING. THERE'S A WHOLE SPECIALIZED SERVICE NETWORK. USE IT. BECAUSE IF NOT IT CAN COST YOU A LOT, A LOT.

MITSUBISHI MOTORS
We put our lives on this.

CHILE
GOLD WORLDMEDAL, SINGLE
BBDO CHILE
SANTIAGO

CLIENT Mitsubishi Chile
CREATIVE DIRECTOR Sebastian Lia/
Hernan Antillo
COPYWRITER Sebastian Lia
ART DIRECTOR Carolina Sanchez
PHOTOGRAPHER Fotobank
ILLUSTRATOR Claudio Ubilla

DO YOU REALLY WANT TO KNOW WHAT THIS SMELLS LIKE?

OF COURSE NOT.

ARBRE MAGIQUE
FRESA

SPAIN
BRONZE WORLDMEDAL, SINGLE
YOUNG & RUBICAM S.A.
MADRID

CLIENT Pinobeto Air Freshener
CREATIVE DIRECTOR Jose Pujol/German Silva
COPYWRITER Jose Pujol/German Silva
ART DIRECTOR Ramon Ruiz De La Prada
PHOTOGRAPHER Fernando Manso

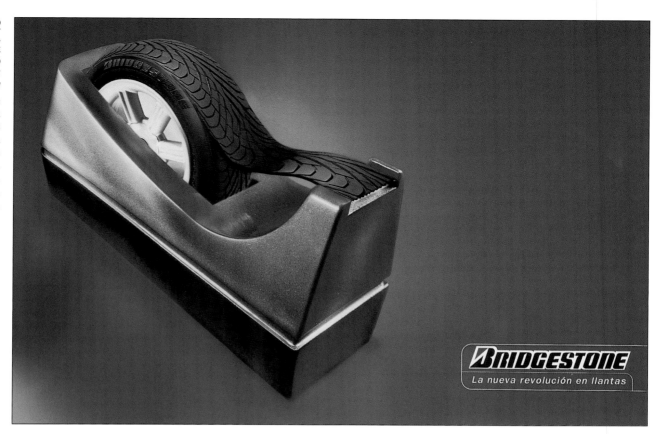

MEXICO

SILVER WORLDMEDAL,
SINGLE
BBDO/MEXICO
MEXICO CITY

CLIENT Bridgestone/
Bridgestone Firestone
CREATIVE DIRECTOR
Carl Jones
COPYWRITER
Jose Rosales
ART DIRECTOR
Alfonso Ochoa
PHOTOGRAPHER
Pep Avila

SWEDEN

FINALIST, SINGLE
AKESTAM. HOLST. MFL
STOCKHOLM

CLIENT OK Winter Tires
COPYWRITER Peter Laurelli
ART DIRECTOR Johan Landin
OTHER Kenneth Adenskog (Account Executive)

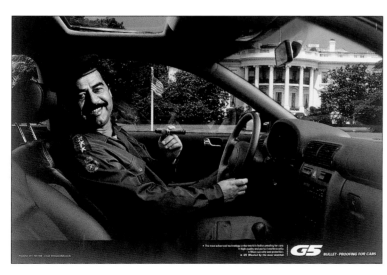

BRAZIL

FINALIST, SINGLE
Z+G GREY - BRAZIL
SAO PAULO

CLIENT Bullet-Proofing for cars
CREATIVE DIRECTOR Zezito Marques da Costa/Marcelo Prista
COPYWRITER Alexandre Scaff
ART DIRECTOR Paulo Pereira
PHOTOGRAPHER Marco Cezar/Hilton Ribeiro/ Sao Paulo

WHEN YOU HIT 30,000 FT. AT 500 MPH

YOU'LL BE GLAD YOU CHOSE GOODYEAR TIRES.

Not only does Goodyear give you excellent value on tires and auto service, we also offer AIR MILES* reward miles on every purchase you make at participating Goodyear outlets across Canada including Fountain Tire in Alberta and B.C. and Coast Tire in the Maritimes. When you need tires or service, come in to Goodyear. Our tires will take you farther than you might think.

GOODYEAR

CANADA
FINALIST, SINGLE
DUE NORTH COMMUNICATIONS, INC.
TORONTO, ONTARIO

CLIENT Goodyear
CREATIVE DIRECTOR Karen Howe
COPYWRITER David Gee
ART DIRECTOR Jeffrey Wilbee

Firestone Uni -T. Powerful grip.

Firestone

MEXICO
FINALIST, SINGLE
BBDO/MEXICO
MEXICO CITY

CLIENT Firestone/Bridgestone /Firestone
CREATIVE DIRECTOR Carl Jones
COPYWRITER Jose Luis Rosales
ART DIRECTOR Alfonso Ochoa

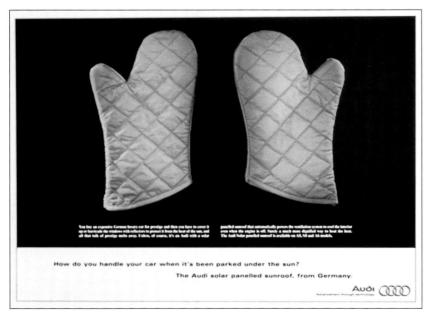

How do you handle your car when it's been parked under the sun?

The Audi solar panelled sunroof. from Germany.

Audi

UNITED ARAB EMIRATES
FINALIST, SINGLE
IMPACT/BBDO
DUBAI

CLIENT Audi
CREATIVE DIRECTOR Ali Azarmi
COPYWRITER Ali Azarmi
ART DIRECTOR Ali Azarmi

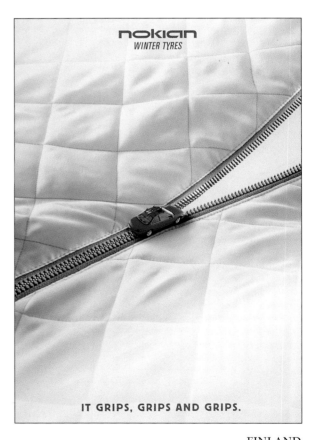

nokian
WINTER TYRES

IT GRIPS, GRIPS AND GRIPS.

FINLAND
FINALIST, SINGLE
PALTEMAA HUTTUNEN SANTALA TBWA
HELSINKI

CLIENT Nokian Tyres
COPYWRITER Kari Eilola
ART DIRECTOR Anu Igoni
PHOTOGRAPHER Markku Lahdesmaki/Los Angeles

GOOD YEAR. Máxima adherencia. Sobre asfalto. Sobre tierra. Sobre agua.

SPAIN
SILVER WORLDMEDAL, CAMPAIGN
McCANN-ERICKSON
MADRID

CLIENT   Good Year
CREATIVE DIRECTOR
Nicolas Hollander/
Andres Martinez

"¿No había curvas por aquí?"

AMORTIGUADORES
MONROE
HACEN TU CAMINO MAS SEGURO

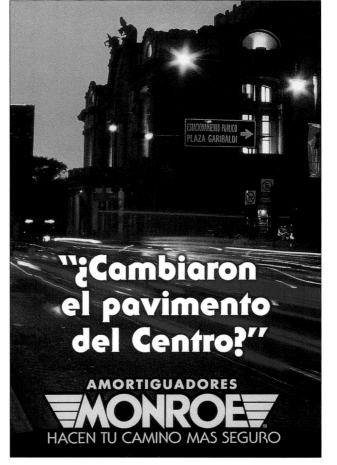

ESTACIONAMIENTO PUBLICO
PLAZA GARIBALDI

"¿Cambiaron el pavimento del Centro?"

AMORTIGUADORES
MONROE
HACEN TU CAMINO MAS SEGURO

MEXICO
FINALIST, CAMPAIGN
J. WALTER THOMPSON MEXICO
MEXICO

CLIENT   Amortiguadores Monroe
CREATIVE DIRECTOR
Shawn McDonough
COPYWRITER   Hector Mireles
ART DIRECTOR   Shawn McDonough
PHOTOGRAPHER   Fabio Foresti/Mexico

THE NETHERLANDS

GOLD WORLDMEDAL, SINGLE

TBWA/CAMPAIGN COMPANY

AMSTERDAM

CLIENT Delta Lloyd
COPYWRITER Poppe van Pelt
ART DIRECTOR Diederick Hillenius
PHOTOGRAPHER Hans Kroeskamp

AUSTRALIA

FINALIST, SINGLE

AMMIRATI PURIS LINTAS

NORTH SYDNEY

CLIENT The Commonwealth Bank Internet Services
CREATIVE DIRECTOR Mel Du Toit
COPYWRITER Tammy Tinkler
ART DIRECTOR John Greig
PHOTOGRAPHER Tim Hizson

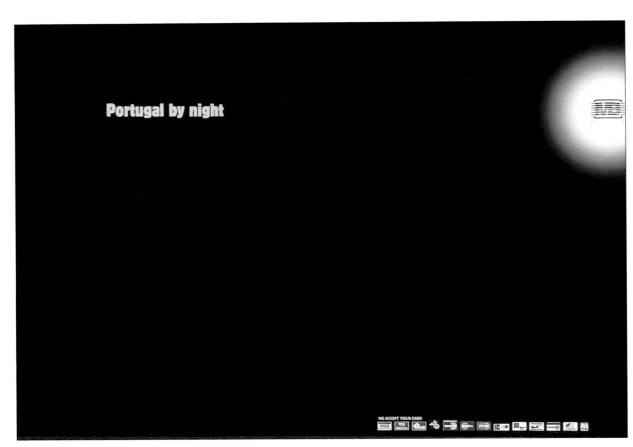

Portugal by night

PORTUGAL
SILVER WORLDMEDAL, SINGLE
NOVA PUBLICIDADE
ALGES
CLIENT SIBS-Sociedade Interbancania Servicos
CREATIVE DIRECTOR Pedro Monteiro
COPYWRITER Alexandre Bezerra
ART DIRECTOR Jose Carlos Fonseca/ Nuno Levezinho

CANADA
BRONZE WORLDMEDAL, SINGLE
YOUNG & RUBICAM TORONTO
TORONTO, ONTARIO
CLIENT AGF Mutual Funds
CREATIVE DIRECTOR David Adams/ John Farguhar
COPYWRITER Tim Kavander
ART DIRECTOR Doug Bramah
PHOTOGRAPHER George Simhoni/Toronto

Turn this page, turn off the light and read this ad.

BANK DRAFTS, APPLICATIONS, REDEMPTIONS, TRANSFERS, PAYMENTS AND ACCOUNT STATEMENTS IN THOUSANDS OF PLACES AROUND THE COUNTRY.

JUST A REMINDER: YOU CAN ALSO DO THIS AT NIGHT.

AUTO-ATENDIMENTO **banespa**. FOR THOSE WHO HAVE TIME TO SAVE TIME.

BRAZIL

FINALIST, SINGLE
GIOVANNI, FCB
RIO DE JANIERO

CLIENT Banespa's Self-Service
CREATIVE DIRECTOR Adilson Xavier/Luiz Lobo
COPYWRITER Lorine Solomonescu
ART DIRECTOR Luiz Lobo

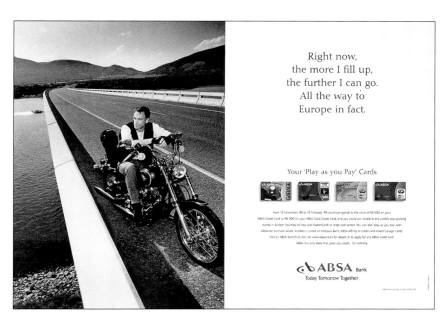

Right now,
the more I fill up,
the further I can go.
All the way to
Europe in fact.

Your 'Play as you Pay' Cards

ABSA Bank
Today Tomorrow Together

SOUTH AFRICA

FINALIST, SINGLE
GITAM/BBDO INTERNATIONAL
WENDYWOOD

CLIENT ABSA - Credit Card
CREATIVE DIRECTOR Dave Renshaw
COPYWRITER Fiona Upton
ART DIRECTOR Evan Sotiropolous
PHOTOGRAPHER Shahn Rowe

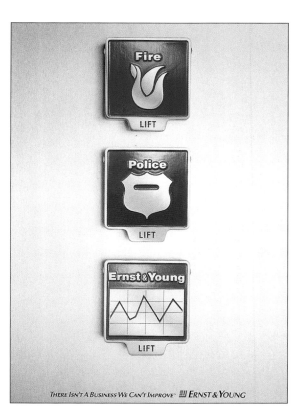

Fire   LIFT

Police   LIFT

Ernst & Young   LIFT

THERE ISN'T A BUSINESS WE CAN'T IMPROVE ᴱᴵᴵ ERNST & YOUNG

USA

FINALIST, SINGLE
GRACE & ROTHSCHILD
NEW YORK, NY

CLIENT Ernst & Young
CREATIVE DIRECTOR Roy Grace
COPYWRITER Kristen Livolsi
ART DIRECTOR Patrick Sutherland
OTHER Abby De Millo(Print Director)

GERMANY

FINALIST, SINGLE

JVM WERBEAGENTUR GMBH
HAMBURG

CLIENT Sixt Leasing
CREATIVE DIRECTOR Frank Dovidat
COPYWRITER Michael Ohanian
ART DIRECTOR Rouven Steinke

ARGENTINA

FINALIST, SINGLE

LEO BURNETT ARGENTINA
BUENOS AIRES

CREATIVE DIRECTOR Boby Ventura/
Gustavo Scarpato/Fabian Bonelli
COPYWRITER Esteban Minoyetti
ART DIRECTOR Ramiro Rodriguez Cohen/
Gustavo Scarpato
PHOTOGRAPHER Daniel Ackerman/
Buenos Aires
ILLUSTRATOR Mario Franco/Buenos Aires

THE NETHERLANDS

FINALIST, SINGLE

LOWE KUIPER & SCHOUTEN
AMSTERDAM

CLIENT KPMG
CREATIVE DIRECTOR Aad Kuiper/Peter van Volsen
COPYWRITER Peter Zeehandelaar
ART DIRECTOR Gerard Foekema
PHOTOGRAPHER Aernout Overbeeke/Amsterdam

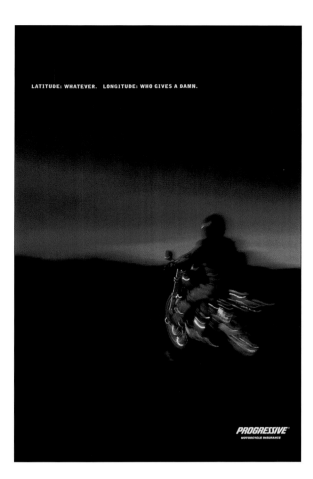

LATITUDE: WHATEVER. LONGITUDE: WHO GIVES A DAMN.

PROGRESSIVE
MOTORCYCLE INSURANCE

... zeker delta lloyd

... zeker delta lloyd

Ready Credit, instant cash from CITIBANK
For more information, call 232-4000.

JAPAN

SILVER WORLDMEDAL, CAMPAIGN

DENTSU, INC.
TOKYO

CLIENT   The Chuo Trust & Banking Co. Ltd.
CREATIVE DIRECTOR   Tatsuya Takeuchi
COPYWRITER   Koichiro Kusaka
ART DIRECTOR   Koichiro Kusaka/Akira Miyashita

AUSTRIA

FINALIST, CAMPAIGN

DEMNER, MERLICEK & BERGMANN
VIENNA

CLIENT   Capital Invest
CREATIVE DIRECTOR   Ernst Baechtold
COPYWRITER   Karin Kammlander/Claude Catsky
ART DIRECTOR   Ernst Baechtold
PHOTOGRAPHER   Kutzler & Wimmer
OTHER   Stela Pancic (Graphics)

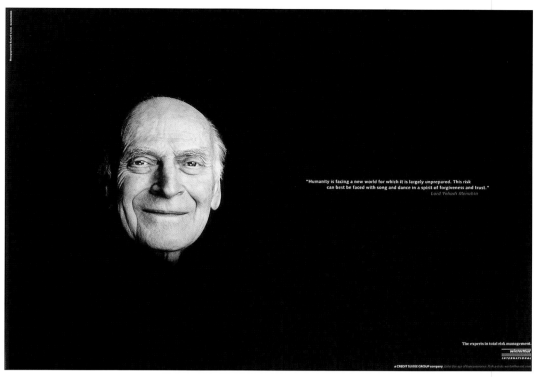

SWITZERLAND

BRONZE WORLDMEDAL, CAMPAIGN
McCANN-ERICKSON
ZURICH

CLIENT Winterthur International
CREATIVE DIRECTOR E. Andrist/D. Comte/
P. Suter/J. Krohn
COPYWRITER Claude Catsky/Joni Muller
ART DIRECTOR Brigit Bauer
PHOTOGRAPHER Richard Avedon/New York
OTHER Verena Rentsh (Art Buyer)

CANADA

FINALIST, CAMPAIGN
GEORGE SIMHONI/WESTSIDE STUDIO
TORONTO, ONTARIO

CLIENT AGF
COPYWRITER Tim Kavander
ART DIRECTOR Doug Bramah
PHOTOGRAPHER George Simhoni

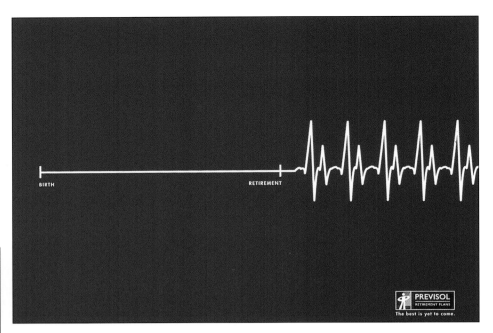

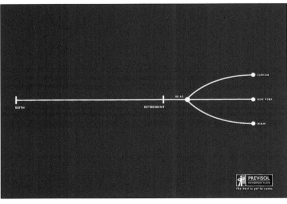

ARGENTINA

FINALIST, CAMPAIGN
SAVAGLIO TBWA
BUENOS AIRES

CLIENT Previsol
CREATIVE DIRECTOR Ernesto Savaglio
COPYWRITER Maria Salaverri
ART DIRECTOR Pepe Balbis/Rodrigo Gorosterrazu

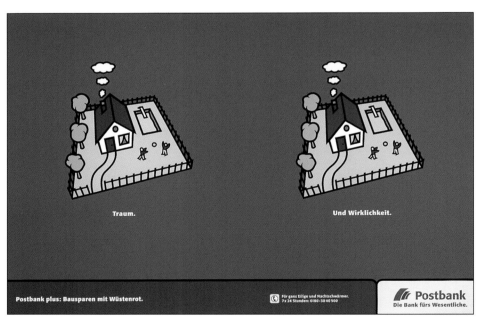

GERMANY

FINALIST, CAMPAIGN
SPRINGER & JACOBY WERBUNG GMBH
HAMBURG

CLIENT Postbank
CREATIVE DIRECTOR Arno Lindemann/Stefan Meske
COPYWRITER A.Aimaq/T.Walter/P.Paetzold/B.Peulecke
ART DIRECTOR Arno Lindemann/Heiko Schmidt/Bert Peulecke
ILLUSTRATOR Stang Gubbels/Rotterdam

SOUTH AFRICA
BRONZE WORLDMEDAL, SINGLE
OGILVY & MATHER RIGHTFORD SEARLE-TRIPP & MAKIN
GAUTENG

CREATIVE DIRECTOR
Brett Wild
COPYWRITER Juan Scott
ART DIRECTOR Brett Wild
PHOTOGRAPHER
Guy Neveling
ILLUSTRATOR
Martin Spencer

Mais um anúncio com demonstração do produto.

BRAZIL
FINALIST, SINGLE
ADD COMUNICACAO
SAO PAULO

CLIENT Helios/Carbex
CREATIVE DIRECTOR Fernando Luna
COPYWRITER Eduardo Di Lascio
ART DIRECTOR Carlos Valle
PHOTOGRAPHER Rodrigo Ribeiro

BRAZIL
FINALIST, SINGLE
ADD COMUNICACAO
SAO PAULO

CLIENT Helios/Carbex
CREATIVE DIRECTOR Fernando Luna
COPYWRITER Fernando Luna
ART DIRECTOR Carlos Valle
PHOTOGRAPHER Rodrigo Ribeiro

ALL THE WISDOM IN ONE BOOK

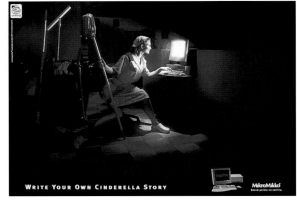

WRITE YOUR OWN CINDERELLA STORY

FINLAND

BRONZE WORLDMEDAL, CAMPAIGN
SEK & GREY OY
HELSINKI

CLIENT MikroMikko Oy

CARGO

You could have sent the whole team by Lufthansa Cargo.

⌒Lufthansa Cargo

ARGENTINA

FINALIST, SINGLE
FOB PUBLICIDAD
BUENOS AIRES

CLIENT Lufthansa Cargo
COPYWRITER Alejandro Egozcue/
Rodolfo Bauza
ART DIRECTOR Alejandro Munoz
ILLUSTRATOR Ruben Leguizamon/
Gabriel Balhinet

GERMANY

FINALIST, SINGLE
JVM WERBEAGENTUR GMBH
HAMBURG

CLIENT Deutsche Post
CREATIVE DIRECTOR Hermann Waterkamp
COPYWRITER Frank Dovidat/
Thorsten Meier
ART DIRECTOR Uli Guertler/Ralf Nolting
PHOTOGRAPHER Oliver Rheindorf

SPAIN

SILVER WORLDMEDAL, CAMPAIGN

BASSAT OGILVY & MATHER

BARCELONA

CLIENT Algida
CREATIVE DIRECTOR Beat Keller
COPYWRITER Felipe Crespo
ART DIRECTOR Beat Keller
PHOTOGRAPHER Jaume Male
OTHER Bettina Farreras (Account Director)

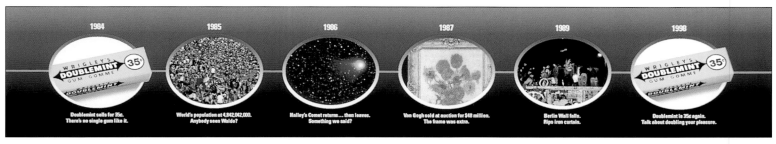

CANADA

BRONZE WORLDMEDAL, CAMPAIGN

BBDO CANADA

TORONTO, ONTARIO

CLIENT Wrigley Canada, Inc.
CREATIVE DIRECTOR Jack Neary/Michael McLaughlin
COPYWRITER Rob Tait
ART DIRECTOR Wally Krysciak

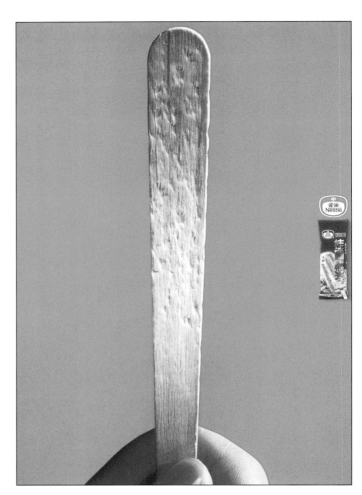

CORPORATE IMAGE

USA

FINALIST, SINGLE
BOZELL WORLDWIDE
SOUTHFIELD, MI

CLIENT House Ad
CREATIVE DIRECTOR Gary Topolewski/
Bill Morden
COPYWRITER Mike Stocker
ART DIRECTOR Robin Chrumka
OTHER Brett Lasko (Producer)

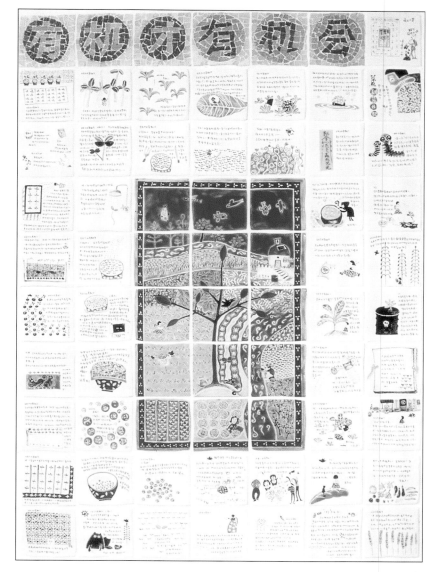

TAIWAN

BRONZE WORLDMEDAL, SINGLE
FUNTASTIC INTERNATIONAL, INC.
TAIPEI

CLIENT Green Formosa Front
CREATIVE DIRECTOR David Sun
COPYWRITER Esther Chen
ART DIRECTOR Kevin Tsia
ILLUSTRATOR Jeff Huang

JAPAN

FINALIST, SINGLE
ASATSU-DK INC.
TOKYO

CLIENT Sony Music Entertainment
CREATIVE DIRECTOR Tsuyoshi Fujimoto
COPYWRITER Hideo Fujimoto
ART DIRECTOR Kazushi Taniichi
PHOTOGRAPHER Akira Kitajima/Tokyo

URUGUAY

FINALIST, SINGLE
CORPORACION/THOMPSON
MONTEVIDEO

CLIENT Image Bank
CREATIVE DIRECTOR Manuel Techera/Marco Caltieri
COPYWRITER Manuel Techera/Marco Caltieri
ART DIRECTOR Manuel Techera/Marco Caltieri

MEXICO

FINALIST, SINGLE
CLEMENTE CAMARA Y ASOCIADOS SA DE CV
MEXICO

CLIENT Asociacion Nacional de la Publicidad
CREATIVE DIRECTOR Eduardo Perez
COPYWRITER Salvador Mejia/Edgar Hernandez
ART DIRECTOR Carla Baeza
ILLUSTRATOR Carla Baeza

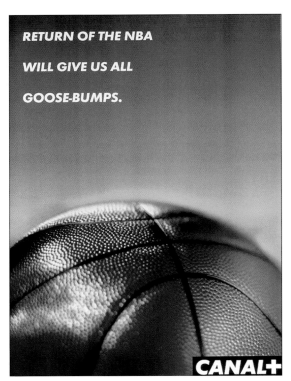

RETURN OF THE NBA
WILL GIVE US ALL
GOOSE-BUMPS.

CANAL+

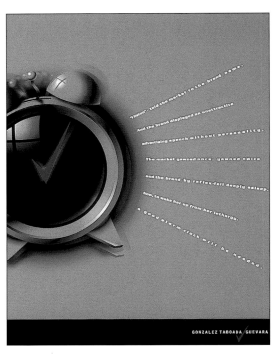

SPAIN

FINALIST, SINGLE
CP COMUNICACION
MADRID

CLIENT CANAL +
CREATIVE DIRECTOR
Gonzalo Figari
COPYWRITER Gonzalo Figari
ART DIRECTOR Chema Bernard/
Ruben Perez
PHOTOGRAPHER Still Life/
Madrid

ARGENTINA

FINALIST, SINGLE
GONZALEZ TABOADA/GUEVARA
BUENOS AIRES

CREATIVE DIRECTOR Guillermo Gonzalez Taboada
COPYWRITER Guillermo Gonzalez Taboada
ART DIRECTOR Alberto Sosa
ILLUSTRATOR Alberto Sosa

ARGENTINA

FINALIST, SINGLE

OGILVY & MATHER ARGENTINA
BUENOS AIRES

CREATIVE DIRECTOR Carlos Torregrosa
COPYWRITER Fernando Belloti
ART DIRECTOR Carlos Torregrosa

ARGENTINA

FINALIST, SINGLE

McCANN-ERICKSON ARGENTINA
BUENOS AIRES

CREATIVE DIRECTOR Sergio Cocu
COPYWRITER Ariel Gil/Daniel Alfieri
ART DIRECTOR Pablo Enriquez/Diego Tuya

ARGENTINA

FINALIST, SINGLE

LAUTREC NAZCA SAATCHI & SAATCHI
BUENOS AIRES

CLIENT Toyota
CREATIVE DIRECTOR Juan Cravero
COPYWRITER Sebastian Castaneda
ART DIRECTOR Maureen Hufnagel
PHOTOGRAPHER Ackerman/Buenos Aires
ILLUSTRATOR Pablo Romanos/Buenos Aires

SEE PAGE 222

ARGENTINA

FINALIST, SINGLE

RATTO/BBDO S.A.
BUENOS AIRES

CLIENT NIKE S.A.
CREATIVE DIRECTOR Juan Manuel Ricciarelli/
Joaquin Molla
COPYWRITER Joaquin Molla
ART DIRECTOR Juan Manuel Ricciarelli
PHOTOGRAPHER Carlos Mainardi

CORPORATE IMAGE **47**

www.swatch.com

BRAZIL

FINALIST, SINGLE

YOUNG & RUBICAM BRASIL
SAO PAULO

CREATIVE DIRECTOR Alexandre Gama/
Atila Francucci
COPYWRITER Erlon Goulart
ART DIRECTOR Erlon Goulart

Stasera la ricerca e la musica avranno grandi sostenitori.

Ecco un concerto che riscuoterà più di un semplice applauso. La musica che ascolteremo questa sera porterà alla ricerca i fondi di cui ha bisogno. Per farlo servirà l'impegno di una grande orchestra. Servirà l'impegno di grandi interpreti. Servirà l'impegno di grandi sostenitori.

ITALY

FINALIST, SINGLE

VERBA SRL.
MILAN

CLIENT Autogerma
CREATIVE DIRECTOR Enrico Bonomini/
Francesco Emiliani
COPYWRITER Dario Alesani
ART DIRECTOR Umberto Mauri
PHOTOGRAPHER Jacopo Cima

Two HEARTS
PERSONAL INTRODUCTION SERVICES SPECIALIZED IN THIRD AGERS.
PHONE: (043) 225 1308

BRAZIL

FINALIST, SINGLE

YOUNG & RUBICAM BRASIL
SAO PAULO

CLIENT Two Hearts Matrimony Agency for Third Age
CREATIVE DIRECTOR Atila Francucci
COPYWRITER Sideny Araujo/Marcos Dyonisio
ART DIRECTOR Sidney Araujo

URUGUAY

SILVER WORLDMEDAL

CORPORACION/THOMPSON

MONTEVIDEO

Client   Image Bank
CREATIVE DIRECTOR   Manuel Techera/
Marco Caltieri
COPYWRITER   Manuel Techera/
Marco Caltieri
ART DIRECTOR   Manuel Techera/
Marco Caltieri
PHOTOGRAPHER   Legum

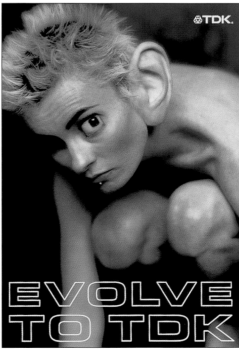

AUSTRALIA

FINALIST, CAMPAIGN

BELGIOVANE WILLIAMS MACKAY

ULTIMO

CLIENT   TDK Australia
CREATIVE DIRECTOR   Rob Belgiovane
COPYWRITER   Rob Belgiovane
ART DIRECTOR   Phil Atkinson
PHOTOGRAPHER   Alister Clark/
Peter Schmidt
DESIGNER/DESIGN   Pulse Design

BELGIUM

FINALIST, CAMPAIGN

BOZELL BRUSSELS

BRUSSELS

CLIENT Chrysler
CREATIVE DIRECTOR Pavone Gerardo
COPYWRITER Alasdhair MacGregor Hastie
ART DIRECTOR John Scully/Joel Lafontaine

BRAZIL

FINALIST, CAMPAIGN

F/NAZCA SAATCHI & SAATCHI

SAO PAULO

CLIENT Research Institute
CREATIVE DIRECTOR Fabio Fernandes
COPYWRITER Eduardo Lima
ART DIRECTOR Luciano Santos
PHOTOGRAPHER Keystone

GERMANY

FINALIST, CAMPAIGN

SPRINGER & JACOBY WERBUNG GMBH
HAMBURG

CLIENT   Daimler Chrysler AG
CREATIVE DIRECTOR   Kurt-Georg Dieckert/
Stefan Schmidt/David Vawter
COPYWRITER   Thomas Chudalla
ART DIRECTOR   Christina Petrich
PHOTOGRAPHER   Hubertus Hamm

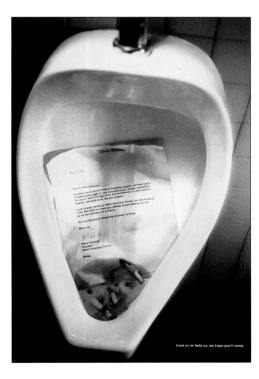

CANADA

FINALIST, CAMPAIGN

TBWA CHIAT/DAY
TORONTO, ONTARIO

CREATIVE DIRECTOR   Duncan Bruce
COPYWRITER   Joe Musicco
ART DIRECTOR   Nathan Montieth
PHOTOGRAPHER   Shin Sugino/
Toronto

SPAIN

GOLD WORLDMEDAL, SINGLE

RUIZ NICOLI

MADRID

CLIENT Vichy/Sliming Gel
CREATIVE DIRECTOR Ana Hidalgo/
Pablo Palazon/Fernando Cerro
COPYWRITER Pablo Palazon
ART DIRECTOR Fernando Cerro

BRAZIL

FINALIST, SINGLE

GIOVANNI, FCB

RIO DE JANIERO

CLIENT Phillips Dental Cream
CREATIVE DIRECTOR Adilson Xavier/ Cristina Amorin
COPYWRITER Adilson Xavier/Felipe Rodrigues
ART DIRECTOR Cristina Amorin
PHOTOGRAPHER Meca

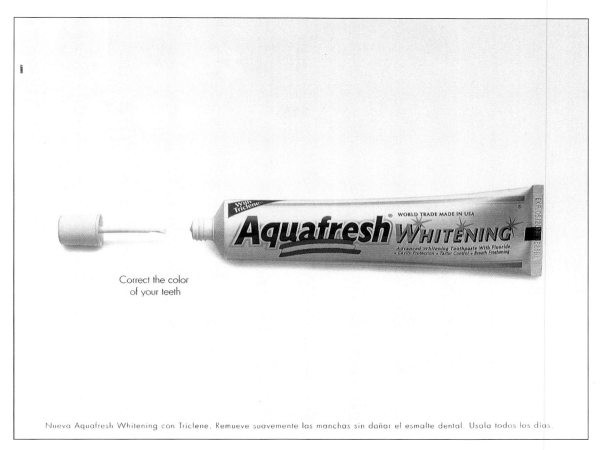

Correct the color
of your teeth

Nueva Aquafresh Whitening con Triclene. Remueve suavemente las manchas sin dañar el esmalte dental. Usala todos los días.

CHILE

BRONZE WORLDMEDAL, SINGLE
GREY CHILE
SANTIAGO

CREATIVE DIRECTOR Calu Sarroca/Victor Mora
COPYWRITER Gabriela Neira
ART DIRECTOR Victor Mora
PHOTOGRAPHER Eseis/Santiago
ILLUSTRATOR Victor Mora
OTHER Patricia Bustos (Agency Producer)

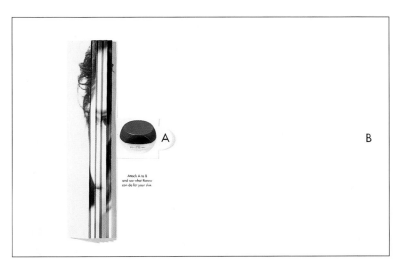

BRAZIL

FINALIST, SINGLE
DPZ PROPAGANDA
SAO PAULO

CLIENT Renew
CREATIVE DIRECTOR Francesc Petit/Carlos
Silverio
COPYWRITER Rui Branquinho
ART DIRECTOR Denise Vendruscolo
PHOTOGRAPHER Tony Stone/Bco. Imagem

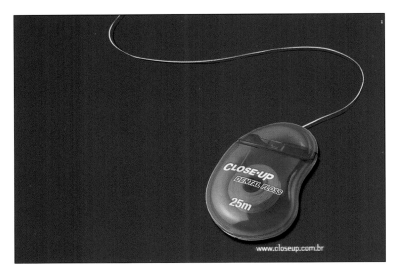

BRAZIL

FINALIST, SINGLE
J. WALTER THOMPSON PUBLIC.
SAO PAULO

CLIENT   Close-Up
CREATIVE DIRECTOR   Andre Pinho
COPYWRITER   Rinaldo Ferrarezi
ART DIRECTOR   Rinaldo Ferrarezi
PHOTOGRAPHER   Generico

VIETNAM

FINALIST, SINGLE
SAATCHI & SAATCHI VIETNAM
HO CHI MINH CITY

CREATIVE DIRECTOR   Mike Sands
COPYWRITER   Paul Vincent Ewen
ART DIRECTOR   Mike Sands/Le Duc Thang
PHOTOGRAPHER   Sebastian Tan/Singapore
OTHER   Hoang Thi Mai Huong/
Phan Hoang Quynh Giao (Translation)

BRAZIL

FINALIST, SINGLE
STANDARD OGILVY & MATHER
SAO PAULO

CLIENT   Baby Dove Soap
CREATIVE DIRECTOR   Camila Franco
COPYWRITER   Rubens Filho
ART DIRECTOR   Teresa Vidigal Guarita

LEBANON

FINALIST, SINGLE
TMI BEIRUT
BIERUT

CLIENT   Schick
CREATIVE DIRECTOR   Georges Joujou
COPYWRITER   Fady Chamaa
ART DIRECTOR   Georges Joujou
PHOTOGRAPHER   Roger Moukarzel

ARGENTINA
FINALIST, SINGLE
YOUNG & RUBICAM
BUENOS AIRES

CLIENT Tulipan
CREATIVE DIRECTOR Pablo Del Campo/
Chanel Basualdo
COPYWRITER Diego Livachoff/Santiago Lucero
ART DIRECTOR Chanel Basualdo
PHOTOGRAPHER Daniel Maestri/Buenos Aires

MEXICO
FINALIST, SINGLE
YOUNG & RUBICAM MEXICO
MEXICO
CLIENT Colgate Palmolive
CREATIVE DIRECTOR Yuri Alvarado
COPYWRITER Yuri Alvarado
ART DIRECTOR Mauricio Castillo
PHOTOGRAPHER Enrique Segarra/Mexico
OTHER Enrique Laguardia Longega
(Vice President & Director of Creative Services)

PORTUGAL
FINALIST, CAMPAIGN
BATES PORTUGAL
LISBOA
CLIENT Artur Barros' Hairdresser
CREATIVE DIRECTOR Pedro Ferreira/
Judite Mota
COPYWRITER Claudia Cristovao
ART DIRECTOR Joao Roque
PHOTOGRAPHER Carlos Ramos/
Paulo Andrade/Lisbon

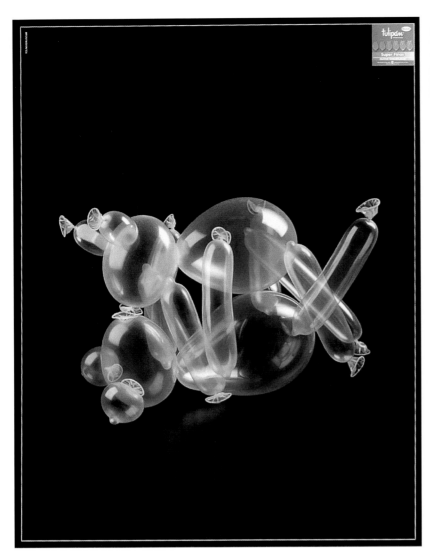

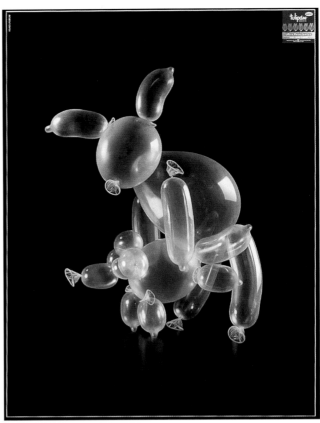

ARGENTINA

SILVER WORLDMEDAL, CAMPAIGN

YOUNG & RUBICAM
BUENOS AIRES

CREATIVE DIRECTOR Pablo Del Campo/Chanel Basualdo
COPYWRITER S.Lucero/D.Livachoff
ART DIRECTOR Chanel Basualdo
PHOTOGRAPHER Daniel Maestri/Buenos Aires

SPAIN

FINALIST, CAMPAIGN

McCANN-ERICKSON
BARCELONA

CLIENT L'Oreal
CREATIVE DIRECTOR Umberto Franca
COPYWRITER Alex Ripolles/Sergi
PHOTOGRAPHER Enric Aromi

BRAZIL

BRONZE WORLDMEDAL, CAMPAIGN
COLUCCI PROPAGANDA
SAO PAULO

CLIENT Phytoervas Shampoo
CREATIVE DIRECTOR Adriana Cury
COPYWRITER Ana Clelia Quarto
ART DIRECTOR Eric Sulzer
PHOTOGRAPHER Paulo Mancini

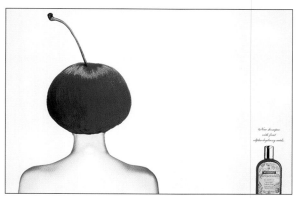

CRAFTS/HOBBIES

JAPAN

FINALIST, CAMPAIGN
DENTSU, INC.
TOKYO

CLIENT Camera
CREATIVE DIRECTOR Masaharu Nakano
COPYWRITER Thom Vanderklipp
ART DIRECTOR Hajime Kaneko/
Kazuyoshi Okuyama/Yuke Fujita
PHOTOGRAPHER Yoshiharu Asayama/
Norito Yoshimura

ENTERTAINMENT PROMOTION

USA

GOLD WORLDMEDAL, SINGLE
IKON CREATIVE
CULVER CITY, CA

CLIENT Sony Pictures Entertainment Services/
Playa Del Rey, CA
CREATIVE DIRECTOR Dana Precious/
Martin Gueulette
COPYWRITER Cari Abraham
ART DIRECTOR Hector Rojas

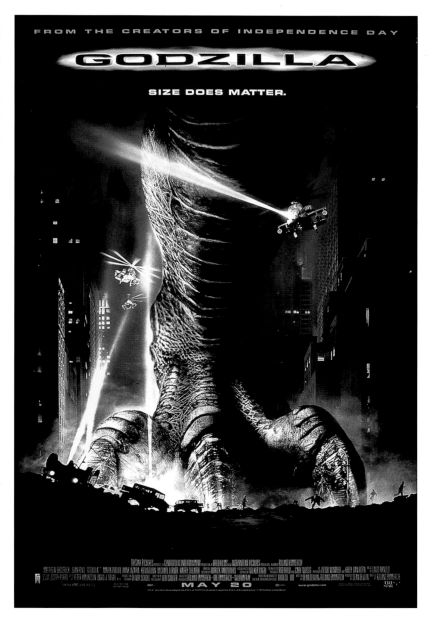

USA

FINALIST, SINGLE
BBDO CHICAGO
CHICAGO, IL

CLIENT: The Rock & Roll Hall of Fame
CREATIVE DIRECTOR Steve Dusenberry
COPYWRITER Derek Sherman
ART DIRECTOR Andy Mamott

JAPAN

PICTO, INC.
OSAKA

ART DIRECTOR Hiroyuki Yamamoto
ILLUSTRATOR Masahiro Fukushima/Osaka
ADVERTISING AGENCY Harpers Planning, Inc./Osaka

THE RED BOOK
ON BRANDS.

(How to build succesful brands)
- *Luis Bassat* -

SPAIN

BASSAT OGILVY & MATHER
BARCELONA

CLIENT The Red Book On Brands
CREATIVE DIRECTOR Oscar Pla
ART DIRECTOR Oscar Pla/Alex Lazaro
PHOTOGRAPHER A. G. Photostock/Horrillo

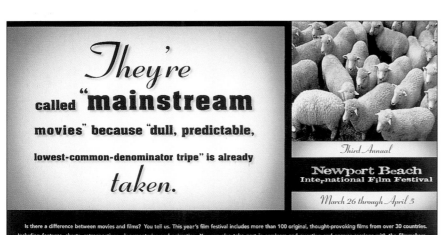

USA

BOZELL WORLDWIDE
COSTA MESA, CA

CLIENT Newport Beach International Film Festival
CREATIVE DIRECTOR Scott Montgomery
COPYWRITER Lauren Gold
ART DIRECTOR Eric Spiegler

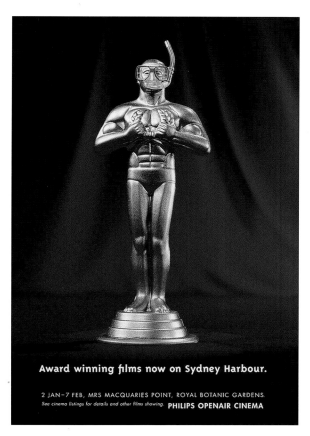

Award winning films now on Sydney Harbour.

2 JAN–7 FEB, MRS MACQUARIES POINT, ROYAL BOTANIC GARDENS.
See cinema listings for details and other films showing. **PHILIPS OPENAIR CINEMA**

AUSTRALIA

FINALIST, SINGLE

CWFS McCANN
NORTH SYDNEY

CLIENT Phillips Open Air Cinema
COPYWRITER Hugh Fitzhardinge
ART DIRECTOR Grant Foster/Sam Simper
PHOTOGRAPHER Andrew Furlong
OTHER Bridget Lenehan (Typographer)

L.A. Summer Film Festival

SINGAPORE

FINALIST, SINGLE

DENTSU, YOUNG & RUBICAM
SINGAPORE

CLIENT L.A. Summer Film Festival
CREATIVE DIRECTOR Patrick Low
COPYWRITER Robert Gaxiola
ART DIRECTOR Jeanie Tan
PHOTOGRAPHER Teo Studio/Singapore

BATTLE OF THE BANDS AT CHIJMES,
THE FORMER CONVENT OF THE HOLY INFANT JESUS.
FOR DETAILS, CALL 3398873.
·C·H·I·J·M·E·S·

SINGAPORE

FINALIST, SINGLE

DMB&B SINGAPORE
SINGAPORE

CLIENT Chijmes
CREATIVE DIRECTOR Curt Detweiler
COPYWRITER Case Deenadayalan
ART DIRECTOR Le Gill
PHOTOGRAPHER The Shooting Gallery/
Wishing Well

Wollen Sie jetzt wirklich einen Orgasmus haben?

OK   Abbrechen   Hilfe

Neue Techniken unter 0-2000°.

GERMANY

FINALIST, SINGLE

**KNSK, BBDO WERBEAGENTUR
GMBH**
HAMBURG

CLIENT EXPO 2000 Hannover,
World Exposition
CREATIVE DIRECTOR Mirko Vasata
COPYWRITER Britta Poetzsch/
Kai Flemming
ART DIRECTOR Michael Barche

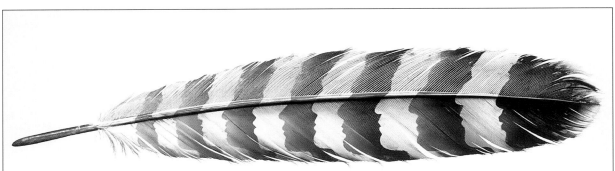

SOUTH AFRICA
FINALIST, SINGLE
OGILVY & MATHER RIGHTFORD
SEARLE-TRIPP & MAKIN
GAUTENG

CLIENT Gay & Lesbian Film Festival
CREATIVE DIRECTOR Brett Wild
COPYWRITER John Smeddle
ART DIRECTOR Sergio Lacueva

JAPAN
FINALIST, SINGLE
PICTO, INC.
OSAKA

ART DIRECTOR Hiroyuki Yamamoto
PHOTOGRAPHER Yasushi Nakamura/Osaka

JAPAN
FINALIST, SINGLE
PICTO, INC.
OSAKA

ADVERTISING AGENCY Narasaki, Inc./Osaka
ART DIRECTOR Hiroyuki Yamamoto
PHOTOGRAPHER Hiroyuki Yamamoto/Osaka
ILLUSTRATOR Takeru Ogawa/Osaka

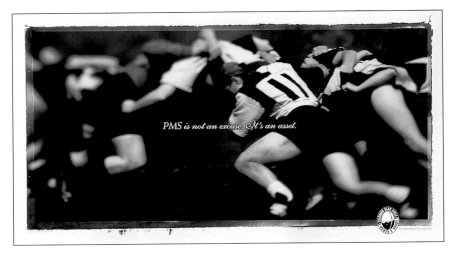

USA

FINALIST, SINGLE

VALENTINE RADFORD
KANSAS CITY, MO

CLIENT Colorado Olde Girls Women's Rugby
CREATIVE DIRECTOR Bob Simon
ART DIRECTOR Trevor Williams
PHOTOGRAPHER Ron Berg

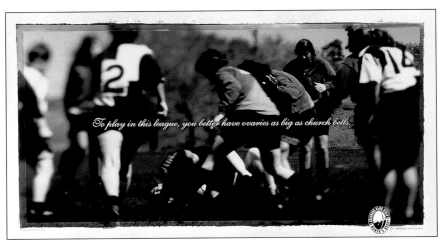

USA

FINALIST, SINGLE

VALENTINE RADFORD
KANSAS CITY, MO

CLIENT Colorado Olde Girls Women's Rugby
CREATIVE DIRECTOR Bob Simon
COPYWRITER Kevin Conard
ART DIRECTOR Trevor Williams
PHOTOGRAPHER Ron Berg

USA

FINALIST, SINGLE

YOUNG & RUBICAM MIAMI
MIAMI, FL

CLIENT Little Cuban Museum
CREATIVE DIRECTOR Armando Hernandez
COPYWRITER Armando Hernandez
ART DIRECTOR Armando Hernandez

No jocks allowed.

USA

GOLD WORLDMEDAL, CAMPAIGN
VALENTINE RADFORD
KANSAS CITY, MO
CLIENT   Colorado Olde Girls Women's Rugby
CREATIVE DIRECTOR   Bob Simon
ART DIRECTOR   Trevor Williams
PHOTOGRAPHER   Ron Berg

Please allow .43 seconds for delivery.

ROGER CLEMENS' FASTBALL

BRING IT ON. 341-1234

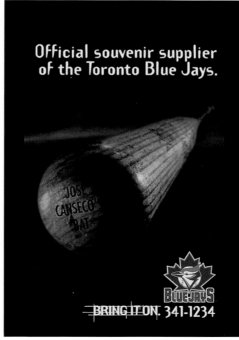

Official souvenir supplier of the Toronto Blue Jays.

JOSE CANSECO'S BAT

BRING IT ON. 341-1234

CANADA

FINALIST, CAMPAIGN
BENSIMON BYRNE DMB&B
TORONTO, ONTARIO

CLIENT   Baseball Team
CREATIVE DIRECTOR   Peter Byrne/
Gerry Monsier
COPYWRITER   Curtis Dufrense
ART DIRECTOR   Amy Morrison
PHOTOGRAPHER   Phillip Rostron

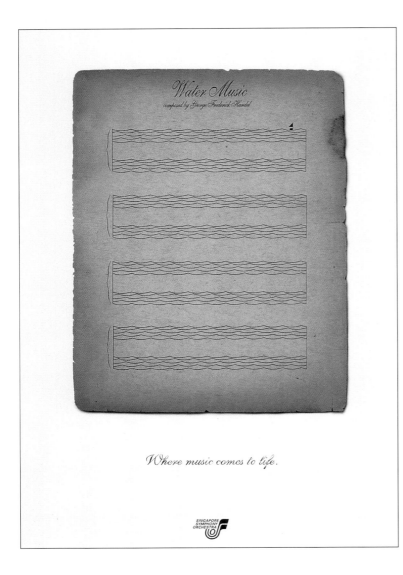

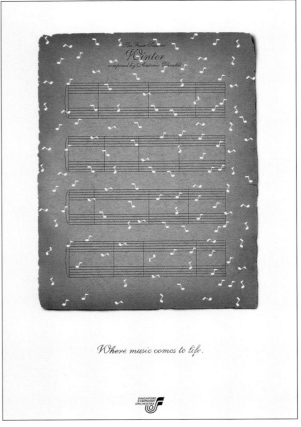

SINGAPORE

SILVER WORLDMEDAL, CAMPAIGN
EURO RSCG PARTNERSHIP
SINGAPORE

CLIENT   Singapore Symphony Orchestra
CREATIVE DIRECTOR   Jeremy Rawle
COPYWRITER   Rambhagat Kapoor
ART DIRECTOR   Keith Loell

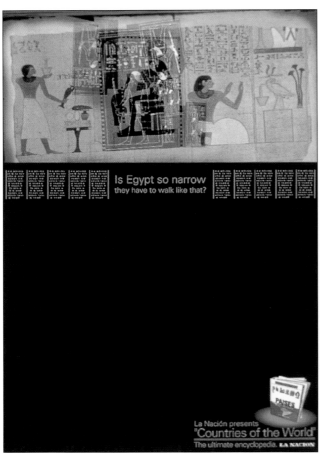

ARGENTINA

FINALIST, CAMPAIGN
VEGAOLMOSPONCE
BUENOS AIRES

CLIENT   Encyclopedia Countries of
The World/La
CREATIVE DIRECTOR   F. Vega Olmos/
H. Ponce/Juarez
COPYWRITER   Hernan Gonzalez
ART DIRECTOR   Hernan Damilano

SPAIN
SILVER WORLDMEDAL, SINGLE
TIEMPO/BBDO
BARCELONA

CLIENT
Ruffles Hot Chili Flavor
CREATIVE DIRECTOR
Siscu Molina
COPYWRITER Siscu Molina
ART DIRECTOR Jordi Comas
PHOTOGRAPHER
Leandre Escorsell
OTHER
Ferran Ramon-Cortes
(Account Director)

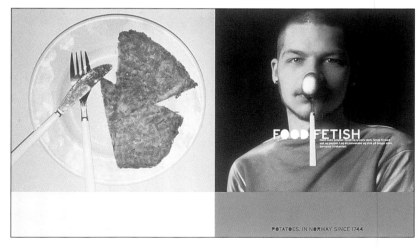

USA

FINALIST, SINGLE
CRAMER-KRASSELT
MILWAUKEE, WI

CLIENT Reddi-wip
CREATIVE DIRECTOR Mike Bednar
COPYWRITER Adam Albrecht
ART DIRECTOR Dan Koel
PHOTOGRAPHER Steve Bronstein/New York

NORWAY

FINALIST, SINGLE
BOLD ADVERTISING
OSLO

COPYWRITER Ragnar Roksvag
ART DIRECTOR Stephanie Dumont
PHOTOGRAPHER Liz Collins/Lars Botten

WEIL MÄNNER IMMER NUR DAS EINE WOLLEN.

agrarfrost
GERMANY

BESSER ISS DAS

GERMANY

BRONZE WORLDMEDAL, SINGLE
TBWA DEUTSCHLAND
HAMBURG

CLIENT RS Markenvertrieb GmbH
CREATIVE DIRECTOR Uwe Gluesing/Thomas Kurzawski
COPYWRITER Peter Zepp
ART DIRECTOR Katja Kroger/Andrea Gritzke
PHOTOGRAPHER Rolf Ozipka

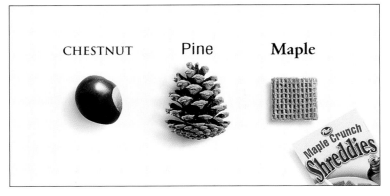

CANADA

FINALIST, SINGLE
BBDO CANADA
TORONTO, ONTARIO

CLIENT Maple Crunch Shreddies Cereal
CREATIVE DIRECTOR Michael McLaughlin
COPYWRITER Rob Tait
ART DIRECTOR Wally Krysciak
PHOTOGRAPHER Garth Grosjean

COLOMBIA

FINALIST, SINGLE
AGUAYO & ASOCIADOS
BOGOTA

CLIENT Chang & Chang
CREATIVE DIRECTOR Nelson Gonzalez
COPYWRITER Nelson Gonzalez
ART DIRECTOR Gabriel Escobar
PHOTOGRAPHER Mario Castillo

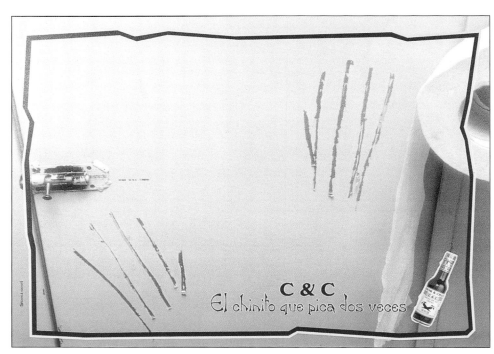

CANADA

FINALIST, SINGLE
BBDO CANADA
TORONTO, ONTARIO

CLIENT Shreddies Cereal
CREATIVE DIRECTOR Michael McLaughlin
COPYWRITER Rob Tait
ART DIRECTOR Wally Krysciak
PHOTOGRAPHER Garth Grosjean

USA
FINALIST, SINGLE
DIESTE & PARTNERS
DALLAS, TX
CLIENT Tabasco
CREATIVE DIRECTOR Aldo Quevedo
COPYWRITER Javier Guemes
ART DIRECTOR Chris Sendra

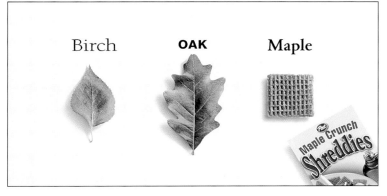

CANADA

FINALIST, SINGLE
BBDO CANADA
TORONTO, ONTARIO

CLIENT Shreddies Cereal
CREATIVE DIRECTOR Michael McLaughlin
COPYWRITER Rob Tait
ART DIRECTOR Wally Krysciak
PHOTOGRAPHER Garth Grosjean

FRANCE
FINALIST, SINGLE
DMB&B
NEUILLY

CLIENT MF Alimentaire
CREATIVE DIRECTOR Gerard Monot
COPYWRITER Herve Bourdon
ART DIRECTOR Christian Picard
PHOTOGRAPHER Jonathan Oakes

Panamá.

MRS BAIRD'S
Queda entre familia.

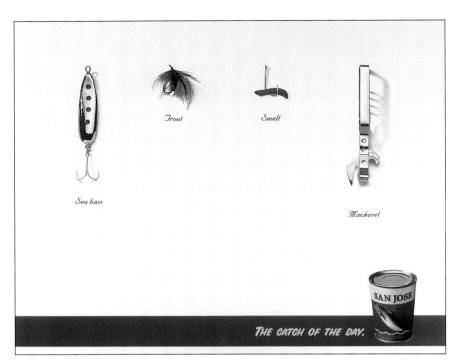

THE CATCH OF THE DAY.

USA

FINALIST, SINGLE
DIESTE & PARTNERS
DALLAS, TX

CLIENT Mrs. Bairds Bread
CREATIVE DIRECTOR Aldo Quevedo
COPYWRITER Javier Guemes
ART DIRECTOR Chris Sendra

CHILE

FINALIST, SINGLE
GREY CHILE
SANTIAGO

CLIENT San Jose
CREATIVE DIRECTOR Rodrigo Gomez/Cristian Samaniego
COPYWRITER Cristian Samaniego
ART DIRECTOR Enrique Belgeri
PHOTOGRAPHER Francisco Krause
ILLUSTRATOR Jaime Millan/Julio Wassaf
OTHER Patricia Bustos (Agency Producer)

When Susan definitely wants a horse.

ARGENTINA

FINALIST, SINGLE
J.WALTER THOMPSON ARGENTINA
BUENOS AIRES

CLIENT Nestle Argentina
CREATIVE DIRECTOR Diego De Pedro
COPYWRITER Yago Fandino
ART DIRECTOR L. Abad/E. Pizzorno

NORWAY

FINALIST, SINGLE
LEO BURNETT
OSLO

CLIENT Happy Meal
COPYWRITER Oystein Halvorsen
ART DIRECTOR Katrine Bervell/Gunhild Sandstad

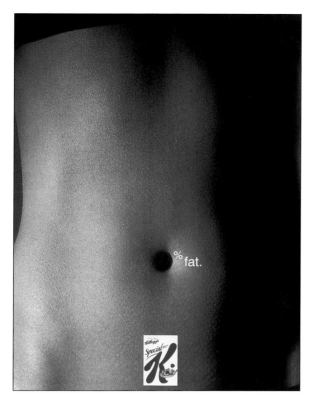

USA

FINALIST, SINGLE

LEO BURNETT SAN JUAN
SAN JUAN, PR

CLIENT Kellogg's Special K
CREATIVE DIRECTOR Carlos Mendez/
Maria del valle
COPYWRITER Maria del Valle
ART DIRECTOR Carlos Mendez
PHOTOGRAPHER Tony Hutchins/London

MEXICO

FINALIST, SINGLE

OGILVY & MATHER MEXICO
MEXICO

CLIENT Pronto gelatines
CREATIVE DIRECTOR L. Lamasney/C. Tourne
COPYWRITER S. Hernandez/Francisco Herran
ART DIRECTOR Adriana Robledo/Mariana Esteva
PHOTOGRAPHER Enrique Covarrubias/Mexico

FINLAND

FINALIST, SINGLE

**PALTEMAA HUTTUNEN SANTALA
TBWA**
HELSINKI

CLIENT Valio Cream
COPYWRITER Kari Eilola
ART DIRECTOR Jyrki Reinikka
ILLUSTRATOR Mikael Eriksson/Stockholm

FINLAND

FINALIST, SINGLE

SEK & GREY OY
HELSINKI

CLIENT Aura Blue Cheese
COPYWRITER Helena Tuomela
ART DIRECTOR Leena Periaho
PHOTOGRAPHER Kalle Helminez
OTHER Paula Rosn (Account Supervisor)

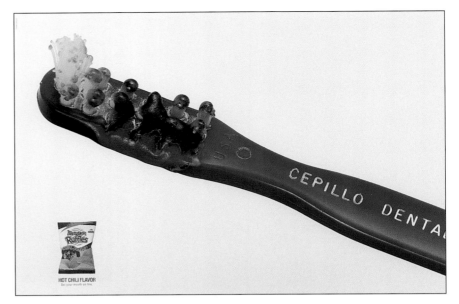

SPAIN
FINALIST, SINGLE
TIEMPO/BBDO
BARCELONA
CLIENT Pepsico/Ruffles
CREATIVE DIRECTOR Siscu Molina
COPYWRITER Siscu Molina
ART DIRECTOR Jordi Comas
PHOTOGRAPHER Leandre Escorsell
OTHER Ferran Ramon-Cortes (Account Director)

ARGENTINA
FINALIST, SINGLE
SOLANAS/GC
BUENOS AIRES
CLIENT Caterplan
CREATIVE DIRECTOR Charly Fiorentino/Federico Teubal
COPYWRITER Oscar Gramajo
ART DIRECTOR Maximiliano Sanchez Correa
PHOTOGRAPHER Gustavo Santos/Estudio Andon
ILLUSTRATOR Maxi/Pata
OTHER Jorge Arance (Production Manager)

We sincerely hope this depiction of fresh, flavorful walnuts makes up for
the tasteless picture on the following page.

USA
FINALIST, SINGLE
**YOUNG & RUBICAM-
SAN FRANCISCO**
SAN FRANCISCO, CA

CLIENT Diamond Walnuts
CREATIVE DIRECTOR Stephen Creet
COPYWRITER Fred Wickham
ART DIRECTOR Melinda Mettler
PHOTOGRAPHER Marshall Gordon

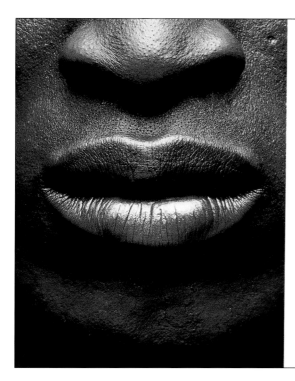

BRAZIL

GOLD WORLDMEDAL, CAMPAIGN
UPGRADE COMUNICACAO TOTAL
SAO PAULO

CLIENT Haagen Dazs
CREATIVE DIRECTOR Ricardo Braga
COPYWRITER Sergio Matsunaga (Jaspion)
ART DIRECTOR Carlos Nunes
PHOTOGRAPHER Willy Biondani/Sao Paulo

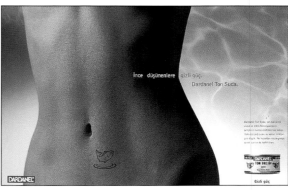

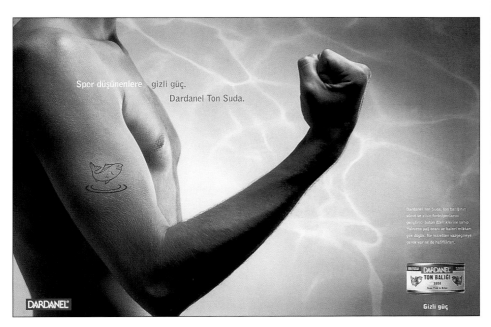

TURKEY

FINALIST, CAMPAIGN
3.KUSAK
ISTANBUL

CLIENT Dardanel Tuna Fish
CREATIVE DIRECTOR Mehmet Ali Turkmen/Dogan Yarici
COPYWRITER Alper Caniguz
ART DIRECTOR Murat Yilmaz
PHOTOGRAPHER Serdar Tanyeli/Istanbul

Cirio tomato sauce.
Everybody attacks.

Experts in tomato sauce prefer Cirio.

BRAZIL

SILVER WORLDMEDAL, CAMPAIGN
YOUNG & RUBICAM BRASIL
SAO PAULO

CLIENT   Cirio/Sauti Tomato Sauce
CREATIVE DIRECTOR   Alexandre Gama/Atila Francucci
COPYWRITER   Atila Francucci
ART DIRECTOR   Alexandre Soares
PHOTOGRAPHER   Mauricio Nahas/Sao Paulo

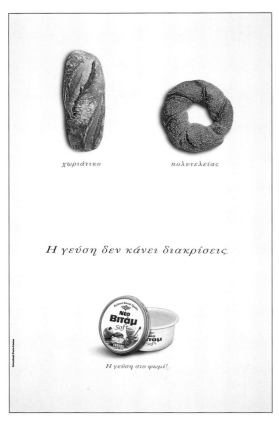

χωριάτικο   πολυτελείας

Η γεύση δεν κάνει διακρίσεις.

Η γεύση στο ψωμί!

άσπρο   μαύρο

Η γεύση δεν κάνει διακρίσεις.

Η γεύση στο ψωμί!

GREECE

FINALIST, CAMPAIGN
AMMIRATI PURIS LINTAS ATHENS
MAROUSI

CLIENT   Neo Vitam Soft - Margarine
CREATIVE DIRECTOR   Theodore Perdikakis
COPYWRITER   Athina Yiannakakis
ART DIRECTOR   Stelios Livanos
PHOTOGRAPHER   IMAGO

How do you weigh your self-worth?

And 12 and 14 and 16...

USA

FINALIST, CAMPAIGN
LEO BURNETT
CHICAGO, IL

CLIENT   Kellogg's Special K
CREATIVE DIRECTOR   Michael Conrad/Mara Fizdale
COPYWRITER   Kerry Keenan
ART DIRECTOR   Marianne Besch

HONG KONG

FINALIST, CAMPAIGN
BBDO HONG KONG LIMITED
HONG KONG

CLIENT   Knorr
CREATIVE DIRECTOR   L. Mee/T. Wong/P. Chan/
K.C. Tsang
COPYWRITER   Eddie Hui/Tony Wong
ART DIRECTOR   Wing Chow/Leslie Mee
PHOTOGRAPHER   Henry Wong, Studio K/
Hong Kong

Available in macaroni

Available in lasagna

CANADA

FINALIST, CAMPAIGN
COSSETTE - MONTREAL
MONTREAL, QUEBEC

CLIENT   Healthy Harvest Pasta
CREATIVE DIRECTOR   Hugues Choquette
COPYWRITER   Martin Rivard
ART DIRECTOR   Nicolas Quintal
ILLUSTRATOR   Studio de la Montagne
OTHER   Creative Vice-Presidents
J. Labelle/F. Forget

CANADA

FINALIST, CAMPAIGN
BBDO CANADA
TORONTO, ONTARIO

CLIENT Cool Whip
CREATIVE DIRECTOR
Michael McLaughlin/Stephen Creet
COPYWRITER Jill Higgins
ART DIRECTOR David Houghton
PHOTOGRAPHER Terry Collier
ILLUSTRATOR Paul Rivoche
OTHER Daryl Aitken
(Account Director)

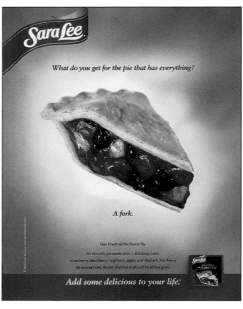

USA

FINALIST, CAMPAIGN
FOOTE CONE & BELDING
CHICAGO, IL

CLIENT Sara Lee
COPYWRITER John Claxton/
Rob White
ART DIRECTOR David Jones

If you can't have Alaska try Philadelphia.

Pure Indulgence

If you can't have Aspen try Philadelphia.

Pure Indulgence

AUSTRALIA
FINALIST, CAMPAIGN
J. WALTER THOMPSON
MELBOURNE, VICTORIA
CLIENT Spreadable Kraft Philadelphia
CREATIVE DIRECTOR Michael Gough
COPYWRITER Tim Shaw
ART DIRECTOR Odette Palmer
PHOTOGRAPHER Chris Budgeon
OTHER Christine McCraith (Typographer)

USA
FINALIST, CAMPAIGN
LEO BURNETT
CHICAGO, IL
CLIENT Pillsbury
CREATIVE DIRECTOR Bill Stone/
Tom Lunt
COPYWRITER Tom Lunt
ART DIRECTOR Bill Stone
PHOTOGRAPHER Chuck Shotwell

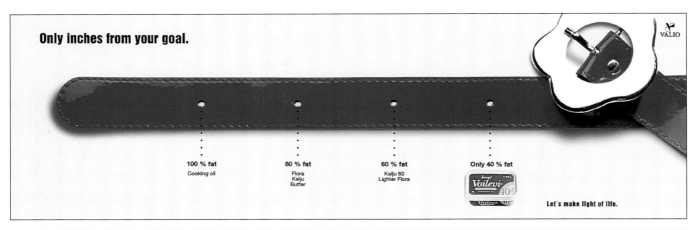

Only inches from your goal.

100 % fat
Cooking oil

80 % fat
Flora
Keiju
Butter

60 % fat
Keiju 60
Lighter Flora

Only 40 % fat

Let´s make light of life.

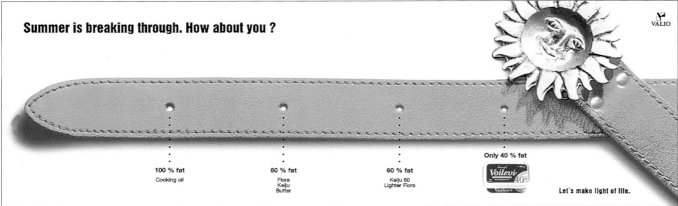

Summer is breaking through. How about you ?

100 % fat
Cooking oil

80 % fat
Flora
Keiju
Butter

60 % fat
Keiju 60
Lighter Flora

Only 40 % fat

Let´s make light of life.

FINLAND

BRONZE WORLDMEDAL, CAMPAIGN
CREATOR-GREY OY
HELSINKI

CLIENT Valio Oy
COPYWRITER Tuija Vesonto
ART DIRECTOR Tuula Karjalainen
PHOTOGRAPHER Ove Tammela/
Helsinki

Nudeln mit Biss **Bernbacher**

Original bayerische Hartweizenqualität. Beißen Sie zu!

Nudeln mit Biss **Bernbacher**

Das Geschmacks-Hai-Light erleben und gewinnen!

GERMANY

FINALIST, CAMPAIGN
**SERVICE PLAN MARKETING GMBH
WERBEAGENTUR**
MUNCHEN

CLIENT Bernbacher Hartweizennudeln
CREATIVE DIRECTOR Ewald Pusch
COPYWRITER Sebastian Schwarzer
ART DIRECTOR Kautrin Burkamp
ILLUSTRATOR Jan Birk

AUSTRALIA

BRONZE WORLDMEDAL, SINGLE
BAM SSB
EAST SYDNEY

CLIENT Australian Therapeutic Supplies
CREATIVE DIRECTOR Darryn Devlin
COPYWRITER Darryn Devlin
ART DIRECTOR Darryn Devlin
PHOTOGRAPHER Sean Izzard/Sydney

AUSTRALIA

FINALIST, SINGLE
BAM SSB
EAST SYDNEY

CLIENT Condom Kingdom
CREATIVE DIRECTOR Darryn Devlin
COPYWRITER Paul Fenton/Rob Martin-Murphy
ART DIRECTOR Paul Fenton
PHOTOGRAPHER Jonathan Clabburn
OTHER Paul Fenton/Rob Martin-Murphy (Writer)

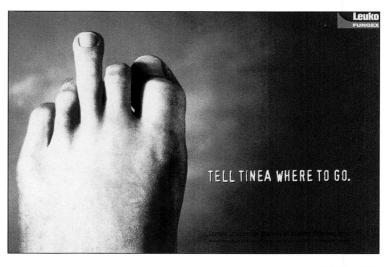

AUSTRALIA

FINALIST, SINGLE
CWFS McCANN
NORTH SYDNEY

CLIENT Fungex
CREATIVE DIRECTOR Madeleine Fairweather
COPYWRITER Hugh Fitzhardinge
ART DIRECTOR Grant Foster
PHOTOGRAPHER Ian Macpherson

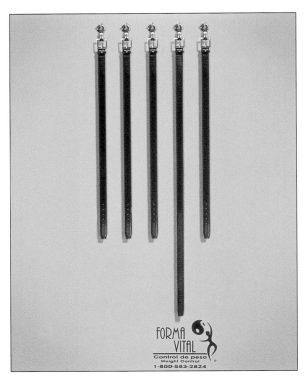

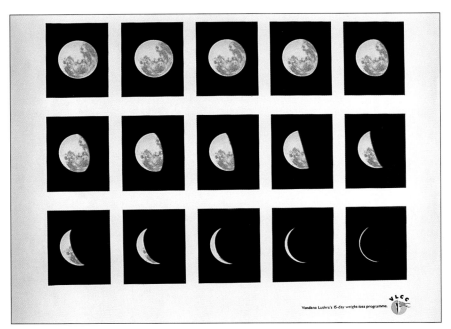

USA

FINALIST, SINGLE

DIESTE & PARTNERS
DALLAS, TX

CLIENT Forma Vital
CREATIVE DIRECTOR Aldo Quevedo/Javier Guemes
COPYWRITER Javier Guemes/Inak/Escudero
ART DIRECTOR Chris Sendra/Patty Marinez

INDIA

FINALIST, SINGLE

ENTERPRISE NEXUS COMMUNICATIONS PVT. LTD.
MUMBAI

CLIENT Vandana Luthra's Curls & Curves
CREATIVE DIRECTOR Mohammed Khan
COPYWRITER Abhijit Avasthi
ART DIRECTOR Raj Kamble
ILLUSTRATOR Shiram Mandale

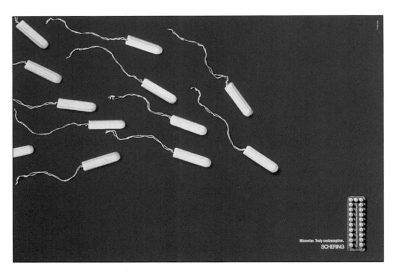

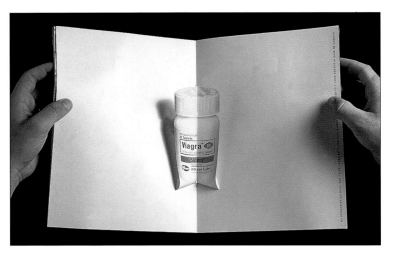

BRAZIL

FINALIST, SINGLE

F/NAZCA SAATCHI & SAATCHI
SAO PAULO, SP

CLIENT Contraceptive Microvlar
CREATIVE DIRECTOR Fabio Fernandes
COPYWRITER Eduardo Lima
ART DIRECTOR Luciano Santos
PHOTOGRAPHER Rodrigo Ribeiro

ARGENTINA

FINALIST, SINGLE

GREY ARGENTINA S.A.
BUENOS AIRES

CLIENT Pfizer Labs
CREATIVE DIRECTOR Carlos Perez/Martin Vinacur
COPYWRITER Gustavo Soria
ART DIRECTOR Gabriel Huici
PHOTOGRAPHER Sergio Assabi

MEXICO

FINALIST, SINGLE
LEO BURNETT MEXICO
MEXICO

CLIENT Pepto Bismol
CREATIVE DIRECTOR Martha Soler/Luis Barbosa
COPYWRITER Larissa Carpinteyro
ART DIRECTOR Juan Angel Rendon

CANADA

FINALIST, SINGLE
TBWA CHIAT/DAY
TORONTO, ONTARIO

CLIENT Life Brand
CREATIVE DIRECTOR Duncan Bruce
COPYWRITER Paul Evans
ART DIRECTOR Daniel Vendramin
PHOTOGRAPHER Philip Rostron

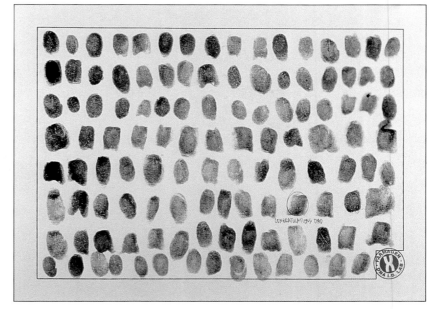

SPAIN

FINALIST, SINGLE
YOUNG & RUBICAM S.A.
MADRID

CLIENT Pharmagen Laboratory Of Genetics
CREATIVE DIRECTOR Jose Maria Pujol
COPYWRITER Jose Maria Pujol
ART DIRECTOR Cassio Moron

GERMANY

SILVER WORLDMEDAL, CAMPAIGN
LUDERS, BBDO
KOLN

CLIENT   Dr. Suwelack Skin & Health Care
CREATIVE DIRECTOR   K. Luders/J. Emonts-pohl
COPYWRITER   J. Strelis
ART DIRECTOR   H. Bergerhoff
PHOTOGRAPHER   Helmut Claus/Cologne

ARGENTINA

FINALIST, CAMPAIGN
GREY ARGENTINA S.A.
BUENOS AIRES

CLIENT   Pfizer Labs
CREATIVE DIRECTOR   Carlos Perez/Martin Vinacur
COPYWRITER   Gustavo Soria/Javier Altholz/
Diego Livachoff
ART DIRECTOR   Gabriel Huici/Geloso
PHOTOGRAPHER   Sergio Assabi
ILLUSTRATOR   Walter Becker

HOME ENTERTAINMENT

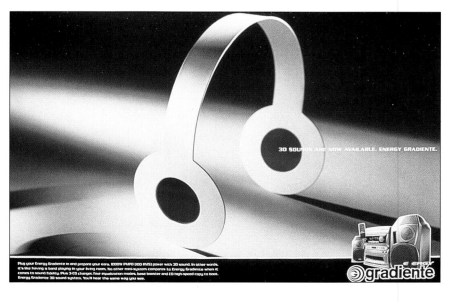

SPAIN

BRONZE WORLDMEDAL, SINGLE
TANDEM CAMPMANY GUASCH DDB, S.A.
BARCELONA

CLIENT Sony Handycam
CREATIVE DIRECTOR J. Rois/J. Krieger
COPYWRITER Evelyn Ribera
ART DIRECTOR J. Krieger

BRAZIL

FINALIST, CAMPAIGN
DPZ PROPAGANDA
SAO PAULO

CLIENT Energizer Max
CREATIVE DIRECTOR Jose Zaragoza/Ruy Lindenberg
COPYWRITER Sidney Braz
ART DIRECTOR Marcos Ribeiro
PHOTOGRAPHER Image Bank/Milenium

JAPAN

SILVER WORLDMEDAL, CAMPAIGN

INTERVISION INC.

TOKYO

CLIENT Sony Headphone MDR-G61
CREATIVE DIRECTOR Toshiro Fumizono
COPYWRITER Kohtaro Shimada
ART DIRECTOR Yutaka Murakoshi
PHOTOGRAPHER Taka Kobayashi/Tokyo

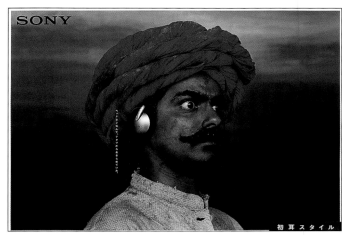

HOUSEHOLD APPLIANCES / FURNISHINGS

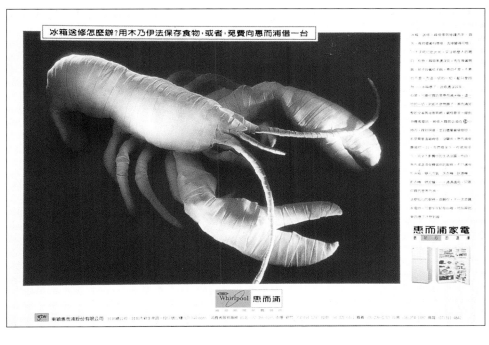

TAIWAN

FINALIST, SINGLE

AMMIRATI PURIS LINTAS TAIWAN

TAIPEI

CLIENT Whirlpool/After Service
CREATIVE DIRECTOR Murphy Chou
COPYWRITER Murphy Chou
ART DIRECTOR Alex Lin

BRAZIL

GOLD WORLDMEDAL, SINGLE
PUBLICIS-NORTON
SAO PAULO

CLIENT Rowenta
CREATIVE DIRECTOR Gilberto Dos Reis
COPYWRITER Wanderley Doro
ART DIRECTOR Jack Ronc
PHOTOGRAPHER Freitas/Sao Paulo

PARADE TAPIJT MOET JE VOELEN

THE NETHERLANDS

FINALIST, SINGLE
BBCW AMSTERDAM
AMSTERDAM

CLIENT Forbo Parade Carpet
CREATIVE DIRECTOR Donald Lopes Cardozo
COPYWRITER Donald Lopes Cardozo
ART DIRECTOR Richard Kuiper
PHOTOGRAPHER Ronald van Teunenbroek/ Amsterdam

SPAIN

SILVER WORLDMEDAL, SINGLE

FCB/TAPSA

MADRID

CLIENT

Roconsa Security Doors

CREATIVE DIRECTOR

Julian Zuazo

COPYWRITER   Oriol Villar

ART DIRECTOR

Yuri Alemany

PHOTOGRAPHER

Eduardo Diaz/Madrid

TRULLY COLD. SAMSUNG AIR CONDITIONER.

ARGENTINA

BRONZE WORLDMEDAL, SINGLE

VEGAOLMOSPONCE

BUENOS AIRES

CLIENT   Samsung Air Conditioner

CREATIVE DIRECTOR   F. Vega Olmos/H. Ponce

COPYWRITER   Luciano Bellelli

ART DIRECTOR   Pablo Izzi

PHOTOGRAPHER   Martin Sigal/Buenos Aires

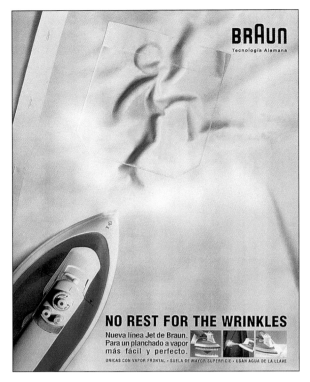

CHILE

FINALIST, SINGLE
McCANN-ERICKSON CHILE
SANTIAGO

CLIENT New Braun Jet Line/Braun
CREATIVE DIRECTOR Jaime Navarro
COPYWRITER Matias Garces
ART DIRECTOR Jaime Navarro
PHOTOGRAPHER Eseis/Santiago
ILLUSTRATOR Jaime Navarrro/Santiago

ARGENTINA

FINALIST, SINGLE
GREY ARGENTINA S.A.
BUENOS AIRES

CLIENT BGH Silent Air
CREATIVE DIRECTOR Carlos Perez/
Fernando Militerno
COPYWRITER Carolina Morano
ART DIRECTOR Fernando Militerno
PHOTOGRAPHER Millennium

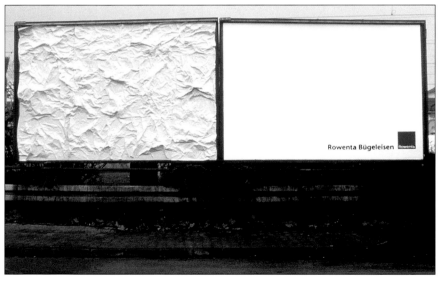

GERMANY

FINALIST, SINGLE
PUBLICIS WERBEAGENTUR GMBH
FRANKFURT

CLIENT Rowenta Iron
CREATIVE DIRECTOR Ljubomir Stoimenoff
COPYWRITER Jochen Leisinger
ART DIRECTOR Jochen Leisinger
GRAPHICS COMPANY Guido Masson

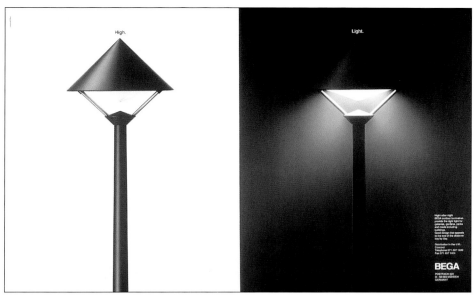

GERMANY

FINALIST, CAMPAIGN
LEONHARDT & KERN WERBUNG GMBH
STUTTGART

CLIENT BEGA Gantenbrink-Leuchten GmbH & Co
CREATIVE DIRECTOR Waldermar Meister
COPYWRITER Waldermar Meister
ART DIRECTOR Waldermar Meister
PHOTOGRAPHER Rolf Herkner

INDIA

FINALIST, CAMPAIGN
SSC&B LINTAS
MUMBAI

CLIENT Formica
CREATIVE DIRECTOR Namita Kuruvilla/
Vikram Gaikund
COPYWRITER Namita Kuruvilla
ART DIRECTOR Vikram Gaikwad

MEXICO

GOLD WORLDMEDAL, SINGLE
LOWE & PARTNERS
MEXICO CITY

CLIENT Polyform
CREATIVE DIRECTOR Norberto Plascencia
COPYWRITER Norberto Plascencia
ART DIRECTOR Rodrigo Munizaga/G. Hernandez
PHOTOGRAPHER Giancarlo Fiorenza
ILLUSTRATOR Arturo Cedillo

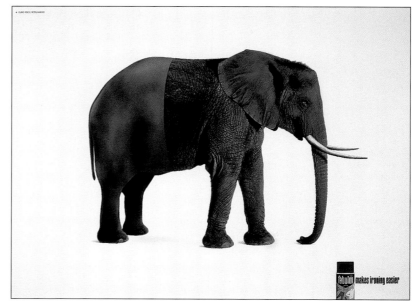

AUSTRALIA

FINALIST, SINGLE
EURO RSCG PARTNERSHIP
SYDNEY

CLIENT Reckitt & Colman
CREATIVE DIRECTOR Danny Higgins
COPYWRITER Julian Horton
ART DIRECTOR Simon Cox
PHOTOGRAPHER Electric Art/Sydney

PORTUGAL
SILVER WORLDMEDAL, SINGLE
BBDO PORTUGAL
LISBON
CLIENT   Whiskas/Effem Portugal
CREATIVE DIRECTOR   Jorge Teixeira
COPYWRITER   Vasco Condessa
ART DIRECTOR   Marco Dias
PHOTOGRAPHER   Miguel Fonseca Da Costa

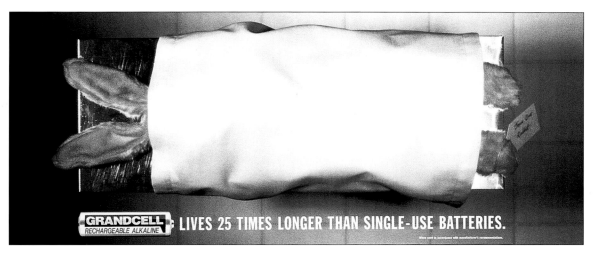

AUSTRALIA
BRONZE WORLDMEDAL, SINGLE
THE EDGE
VICTORIA
CLIENT   Grandcell Batteries
CREATIVE DIRECTOR   Stephen Fisher
COPYWRITER   Steve Wooster/Nick Weller
ART DIRECTOR   Steve Wooster/Stephen Fisher
PHOTOGRAPHER   Jaime MacFadyen

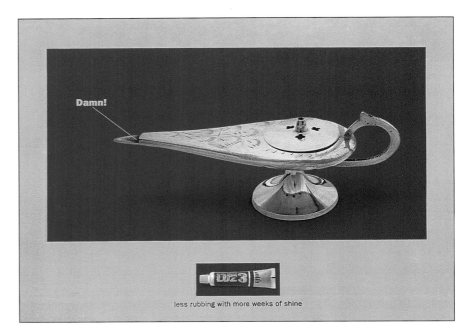

COLOMBIA

FINALIST, SINGLE

LOWE & PARTNERS /SSPM S.A.
BOGOTA

CREATIVE DIRECTOR H. Polar/J. Sokoloff/L. Correa
COPYWRITER Eduardo Vargas
ART DIRECTOR Lucho Correa
PHOTOGRAPHER Jorge Gamboa

ARGENTINA

FINALIST, SINGLE

RATTO/BBDO S.A.
BUENOS AIRES

CLIENT Alba S.A. - Albatros Double Line
CREATIVE DIRECTOR Daniel Gandini
COPYWRITER Ariel Dress
ART DIRECTOR Matias Aubi
PHOTOGRAPHER Sergio Belintende

CHILE

FINALIST, SINGLE

LOWE PORTA
SANTIAGO

CLIENT Talvox
CREATIVE DIRECTOR Kiko Carcavilla
COPYWRITER Kiko Carcavilla
ART DIRECTOR Alejandro Armstrong

ARGENTINA

FINALIST, SINGLE

PRAGMA/FCB
BUENOS AIRES

CLIENT Fuyi
COPYWRITER Esteban Seimandi
ART DIRECTOR Gaston Castanares

SPAIN

FINALIST, SINGLE

TBWA

BARCELONA

CLIENT Enervit
CREATIVE DIRECTOR Xavi Munill
COPYWRITER Xavi Munill
ART DIRECTOR Tomas Descals

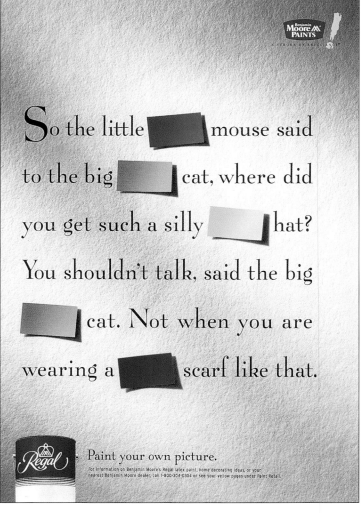

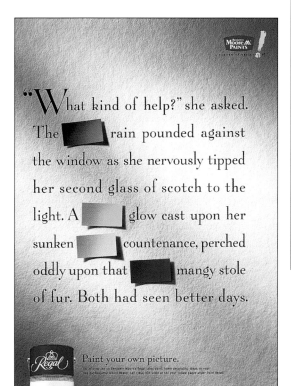

CANADA

FINALIST, CAMPAIGNE

COMMUNIQUE GROUP

TORONTO, ONTARIO

CLIENT Benjamin Moore Paint
CREATIVE DIRECTOR Bill Keenan
COPYWRITER Ron McDonald
ART DIRECTOR Clark Smith

MEDIA PROMOTION: PRINT

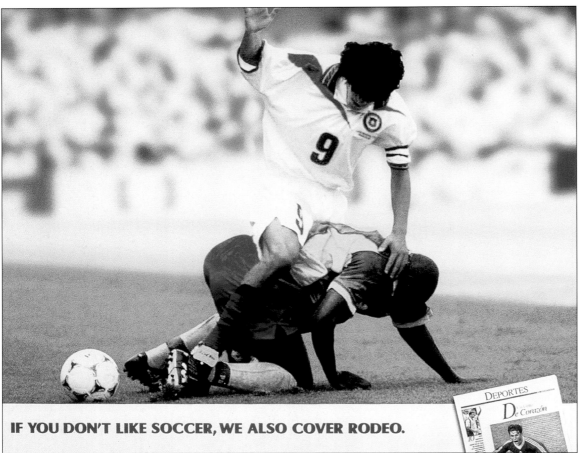

IF YOU DON'T LIKE SOCCER, WE ALSO COVER RODEO.

CHILE

BRONZE WORLDMEDAL, SINGLE
LEO BURNETT CHILE
SANTIAGO

CLIENT   El Grafico Magazine
CREATIVE DIRECTOR   Jaime Atria
COPYWRITER   Jaime Atria
ART DIRECTOR   Javier Ugarte

Hundreds of stars and just one wish: Peace.
To all our readers, its Christmas Greetings from Las Ultimas Noticias.

CHILE

FINALIST, SINGLE
BBDO CHILE
SANTIAGO

CREATIVE DIRECTOR   Claudio Bustamante
COPYWRITER   Claudio Bustamante
ART DIRECTOR   Ricardo Chavez
OTHER   Hernan Antillo

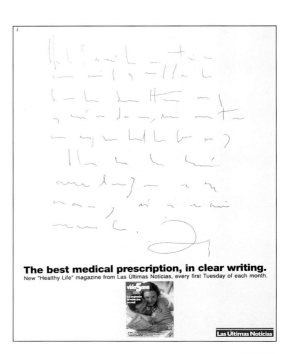

The best medical prescription, in clear writing.
New "Healthy Life" magazine from Las Últimas Noticias, every first Tuesday of each month.

CHILE

FINALIST, SINGLE
BBDO CHILE
SANTIAGO

CLIENT   Healthy Life
CREATIVE DIRECTOR   Claudio Bustamante
COPYWRITER   Claudio Bustamante
ART DIRECTOR   Ricardo Chavez
ILLUSTRATOR   Claudio Bustamante/Santiago
OTHER   Hernan Antillo

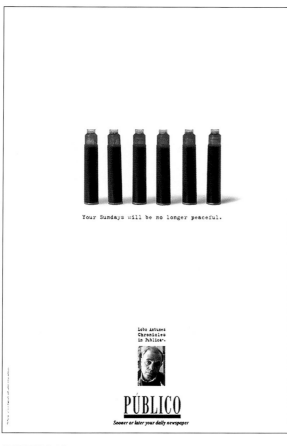

Your Sundays will be no longer peaceful.

Lobo Antunes
Chronicles
in Publico.

PÚBLICO
Sooner or later your daily newspaper

PORTUGAL
FINALIST, SINGLE
EURO RSCG
OEIRAS
CLIENT Jornal O Publico
CREATIVE DIRECTOR Paulo Monteiro
COPYWRITER Nuno Cardoso
ART DIRECTOR Rui Miguel
PHOTOGRAPHER Carlos Martins/Lisbon

BRAZIL
FINALIST, SINGLE
HEADS PROPAGANDA LTDA.
CURITIBA
CREATIVE DIRECTOR Jose Buffo
COPYWRITER Juliano Barcella
ART DIRECTOR Kleber Menezes
PHOTOGRAPHER Photomakers/Curitiba

GERMANY
FINALIST, SINGLE
KNSK, BBDO ADVERTISING AGENCY GMBH
HAMBURG
CLIENT Stern
CREATIVE DIRECTOR Beat Nageli/Wolfgang Sasse
COPYWRITER Kai Flemming/Stephan Garbe
ART DIRECTOR Jurgen Florenz/Rene Wold

Because fences
make
uncomfortable seats.

The
Economist

HONG KONG
FINALIST, SINGLE
OGILVY & MATHER ADVERTISING
HONG KONG
CLIENT The Economist
CREATIVE DIRECTOR John Weston
COPYWRITER John Weston
ART DIRECTOR Andrew Charles
OTHER Sarah Hale/Kara Cartin

COLOMBIA

FINALIST, SINGLE

LOWE & PARTNERS /SSPM S.A.
BOGOTA

CLIENT Revista Jet Set
CREATIVE DIRECTOR H. Polar/J.M.
Sokoloff/L. Correa
COPYWRITER Eduardo Vargas
ART DIRECTOR Ivan Onatra/L. Correa

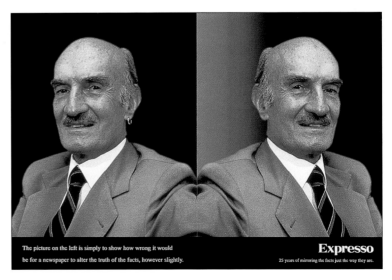

FINLAND

FINALIST, SINGLE

PALTEMAA HUTTUNEN SANTALA TBWA
HELSINKI

CLIENT Helsingin Sanomat - Newspaper
COPYWRITER Antti Einio/Markku Ronkko
PHOTOGRAPHER Markku Lahdesmaki/Los Angeles

PORTUGAL

FINALIST, SINGLE
W/PORTUGAL
LISBOA

CLIENT Newspaper O Independente
CREATIVE DIRECTOR Jaime Mourao-Ferreira
COPYWRITER Flavio Waiteman
ART DIRECTOR Giancarlo Ricci/Ricardo Bueno
PHOTOGRAPHER Joao Palmeiro/Lisbon

PORTUGAL

FINALIST, SINGLE
W/PORTUGAL
LISBOA

CLIENT Newspaper - Expresso
CREATIVE DIRECTOR Jaime Maurao-Ferreira
COPYWRITER Flavio Waiteman
ART DIRECTOR Ricardo Bueno

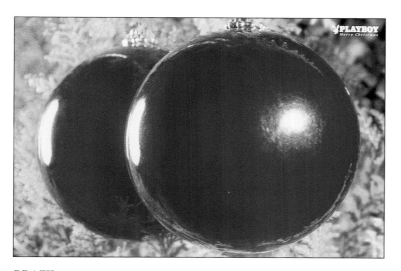

BRAZIL

FINALIST, SINGLE

YOUNG & RUBICAM BRASIL
SAO PAULO

CLIENT Corporate Playboy Magazine
CREATIVE DIRECTOR Alexandre Gama/
Atila Francucci
COPYWRITER Erlon Goulart
ART DIRECTOR Erlon Goulart
PHOTOGRAPHER Mario Fontes/Sao Paulo

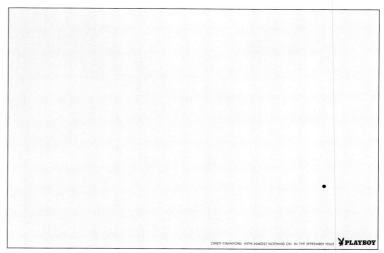

BRAZIL

FINALIST, SINGLE

YOUNG & RUBICAM BRASIL
SAO PAULO

CLIENT Playboy - Magazine
CREATIVE DIRECTOR Alexandre Gama
COPYWRITER Gustavo Gusmao
ART DIRECTOR Sidney Araujo

BRAZIL

FINALIST, CAMPAIGN

F/NAZCA SAATCHI & SAATCHI
SAO PAULO

CLIENT Magazine
CREATIVE DIRECTOR Fabio Fernandes
COPYWRITER Joao Livi
ART DIRECTOR Sergio Barros
PHOTOGRAPHER Mauricio Nahas

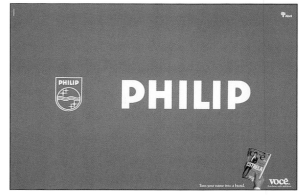

»D'you know what happens when a guy gets an erection? Medically speaking, an erection is nothing more than an acute build-up of blood. Which means it needs lots and lots of blood. Loads and loads, in fact. And obviously these huge amount of blood has to come from somewhere. The brain for example. You see? I told you I could give you a damn good reason why boys don't think with their heads when it comes to cheating on their girlfriends.«

Okay guys, trousers down: What boys really think about being faithful. Plus: a special book feature on the autumn's essential reading. It's all in the new YOUNG MISS. THE MONTHLY PICK ME UP.

GERMANY

SILVER WORLDMEDAL, CAMPAIGN

GRABARZ & PARTNER WERBEAGENTUR GMBH
HAMBURG

CLIENT   Young Miss Magazine
CREATIVE DIRECTOR   Ralf Heuel/Henner Kronenberg
COPYWRITER   Ralf Heuel
ART DIRECTOR   Nicola Fromm
PHOTOGRAPHER   Chon Choi

»I haven't slept for days now. I lie awake, gazing at the ceiling, unable to stop thinking about you. About how, when you and me wander round town, the people turn and stare. About how my boyfriend looks so jealous and my mom goes so pale whenever we are together. But I feel so very sure that you and me are meant for each other. After all, I am young and a girl. And you are a purple narrow-cord jacket with sequins and dark green buttons.«

GERMANY

FINALIST, CAMPAIGN

OGILVY & MATHER FRANKFURT
FRANKFURT

CLIENT   rtv magazine
CREATIVE DIRECTOR   Johannes Krempl
COPYWRITER   Johannes Krempl/Anna Kohlhaupt
ART DIRECTOR   Patrick They
ILLUSTRATOR   Fred Burg/Marc Oliver/Pierre Dalla Palma

Wer nah am Menschen ist, ist nah an der Wahrheit.

1 Von Michael Stoessinger und
2 Sebastian Lehmann und Gerhard Hagen
3 (Foto)
4
5 (...) »Ich kenne die Leute hier. Das
6 sind Menschen, mit denen du jahrelang
7 zusammengearbeitet hast. Und jetzt
8 triffst du sie schon morgens alkoholi-
9 siert. Aus lauter Scham grüßen die
10 dich nicht mal mehr.« (...) Da ist
11 nicht die Braune Armee Fraktion unter-
12 wegs, sondern es sind Tausende kleiner
13 Cliquen, die einen von der Öffentlich-
14 keit kaum wahrgenommenen Kampf führen
15 um die Disco, den Bahnhofsvorplatz,
16 den Parkplatz vor dem Supermarkt.
17 (...)

Stern-Redakteur Michael Stoessinger
hat den Umbruch im Osten zwischen '89
und '91 u.a. in Moskau und Leipzig
hautnah miterlebt. Volontär Sebastian
Lehmann ist Student der Henri-Nannen-
Journalistenschule.

Der Stern bewegt.

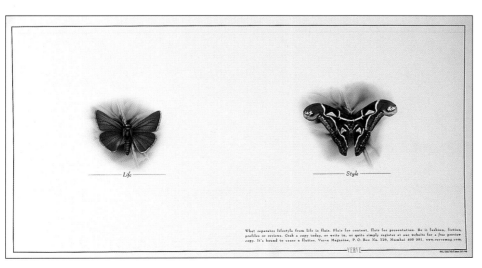

Wer verstehen will, muß fühlen können.

1 Von Teja Fiedler und
2 Pierre St. Jacques (Foto)
3
4 Wenn die Hölle einen irdischen
5 Vorposten hat, dann ist es die
6 Leichenhalle von Port-au-Prince
7 auf Haiti. Menschliche Kadaver,
8 nackt oder in Lumpen und in ver-
9 schiedenen Graden des Zerfalls,
10 liegen übereinandergestapelt wie
11 Sandsäcke. Trotz der tropischen
12 Hitze gibt es keine Kühlanlage.
13 Der Gestank ist entsetzlich.
14 Keine Zeichen von Mitgefühl bei
15 den Wärtern, obwohl die meisten
16 dieser Bündel aus Fleisch, Knochen
17 und Verwesung die Leichen von
18 Kindern sind. Inmitten des grauen-
19 haften Stillebens steht eine
20 Frau mit blonden Haaren und ver-
21 störten Gesicht. (...)

Stern-Korrespondent Teja Fiedler
bewegte die Stern-Leser mit seiner
Geschichte über Susan Scotts
Hilfsprojekt zu Spenden von über
90.000 Mark. »Hilferuf Haiti«,
Spendenkonto 22002000, Sparkasse
Warendorf, BLZ 40051475.

Der Stern bewegt.

GERMANY

BRONZE WORLDMEDAL, CAMPAIGN

KNSK, BBDO ADVERTISING AGENCY GMBH
HAMBURG

CLIENT Stern
CREATIVE DIRECTOR Beat Nageli/Wolfgang Sasse
COPYWRITER Kai Flemming
ART DIRECTOR Jurgen Florenz/Rene Wolf

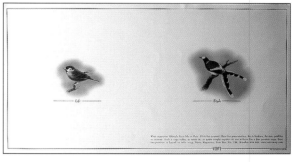

INDIA

FINALIST, CAMPAIGN

PSL ERICKSON
MUMBAI

CLIENT Verve Magazine
CREATIVE DIRECTOR C. Gangadharan/
Nalesh Patil
COPYWRITER C. Gangadharan
ART DIRECTOR Ajay Takalkar
ILLUSTRATOR Rajendra Vanmali/Mumbai

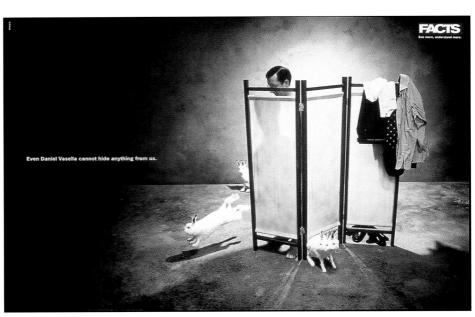

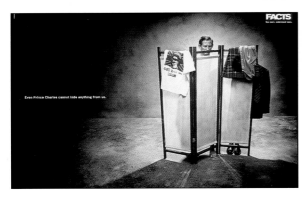

MEDIA PROMOTION   BROADCAST

USA

GOLD WORLDMEDAL, SINGLE
THE HISTORY CHANNEL
NEW YORK, NY
CREATIVE DIRECTOR Artie Scheff/
The History Channel
CREATIVE DIRECTOR Rick Beyer/Smash
ART DIRECTOR Kevin Grady/Smash
ADVERTISING AGENCY Smash/Boston
OTHER Deanne Josephson/David Corey/
Bob Hoffman/David Cianciarulo/
Lea Todisco/Amy Frith

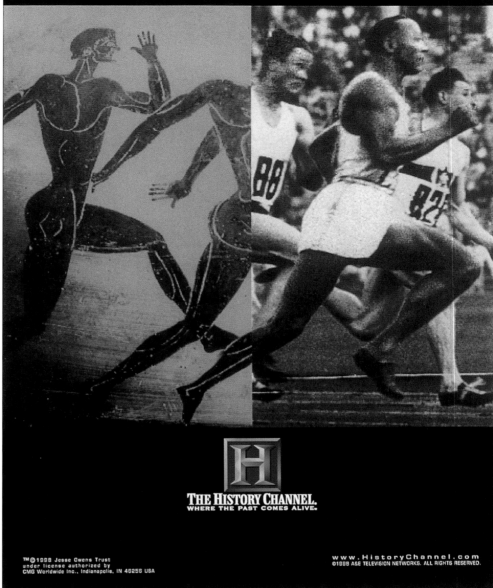

USA

FINALIST, CAMPAIGN
**INGALLS MORANVILLE
ADVERTISING**
SAN FRANCISCO, CA

CLIENT Infoseek
CREATIVE DIRECTOR
Rob Ingalls/
David Moranville
COPYWRITER
Jason Siciliano
ART DIRECTOR Peter Judd

Because Your World Changes Every Day

CNN

THE WORLD'S NEWS LEADER

USA

SILVER WORLDMEDAL, SINGLE
CNN
ATLANTA, GA

CREATIVE DIRECTOR Gregg Bauer
ILLUSTRATOR Ron Silvers/Boston
ADVERTISING AGENCY Zoom Design/Atlanta
OTHER Jennifer Boardman

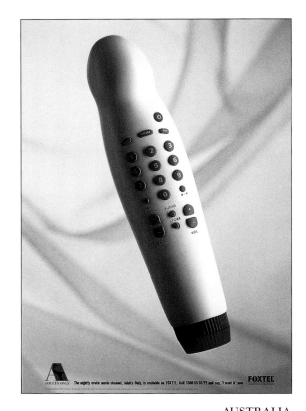

AUSTRALIA

FINALIST, SINGLE
WHYBIN LAWRENCE TBWA
PYRMONT

CLIENT Adult Channel
CREATIVE DIRECTOR Neil Lawrence
COPYWRITER Jon Skinner
ART DIRECTOR Christian Finucane
PHOTOGRAPHER Michael Corredore

MEXICO

BRONZE WORLDMEDAL, CAMPAIGN
LOWE & PARTNERS
MEXICO

CLIENT The Weather Channel
CREATIVE DIRECTOR Alfredo Ruiz
COPYWRITER Alfredo Ruiz
ART DIRECTOR Rodrigo Munizaga/
Gabriel Hernandez

SPAIN

FINALIST, SINGLE
CONTRAPUNTO
MADRID

CLIENT Pay TV Channel (NBA)
CREATIVE DIRECTOR Antonia Montero
COPYWRITER Rosa Garcia
ART DIRECTOR Gemma Guio

AUSTRALIA

FINALIST, SINGLE
BAM SSB
EAST SYDNEY

CLIENT SBS Television
CREATIVE DIRECTOR Darryn Devlin
ART DIRECTOR Darryn Devlin/Dave Heytman
PHOTOGRAPHER Julian Watt/Sydney
OTHER Rob Martin-Murphy (Writer)

AUSTRALIA

FINALIST, CAMPAIGN
BAM SSB
EAST SYDNEY

CLIENT SBS Television
CREATIVE DIRECTOR
Darryn Devlin
ART DIRECTOR Darryn Devlin/
Lisa Jelliffe/Dave Heytman
PHOTOGRAPHER Julian Watt/
Sydney
OTHER Ilana Einfeld/
Rob Martin-Murphy/
Lisa Jelliffe (Writer)

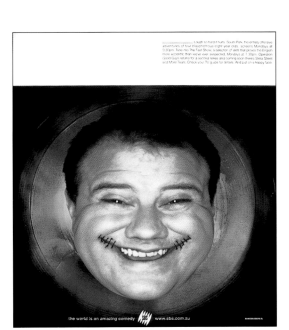

Soon, the sentence will come to an end.

DIRECTV arrives. Superior entertainment.

DIRECTV

Your eyes will be DIRECTV fans.

DIRECTV arrives. Superior entertainment.

DIRECTV

ARGENTINA

FINALIST, CAMPAIGN
J.WALTER THOMPSON ARGENTINA
BUENOS AIRES

CLIENT DirecTV
CREATIVE DIRECTOR Oscar Cerutti
COPYWRITER B. Bernardo/ M. Maggi/M. Corbelle
ART DIRECTOR Pablo Steinberg
ILLUSTRATOR Carlos Baragli

Larry's last chance to take home the woman he really wants

THE LARRY SANDERS SHOW
FOR YOUR EMMY CONSIDERATION IN ALL CATEGORIES HBO

USA

FINALIST, CAMPAIGN
PITTARD SULLIVAN
CULVER CITY, CA

CLIENT Larry Sander Show
CREATIVE DIRECTOR Ron Taft
COPYWRITER Ron Taft
PHOTOGRAPHER Marcelo Coelho/Los Angeles
OTHER Ron Taft (Designer)

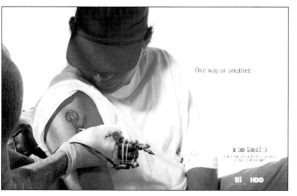

One way or another.

MEXICO

SILVER WORLDMEDAL, SINGLE

LOWE & PARTNERS

MEXICO

CLIENT Marcas Mundiales
CREATIVE DIRECTOR N. Plascencia/
Rodrigo Munizaga
COPYWRITER Norberto Plascencia
ART DIRECTOR Rodrigo Munizaga
PHOTOGRAPHER Giancarlo Fiorenza

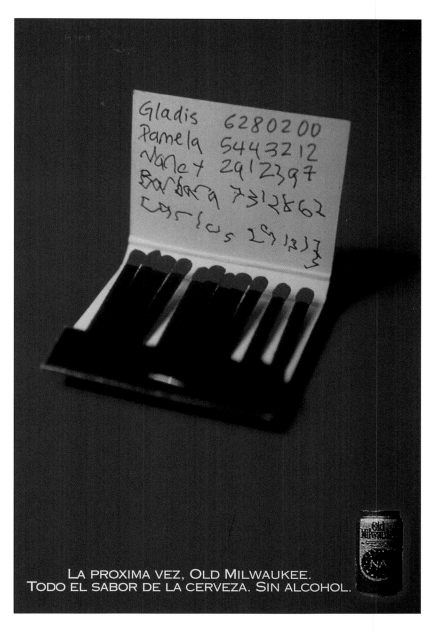

CHILE

FINALIST, SINGLE

LOWE PORTA

SANTIAGO

CLIENT Cachantun Mineral Water
CREATIVE DIRECTOR Kiko Carcavilla
COPYWRITER Rene Moraga
ART DIRECTOR Kiko Carcavilla
ILLUSTRATOR Cristian Stella/Santiago

SPAIN

BRONZE WORLDMEDAL, SINGLE
McCANN-ERICKSON
BARCELONA

CLIENT Nestle/Nescafe Decaffeinated
CREATIVE DIRECTOR Josep M. Ferrara
COPYWRITER Josep M. Ferrara/Sergi Zapater
ART DIRECTOR Xavi Cubero
PHOTOGRAPHER Josep Roca/Barcelona

VENEZUELA

FINALIST, SINGLE
FISCHER GREY
CARACAS

CLIENT Gatorade
CREATIVE DIRECTOR Eduardo Capuano
COPYWRITER Eduardo Capuano
ART DIRECTOR Christian Gonzalez
PHOTOGRAPHER G. Dao/A. Rodriguez
OTHER Vito Fumai

BELGIUM

FINALIST, SINGLE
EQUATION
BRUSSELS

CLIENT White Night Energy Drink
CREATIVE DIRECTOR Marc Weymeers
ILLUSTRATOR Chris Mascarello/Brussels

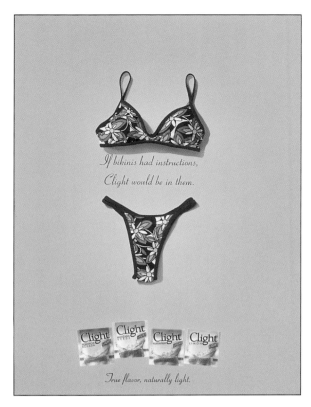

BRAZIL
FINALIST, SINGLE
YOUNG & RUBICAM BRASIL
SAO PAULO
CLIENT Diet Shake
CREATIVE DIRECTOR Rita Corradi/
J.R. D'Elboux/Alexandre Gama
COPYWRITER Isabella Paulelli
ART DIRECTOR Rogerio Lima
PHOTOGRAPHER Felipe Hellmeister/
Sao Paulo

MEXICO
FINALIST, SINGLE
OGILVY & MATHER MEXICO
MEXICO
CLIENT Clight
CREATIVE DIRECTOR Lourdes Lamasney
COPYWRITER Rafael Gomez
ART DIRECTOR Thaina Garza
ART DIRECTOR Miguel A. Muniz
PHOTOGRAPHER Enrique Covarrubias
OTHER Jose Luis Garcia

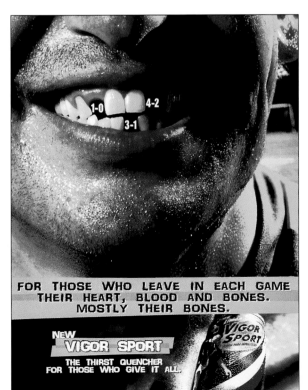

MEXICO
FINALIST, SINGLE
**TERAN TBWA, S.A. DE
C.V.**
MEXICO
CLIENT Vigor Sport
CREATIVE DIRECTOR
Ana Ma. Olabuenaga/
Gonzalo Munoz
COPYWRITER Diego Gonzales
ART DIRECTOR Jose Brousset
PHOTOGRAPHER
Flavio Bizzarri

MEXICO
FINALIST, SINGLE
OGILVY & MATHER MEXICO
MEXICO
CLIENT Clight
CREATIVE DIRECTOR Lourdes Lamasney
COPYWRITER Rafael Gomez
ART DIRECTOR Miguel A. Muniz/Thaina Garza
PHOTOGRAPHER Enrique Covarrubias
OTHER Jose Luis Garcia

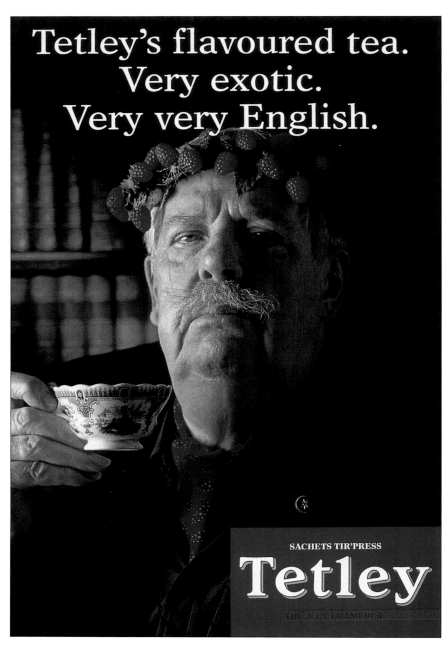

Tetley's flavoured tea.
Very exotic.
Very very English.

SACHETS TIR'PRESS

Tetley

THÉ À LA FRAMBOISE

FRANCE

GOLD WORLDMEDAL, CAMPAIGN

DMB&B
NEUILLY

CLIENT Tetley
CREATIVE DIRECTOR Gerard Monot
COPYWRITER Christophe Corsand
ART DIRECTOR Marc Collombet
PHOTOGRAPHER Rolph Gobits/London

Tetley's flavoured tea.
Very exotic.
Very very English.

SACHETS TIR'PRESS

Tetley

THÉ À L'ORANGE SANGUINE

ARGENTINA

FINALIST, SINGLE

LAUTREC NAZCA SAATCHI & SAATCHI
BUENOS AIRES

CLIENT Resero/Villavicencio Mineral Water
CREATIVE DIRECTOR Juan Cravero/Esteban Pigni
COPYWRITER Esteban Pigni
ART DIRECTOR Toto Marelli
PHOTOGRAPHER Freddy Fabris/Buenos Aires
ILLUSTRATOR Victor Bustos/Buenos Aires

SEE PAGE 204

CHILE

GOLD WORLDMEDAL, SINGLE

BBDO CHILE
SANTIAGO

CLIENT Swatch
CREATIVE DIRECTOR Sebastian Lia/
Hernan Antillo
COPYWRITER Rodrigo Duarte
ART DIRECTOR Carolina Sanchez
PHOTOGRAPHER Eduardo Nunez/Santiago
ILLUSTRATOR Claudio Ubilla/Santiago

SEE GRAND AWARD PAGE 3

USA

SILVER WORLDMEDAL, SINGLE

LEO BURNETT
CHICAGO, IL

CLIENT Hallmark Cards
CREATIVE DIRECTOR
Greg Taubeneck/Tim Pontarelli
COPYWRITER Tim Pontarelli
ART DIRECTOR Jim Bruch

JAPAN

FINALIST, CAMPAIGN

HAKUHODO INCORPORATED
TOKYO

CLIENT Citta International
CREATIVE DIRECTOR Akira Kurosawa
COPYWRITER Tomomi Maeda
ART DIRECTOR Gen Ishii
PHOTOGRAPHER Hibiki Kobayashi/Tokyo

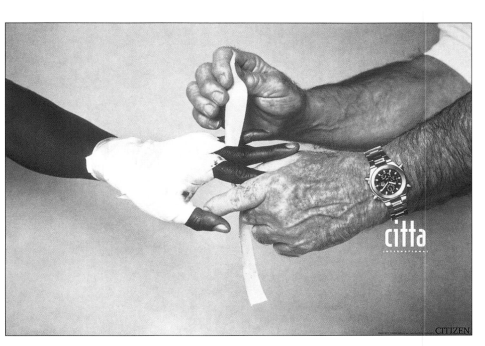

He didn't say anything, but somehow I knew that for the first time in years we were talking again.

When you care enough to send the very best.

He says he loves the place. He loves the people. Loves the food. I just wanted to remind him of someone he loves back home.

With you care enough to send the very best.

AUSTRALIA
BRONZE WORLDMEDAL, CAMPAIGN
LEO BURNETT CONNAGHAN & MAY
MELBOURNE

CLIENT Hallmark
CREATIVE DIRECTOR Shapoor Batliwalla
COPYWRITER Derek Craig/Shapoor Batiwalla
ART DIRECTOR Tone Walde/David Lack
PHOTOGRAPHER Tomek Sikora/Melbourne

PROFESSIONAL SERVICES

Guillermo Forero • ADIESTRADOR DE PERROS • 268 36 66

COLOMBIA
FINALIST, SINGLE
AGUAYO & ASOCIADOS
BOGOTA

CLIENT Guillermo Forero
CREATIVE DIRECTOR David Cabezas
COPYWRITER David Cabezas
ART DIRECTOR Gabriel Escobar
PHOTOGRAPHER Miguel Angel Moreno

GERMANY
FINALIST, SINGLE
LOWE & PARTNERS GMBH
FRANKFURT

CLIENT Marcus Kaufhold
CREATIVE DIRECTOR Christian Daul
COPYWRITER Lars Huvart
ART DIRECTOR Norbert Hubner
PHOTOGRAPHER NASA

UNITED ARAB EMIRATES

GOLD WORLDMEDAL, SINGLE

YOUNG & RUBICAM TEAM, DUBAI

DUBAI

CLIENT: Helen Keeney
COPYWRITER: Shahir Ahmed
ART DIRECTOR: Sameer Ahmed
PHOTOGRAPHER: Tejal Patni
ILLUSTRATOR: Anil Palyekar

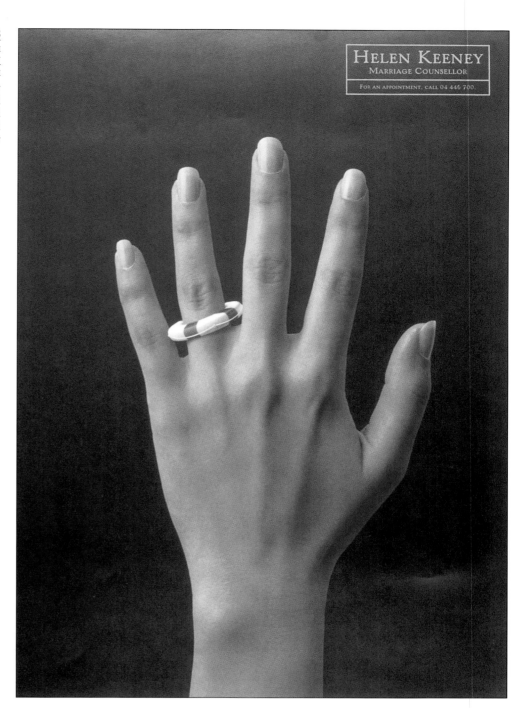

PORTUGAL

FINALIST, SINGLE

YOUNG & RUBICAM, PORTUGAL

LISBON

CREATIVE DIRECTOR Elisabete Vaz Meena/
Cristiano Zancuoghi
COPYWRITER Joao Castanho
ART DIRECTOR Marcelo Medeiros
ILLUSTRATOR Marcelo Medeiros

GERMANY

SILVER WORLDMEDAL, SINGLE

SCHOLZ & FRIENDS GMBH

HAMBURG

CLIENT   Faith. Professional Personal Protection
CREATIVE DIRECTOR   Richard Jung/Christian Storck
COPYWRITER   Bernd Huesmann
ART DIRECTOR   Arwed Berendts
PHOTOGRAPHER   Richard Jung/Hamburg
OTHER   Feodor von Wedel

SINGAPORE

FINALIST, SINGLE

WUNDERMAN CATO JOHNSON

SINGAPORE

CLIENT   National University Hospital
CREATIVE DIRECTOR   Mike Sutcliffe
COPYWRITER   Eliot Powell
ART DIRECTOR   Koh Kuan Eng
PHOTOGRAPHER   Clang
OTHER   Alvin Lee/Joanna Leong

Sí. La justicia es un cachondeo. Pero sólo del 18 al 24 de Enero. Celebraciones de Sant Raimon de Penyafort '99. LA FIESTA DEL DERECHO.

tennis school for childrens

CHILE

SILVER WORLDMEDAL, SINGLE

LOWE PORTA

SANTIAGO

CLIENT Patricio Cornejo
Tennis Club

CREATIVE DIRECTOR
Ignacio Armstrong/
Francisco Guarello

COPYWRITER
Francisco Guarello/
Rafael Saits

ART DIRECTOR
Fernando Riveros

PHOTOGRAPHER
Factory/Santiago

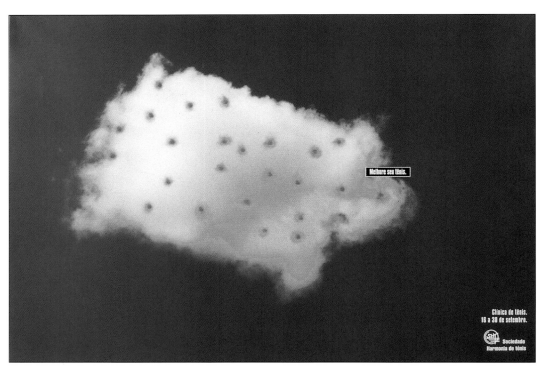

BRAZIL

BRONZE WORLDMEDAL, SINGLE

F/NAZCA SAATCHI & SAATCHI

SAO PAULO

CLIENT Sociedade Harmonia de Tenis
CREATIVE DIRECTOR Fabio Fernandes
COPYWRITER Eduardo Lima
ART DIRECTOR Luciano Santos
PHOTOGRAPHER Get Images/Keystone

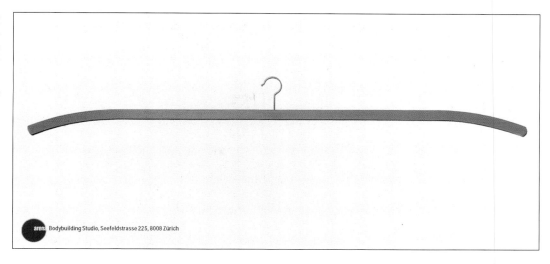

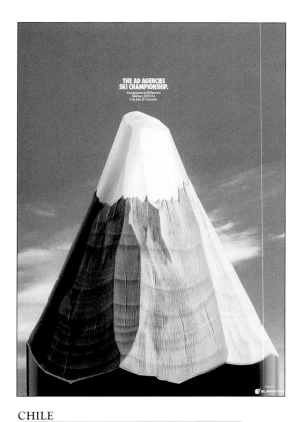

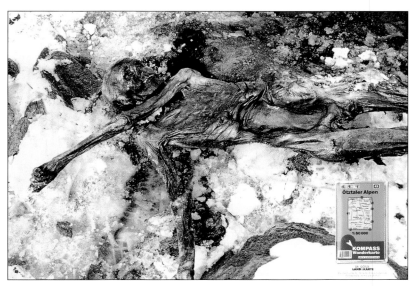

SPAIN

GOLD WORLDMEDAL, CAMPAIGN
McCANN-ERICKSON
BARCELONA

CLIENT   Mares
CREATIVE DIRECTOR   Josep Ferrara
COPYWRITER   Josep Ferrara/Sergi Zapater
ART DIRECTOR   Xavi Cubero
ILLUSTRATOR   Joan Rigau/Barcelona

USA

FINALIST, CAMPAIGN
CRAMER-KRASSELT
MILWAUKEE, WI

CLIENT   Slammer
CREATIVE DIRECTOR   Neil Casey
COPYWRITER   Dan Ames
ART DIRECTOR   Matt Hermann
PHOTOGRAPHER   Dave Gilo/Milwaukee

SPAIN

FINALIST, SINGLE
TANDEM CAMPMANY GUASCH DDB, S.A.
BARCELONA

CLIENT   School Of Drama
CREATIVE DIRECTOR   F. Macia/J.M. Roca
COPYWRITER   D. Guirmaraes/D. Campmany
ART DIRECTOR   A. Giralt/J.R. Alfaro

SINGAPORE

SILVER WORLDMEDAL, CAMPAIGN
TBWA SINGAPORE
SINGAPORE

CLIENT Ritz-Carlton Fitness Centre
CREATIVE DIRECTOR Michael Fromowitz
COPYWRITER Justin Lim
ART DIRECTOR Gregory Yeo
ILLUSTRATOR Yau Wai Kin

ARGENTINA

FINALIST, CAMPAIGN
GRAFFITI DMB&B
BUENOS AIRES

CLIENT Gran Premio Nacional
CREATIVE DIRECTOR Alvaro Fernandez Mendy
COPYWRITER Fernando Gonzalez
ART DIRECTOR Artemio Buneta
ILLUSTRATOR Artemio Buneta

A dream is chasing me. Even if I run, I can't leave it behind. Because this dream lives in me. Today I came out onto the track determined to make it and raced. Raced until I got here. Because I know that here played Maradona. And I am as big as him, I'm the best. But I was born a horse and that's why only some people know me. Came here for people to know who I am. Came to fulfill this dream that has been chasing me, even if I run faster, I can't leave it behind.

14th November "National Award" Palermo Race Track. The best Argentine horses will run. And for being the best, they deserve to be known.

SINGAPORE

GOLD WORLDMEDAL, CAMPAIGN
TBWA SINGAPORE
SINGAPORE

CLIENT TBWA House Ads
CREATIVE DIRECTOR Michael Fromowitz
COPYWRITER Benjamin Baron Hunt
ART DIRECTOR Adrian An/Michael Fromowitz

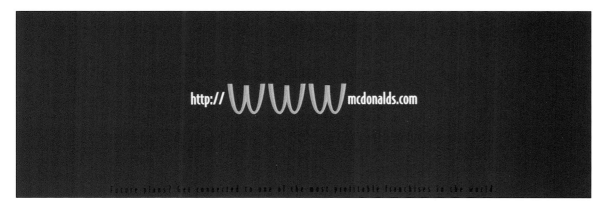

SPAIN

FINALIST, SINGLE
VITRUVIO/LEO BURNETT
MADRID

CLIENT McDonald's
CREATIVE DIRECTOR Rafa Anton
COPYWRITER Alejandro Henche
ART DIRECTOR Kike Mingo

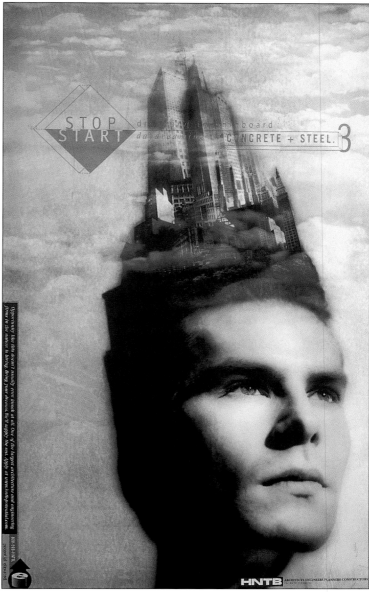

USA

SILVER WORLDMEDAL, CAMPAIGN
NKH&W INC.
KANSAS CITY, MO

CLIENT   HNTB Recruitment Ads
CREATIVE DIRECTOR   John Harrington
COPYWRITER   Trent Patterson
ART DIRECTOR   John Stewart
PHOTOGRAPHER   Pete Kelly/New York

THE NETHERLANDS

FINALIST, CAMPAIGN
PMSVW/Y&R
AMSTERDAM

CLIENT   DAF Trucks NV
CREATIVE DIRECTOR   Karel Beyen
COPYWRITER   Maurice van Gijzelen
ART DIRECTOR   Rob van Gijzelen
ILLUSTRATOR   Rob van Gijzelen

DIE HARD. BUT FAMOUS.

SWITZERLAND

GOLD WORLDMEDAL, SINGLE

HONEGGER/VON MATT

ZURICH

CLIENT Zelo Hairstylist

CREATIVE DIRECTOR
David Honegger

COPYWRITER
Christoph Hess

ART DIRECTOR
Patrick Rychner

PHOTOGRAPHER
Georgina Wilson/Zurich

RETAIL DEALERS: NON-FOOD-REGIONAL / NATIONAL MARKET

SPAIN

SILVER WORLDMEDAL, SINGLE

GREY TRACE

BARCELONA

CLIENT Byzantia

CREATIVE DIRECTOR
A. Vaquerut/
Pablo Torre Blanca/
Gerardo Silva

COPYWRITER
Susana Biedma

ART DIRECTOR
Henak Jimenez de Munana

PHOTOGRAPHER
Angel Almena

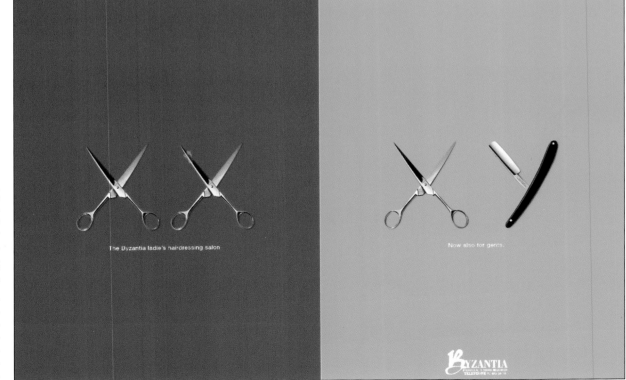

MEXICO

FINALIST, SINGLE
LOWE & PARTNERS
MEXICO

CLIENT Liverpool/Fabricas de Francia
CREATIVE DIRECTOR Rodrigo Munizaga
COPYWRITER Norberto Plascencia
ART DIRECTOR Rodrigo Munizaga/
Gabriel Hernandez
ILLUSTRATOR Arturo Cedillo

GERMANY

FINALIST, SINGLE
**SPRINGER & JACOBY WERBUNG
GMBH**
HAMBURG

CLIENT Endless Pain
CREATIVE DIRECTOR Arndt Dallmann/
Guido Heffels
COPYWRITER Rafael Knuth
ART DIRECTOR Oliver Haupt
PHOTOGRAPHER Gerd George/Hamburg
OTHER Ulrike Letule (Design)

SPAIN

FINALIST, SINGLE
VALVERDE/DE MIQUEL
BARCELONA

CLIENT Probike
CREATIVE DIRECTOR Jaume Garcia
COPYWRITER Gregori Saavedra
ART DIRECTOR Toni Agelet
PHOTOGRAPHER Fototeca Stone

MALAYSIA

SILVER WORLDMEDAL, CAMPAIGN

McCANN-ERICKSON MALAYSIA

KUALA LUMPUR

CLIENT   Harley Davidson Motor Clothes
CREATIVE DIRECTOR   Paul Grezoux
COPYWRITER   Scott Isaac
ART DIRECTOR   Peter Wong
PHOTOGRAPHER   Stills Photography/Kuala Lumpur
ILLUSTRATOR   Chan Choon Ming
OTHER   Low Aik Hoon (Designer)

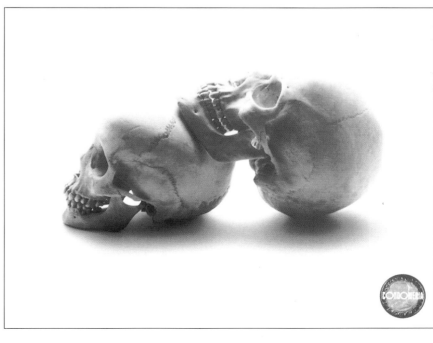

SWITZERLAND

FINALIST, CAMPAIGN

McCANN-ERICKSON

GENEVA

CLIENT   Condomeria
CREATIVE DIRECTOR   Frank Bodin
COPYWRITER   Claude Catsky
ART DIRECTOR   Alvaro F. Maggini
PHOTOGRAPHER   Mathia Zuppiger/Andy Howald

Just arrived. Pullover 69.-

Just arrived. Pullover 69.-

THE NETHERLANDS

FINALIST, CAMPAIGN

TBWA/CAMPAIGN COMPANY
AMSTERDAM

CLIENT We Communications Europe
COPYWRITER Gregg Wasiak
ART DIRECTOR Ray Mendez
PHOTOGRAPHER Hans Kroeskamp

RETAIL RESTAURANTS / SPECIALTY FOOD STORES–LOCAL MARKET

The Chinese Seafood Festival.

House Of Ming

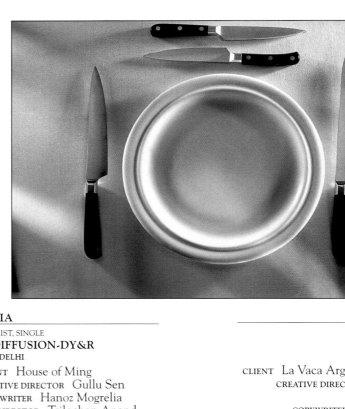

INDIA

FINALIST, SINGLE

REDIFFUSION-DY&R
NEW DELHI

CLIENT House of Ming
CREATIVE DIRECTOR Gullu Sen
COPYWRITER Hanoz Mogrelia
ART DIRECTOR Trilochan Anand
PHOTOGRAPHER Sanjeev Sen/Delhi
OTHER Pavita Puri/Swati Akhouri

SPAIN

FINALIST, SINGLE

RUIZ NICOLI
MADRID

CLIENT La Vaca Argentina/Restaurants
CREATIVE DIRECTOR Ana Hidalgo/
Arturo Lopez
COPYWRITER Paco Ruiz Nicoli
ART DIRECTOR Laura Parias
PHOTOGRAPHER Alfonso Zubiaga

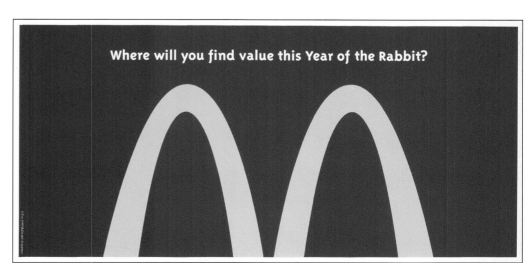

PORTUGAL

GOLD WORLDMEDAL, SINGLE

ABRINICIO PUBLICIDADE
& COMUNICACAO LTDA.
LISBON

CLIENT Mexico House
CREATIVE DIRECTOR
Anselmo Candido
COPYWRITER Jorge Coelho
ART DIRECTOR Ana Vieira
PHOTOGRAPHER
Miguel Fonseca da Costa

FINLAND

BRONZE WORLDMEDAL, SINGLE

PALTEMAA HUTTUNEN
SANTALA TBWA
HELSINKI

CLIENT Kotipizza Restaurant Chain
COPYWRITER Markku Ronkko
ART DIRECTOR Jukka Rosti

McDonald's. Irresistible.

INDIA

SILVER WORLDMEDAL, SINGLE
MUDRA COMMUNICATIONS
MUMBAI

CLIENT McDonald's
CREATIVE DIRECTOR B. Ramnathkar/
Maia Katrak
COPYWRITER Maia Katrak
ART DIRECTOR B. Ramnathkar
PHOTOGRAPHER Sanjeev Angne
ILLUSTRATOR Ajay Bhatkar/
Virendra V
OTHER Bipin S./
S. Deshmukh (Production)

Nicer buns and tastier meat than Baywatch.

USA

FINALIST, SINGLE
ALCONE MARKETING GROUP
IRVINE, CA

CLIENT Burger King
CREATIVE DIRECTOR Luis Camano
COPYWRITER Cameron Young
ART DIRECTOR Luis Camano
OTHER Kevin Favell (VP CD)

RETAIL SUPERMARKETS / MINI MARTS / SHOPPING CENTERS

BRAZIL
FINALIST, SINGLE
STANDARD OGILVY & MATHER
SAO PAULO

CLIENT Morumbifashion Brasil
CREATIVE DIRECTOR Camila Franco
COPYWRITER Gabriela Hunnicutt
ART DIRECTOR Teresa Vidigal Guarita
PHOTOGRAPHER Luis Crispino

SOFT DRINKS

BELGIUM
SILVER WORLDMEDAL, SINGLE
OGILVY & MATHER
BRUSSELS

CLIENT Perrier
CREATIVE DIRECTOR Mark Hilltout
COPYWRITER Olivier Roland
ART DIRECTOR Marc Thomasset
PHOTOGRAPHER Frank Uyttenhove
OTHER Valerie Paul (Typographer)
OTHER David Grunewald
(Account Executive)

CHILE
FINALIST, SINGLE
BBDO CHILE
SANTIAGO

CLIENT Pepsi Light
CREATIVE DIRECTOR Sebastian Lia/Hernan Antillo
COPYWRITER Rodrigo Duarte
ART DIRECTOR Carolina Sanchez
PHOTOGRAPHER Eduardo Nunez/Santiago

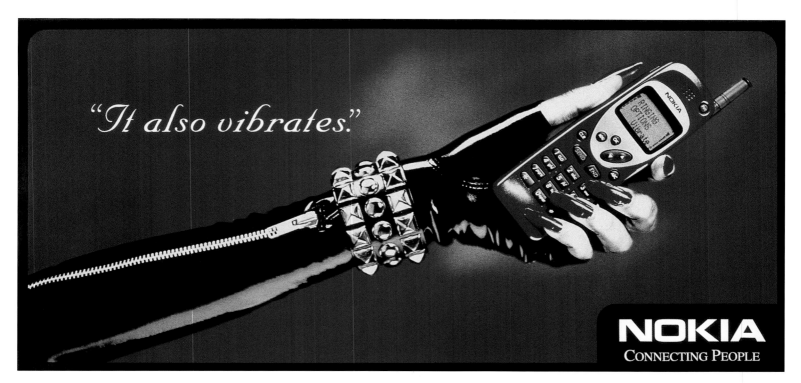

SILVER WORLDMEDAL, SINGLE
CANADA
TBWA CHIAT/DAY
TORONTO, ONTARIO
CLIENT Nokia Cellular Phones
CREATIVE DIRECTOR Duncan Bruce
COPYWRITER Paul Evans
ART DIRECTOR Daniel Vendramin
PHOTOGRAPHER Chris Nicholls/Toronto

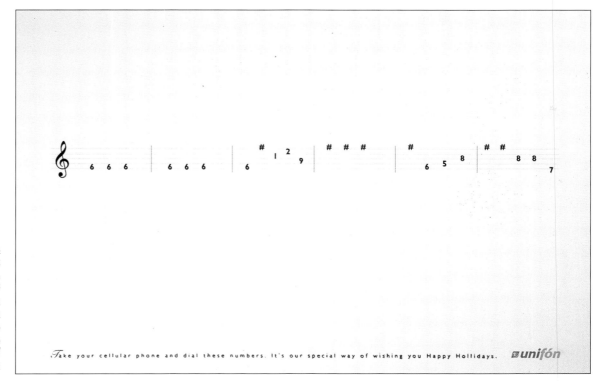

ARGENTINA
BRONZE WORLDMEDAL, SINGLE
SAVAGLIO TBWA
BUENOS AIRES

CLIENT Unifón
CREATIVE DIRECTOR
Ernesto Savaglio
COPYWRITER Diego Donato
ART DIRECTOR Inaqui/Marcelo/
Virgillito/Demian Velda

CANADA

COSSETTE - MONTREAL
MONTREAL, QUEBEC

CLIENT   Bell Mobility Cellular Phones Network
CREATIVE DIRECTOR   Martin Gosselin
COPYWRITER   Martin Rivard
ART DIRECTOR   Nicolas Quintal
PHOTOGRAPHER   Jean-Francois Gratton/Montreal
OTHER   Jacques LaBelle/Francois Forget
(Creative Vice Presidents)

CANADA

SAINT-JACQUES VALLEE
YOUNG & RUBICAM
MONTREAL/QUEBEC

CLIENT
Radio Communications
Network
CREATIVE DIRECTOR
Caroline Jarvis
COPYWRITER
Alexandre Gadoua
ART DIRECTOR
Francois Vaillancourt

THE NETHERLANDS

LOWE KUIPER & SCHOUTEN
AMSTERDAM

CLIENT   Dutchtone
CREATIVE DIRECTOR
Aad Kuijper/Pieter van Velsen
COPYWRITER   Aad Kuijper
ART DIRECTOR   Pieter van Velsen
PHOTOGRAPHER
Hans Kroeskamp/Amsterdam

SOME OF OUR CUSTOMERS

USE OUR RADIO COMMUNICATIONS NETWORK

TO DODGE BULLETS.

REAL ONES.

Recently, we were chosen to design and build private radio networks
for the RCMP in St. John's and the new Emergency Communications
Centre for South west British Columbia. And the reason is crystal clear.
Ericsson communications simply perform better under fire. If this
kind of reliability is critical to your business, let's talk.

 ERICSSON

SPAIN

GOLD WORLDMEDAL, SINGLE

FCB/TAPSA
MADRID

CLIENT Nintendo Playgames
CREATIVE DIRECTOR Julian Zuazo
COPYWRITER Oriol Villar/Martin Ostiglia
ART DIRECTOR Eduardo Martinez Gil

BRAZIL
FINALIST, SINGLE
F/NAZCA SAATCHI & SAATCHI
SAO PAULO
CLIENT Nintendo 64
CREATIVE DIRECTOR Fabio Fernandes
COPYWRITER Eduardo Lima
ART DIRECTOR Luciano Santos
PHOTOGRAPHER Rodrigo Ribeiro

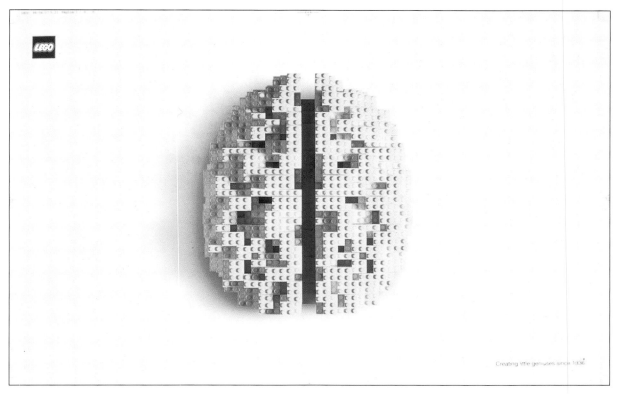

PORTUGAL

SILVER WORLDMEDAL, SINGLE
J. WALTER THOMPSON PUBLICIDADE
ALGES

CLIENT Lego
CREATIVE DIRECTOR Jose Campos/
Anselmo Candido
COPYWRITER Ricardo Adolfo
ART DIRECTOR Miguel Coimbra
PHOTOGRAPHER Chito Prata/Lisbon

BRAZIL

FINALIST, SINGLE
F/NAZCA SAATCHI & SAATCHI
SAO PAULO

CLIENT Football for Nintendo 64
CREATIVE DIRECTOR Fabio Fernandes
COPYWRITER Eduardo Lima
Luciano Santos

SPAIN

FINALIST, SINGLE
FCB/TAPSA
MADRID

CLIENT Ninendo Playgames
CREATIVE DIRECTOR Julian Zuazo
COPYWRITER Oriol Villar/Martin Ostiglia
ART DIRECTOR Eduardo Martinez Gil

Now in 3D.

BRAZIL

BRONZE WORLDMEDAL, SINGLE
F/NAZCA SAATCHI & SAATCHI
SAO PAULO

CLIENT Nintendo
CREATIVE DIRECTOR Fabio Fernandes
COPYWRITER Eduardo Lima
ART DIRECTOR Luciano Santos
PHOTOGRAPHER Client file

SPAIN

FINALIST, SINGLE
GREY TRACE
BARCELONA

CLIENT Sega Saturn
CREATIVE DIRECTOR A. Vaquero/
Pablo Torre Blanca/Gerardo Silva
COPYWRITER Eduardo Giuerrero
ART DIRECTOR Pablo Rodriguez
PHOTOGRAPHER Manuel Alvarez

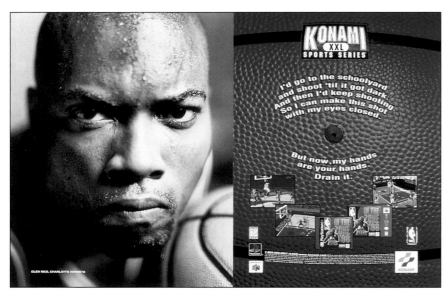

USA

FINALIST, SINGLE
GREY ADVERTISING
NEW YORK, NY

CLIENT Konami of America, Inc.
CREATIVE DIRECTOR Glenn Batkin
COPYWRITER Doug Kagan
ART DIRECTOR Glenn Batkin
PHOTOGRAPHER Sandro

NORWAY
SILVER WORLDMEDAL, SINGLE
BOLD ADVERTISING
OSLO
CLIENT Icelandair
COPYWRITER
Ragnar Roksvag
ART DIRECTOR
Stephanie Dumont

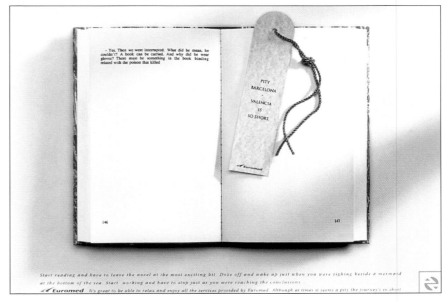

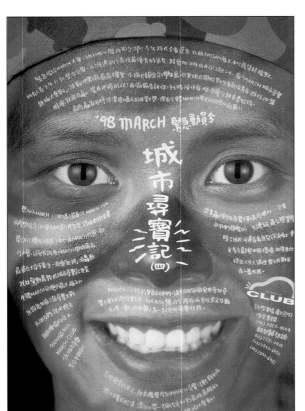

SPAIN
FINALIST, SINGLE
FCB/TAPSA
MADRID
CLIENT Euromed
CREATIVE DIRECTOR Julian Zuazo
COPYWRITER Jose Carnero
ART DIRECTOR Carlos Spottorno
PHOTOGRAPHER Inaki Preysler/Madrid

TAIWAN
FINALIST, SINGLE
**FUNTASTIC
INTERNATIONAL, INC.**
TAIPEI
CLIENT March
CREATIVE DIRECTOR David Sun
COPYWRITER Ashley Yang
ART DIRECTOR Bird

PERU

FINALIST, SINGLE

QUORUM/NAZCA S&S

LIMA

CLIENT Delta Airlines
CREATIVE DIRECTOR Gustavo Rodriguez
COPYWRITER Gustavo Rodriguez
ART DIRECTOR Socorro Llaury

SPAIN

BRONZE WORLDMEDAL, SINGLE

YOUNG & RUBICAM S.A.

MADRID

CLIENT Lufthansa Airline
CREATIVE DIRECTOR Jose Maria Pujol/German Silva/
Manolo Moreno Marquez
COPYWRITER J.M. Pujol/G. Silva/M. Moreno
ART DIRECTOR Ramon Ruiz de la Prada
PHOTOGRAPHER Alfonso Zubiaga

ARGENTINA

FINALIST, SINGLE

GOWLAND S,A,

BUENOS AIRES

CLIENT Aeroperu
CREATIVE DIRECTOR
Fernando Manzanal/Sergio Protta
COPYWRITER Marcelo Montes
ART DIRECTOR Omar Pietrasek
PHOTOGRAPHER Rodolfo Parra

HONG KONG

FINALIST, SINGLE

OGILVY & MATHER ADVERTISING

HONG KONG

CLIENT KCR East Rail
CREATIVE DIRECTOR Raymond Chau
COPYWRITER Louie Hui
ART DIRECTOR Ng Fan
OTHER Grace Loong (A/S)

USA

FINALIST, SINGLE

FJCANDN
SALT LAKE CITY, UT

CLIENT   Samtrans
CREATIVE DIRECTOR
Dave Newbold
COPYWRITER
Bryant Marcum
ART DIRECTOR   Matt Manfull

AUSTRALIA

FINALIST, SINGLE

McCANN-ERICKSON
SYDNEY
NORTH SYDNEY

CLIENT   Cathay Pacific
CREATIVE DIRECTOR
Trevor Purvis
COPYWRITER
Samantha Begg
ART DIRECTOR   Paul Rauch
OTHER   Pino Sellaro/
Anton Pardavi

USA

FINALIST, SINGLE

TEMERLIN McCLAIN
IRVING, TX

CLIENT   American Airlines
CREATIVE DIRECTOR   Matt Manroe/Vinny Minchillo
COPYWRITER   Vinny Minchillo
ART DIRECTOR   Barbara Stampley
PHOTOGRAPHER   Richard Berenholtz/New York

DENMARK

FINALIST, SINGLE

GREY COPENHAGEN
COPENHAGEN

CLIENT   SAS Youth
COPYWRITER   Niels Thomsen
ART DIRECTOR   Mikkel Jangaard

SINGAPORE

BRONZE WORLDMEDAL, CAMPAIGN
BOZELL WORLDWIDE SINGAPORE
SINGAPORE

CLIENT   All Nippon Airways
CREATIVE DIRECTOR   Allein Moore
COPYWRITER   Xavier Kiat
ART DIRECTOR   Kenny Choo
ILLUSTRATOR   Phenonmenon

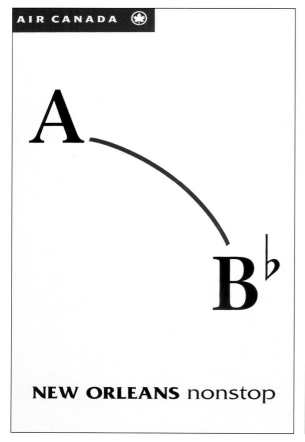

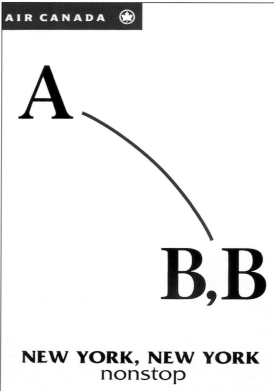

CANADA

FINALIST, CAMPAIGN
**MARKETEL McCANN
ERICKSON**
MONTREAL, QUEBEC

CLIENT   Air Canada
CREATIVE DIRECTOR   Maico Meier
COPYWRITER   Andrew Morgan/
Jennifer Goddard
ART DIRECTOR   Lizanne L'Africain

TRAVEL/TOURISM

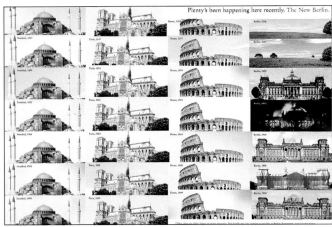

GERMANY

SILVER WORLDMEDAL, CAMPAIGN
SCHOLZ & FRIENDS BERLIN
BERLIN

CLIENT   Initiative Freunde Fur Berlin
CREATIVE DIRECTOR   Sebastian Turner
COPYWRITER   Robert Krause/Nina Havlicek
ART DIRECTOR   Lutz Plumecke

GERMANY

BRONZE WORLDMEDAL, SINGLE
SPRINGER & JACOBY WERBUNG GMBH
HAMBURG

CLIENT   Sunway Travel
CREATIVE DIRECTOR   Arno Lindemann/
Stefan Meske
COPYWRITER   Amir Kassaei
ART DIRECTOR   Florian Grimm
ILLUSTRATOR   Jens Grummich/Hamburg

Isn't it time you changed your boiler?
Call for a great finance deal.

SPAIN

BRONZE WORLDMEDAL, SINGLE
YOUNG & RUBICAM S.A.
MADRID

CLIENT Repsol Butane Gas
CREATIVE DIRECTOR Jose Maria Pujol
COPYWRITER Felix Del Valle
ART DIRECTOR Vicente Navarro

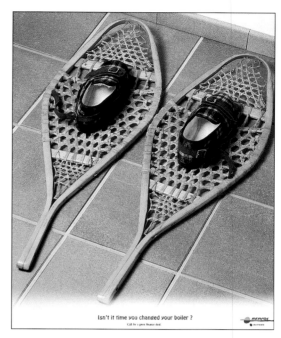

Isn't it time you changed your boiler?

SPAIN

FINALIST, SINGLE
YOUNG & RUBICAM S.A.
MADRID

CLIENT Repsol Butane Gas
CREATIVE DIRECTOR Jose Maria Pujol
COPYWRITER Felix Del Vallle
Art Director Vicente Navarro

More and more fish are returning to the cleaner Thames Estuary.

The waters of the Thames Estuary are just like one big nursery for an enormous variety of young sea fish.

As a result of Thames Water's efforts to keep the waters of the estuary clean, we're glad to say more and more fish are thriving there.

Sole, bass, plaice and dab all find that the abundance of food, shelter

and the warmer water help them grow faster, before they swim out to join the shoals in the North Sea.

Many long-absent species of fish are returning to the estuary and making a home there, too. (Welcome back, the pogge, the scad, the leopard goby and the straight-nosed pipefish!)

There are now, in fact, 115 species of fish in the estuary as a result of the cleaner waters there. (Not to mention many more species of birds, and invertebrates such as the sea anemone.)

It's just one aspect of Thames Water's determination to invest in a better environment. For fish-lovers everywhere.

A flow of good ideas.

We renewed the water main while keeping the traffic flowing.

The A3 is one of the busiest trunk roads out of London. Hundreds of cars and trucks use it every hour between the capital and Portsmouth.

Recently, we found that one of the water mains under the dual carriageway badly needed renewing. Digging up the road would have been out of the question. It would have meant miles of tailbacks and angry drivers.

And turning off the water on both sides of the road for very long would have interrupted the supply to thousands of our customers.

Fortunately, we found an ingenious and permanent solution. We introduced a motorised 'mole' into the pipe to reline it with a tough new plastic coating.

Thus, we ensured an uninterrupted supply of water without interrupting the flow of traffic.

It's this sort of flexible thinking that is helping us at

Thames Water to restore and refurbish our whole pipe system.

Something else we're absolutely committed to tackling is leakage. We're investing £200 million to halve leakage within the next three years.

With over 20,000 miles of mains and 18 million joints in the Thames Water region, the task facing our detection teams is huge.

Many leaks can't be seen, lying deep down under streets and buildings, so we're using a combination of high-tech equipment to find them.

Radar, electronic correlators, flow-meters in the mains and tighter zoning are just some of the techniques that are helping to pin-point where these leaks lie.

If you'd like to help us by reporting a leak, ring Thames Water on our free 24-hour Leakline. Just call us on 0800 714614.

A flow of good ideas.

ENGLAND

BRONZE WORLDMEDAL, CAMPAIGN
ARC ADVERTISING
LONDON

CLIENT Thames Water
CREATIVE DIRECTOR Ray Hearder
COPYWRITER Peter Little
ART DIRECTOR Jim Robertshaw
PHOTOGRAPHER Neil Bairstow/Desmond Burdon
OTHER Ray Craigie (Typographer)

BUSINESS SERVICES/EQUIPMENT

ARGENTINA

GOLD WORLDMEDAL, SINGLE

AGULLA Y BACCETTI
BUENOS AIRES

CLIENT Raya Jingle
CREATIVE DIRECTOR R. Agulla/C. Baccetti/
S. Wilhelm/M. Anselmo/L. Raposo
COPYWRITER Sebastian Wilhelm
ART DIRECTOR Maximiliano Anselmo
ILLUSTRATOR Roy Garcia

THE NETHERLANDS

FINALIST, SINGLE

ANDERSON & LEMBKE
AMSTERDAM

CLIENT Ericsson
CREATIVE DIRECTOR Tore Claesson
COPYWRITER Harald Bugge
ART DIRECTOR Tore Claesson
PHOTOGRAPHER Charles Liddall/
Kuala Lumpur

CANADA

SILVER WORLDMEDAL, SINGLE

BBDO CANADA
TORONTO, ONTARIO

CLIENT Federal Express
CREATIVE DIRECTOR Michael McLaughlin/
Jack Neary
COPYWRITER Ian MacKellar
ART DIRECTOR Scott Dube
PHOTOGRAPHER Philip Rostron

FedEx: Proud shipper of portfolios to the 1998 Strategy Magazine Agency of the Year Competition.

SWEDEN

FINALIST, CAMPAIGN

JERLOV & COMPANY
GOTEBORG

CLIENT Xerox
CREATIVE DIRECTOR Fredrik Jerlov
COPYWRITER Patrik Andreasson
ART DIRECTOR Madeleine Wallstrom
PHOTOGRAPHER Carl Swensson/Goteborg

DENMARK

BRONZE WORLDMEDAL, CAMPAIGN
DDB NEEDHAM DENMARK
COPENHAGEN

CLIENT   Sony Nordic
CREATIVE DIRECTOR   Paul Mikkelsen
COPYWRITER   Tom Olsen
ART DIRECTOR   Robert Lerkez

MEDICAL/PHARMACEUTICAL

CHILE

BRONZE WORLDMEDAL, SINGLE
ZEGERS DDB
SANTIAGO

CLIENT   Laboratorio Maver
CREATIVE DIRECTOR   Jorge Leiva
COPYWRITER   Hermes Drago
ART DIRECTOR   Pablo Leiva
PHOTOGRAPHER   Ricardo Salamanca/
J. Carlos Soto

SPAIN

SILVER WORLDMEDAL, SINGLE

SAATCHI & SAATCHI

MADRID

CLIENT
Dental Clinic Bravo

CREATIVE DIRECTOR
Miguel Roig/Cesar Garcia

COPYWRITER Miguel Roig

ART DIRECTOR
Anaki Barreiro

PHOTOGRAPHER
Pablo Cruz/Madrid

OTHER Rafael Silvela
(Acount Director)

BRAVO DENTAL CLINIC.
RAMBLA JUSTO OLIVERAS, 56, 2ª-2ª. - TEL.: 93 337 77 14. - 08091 HOSPITALET DEL LLOBREGAT.

SINGAPORE

BRONZE WORLDMEDAL, SINGLE

THE ASYLUM

SINGAPORE

CLIENT Gayathiri Pte. Ltd

COPYWRITER Mahesan M./Anand A.

ART DIRECTOR Zainal Y.

PHOTOGRAPHER Lee Jen/Singapore

NEW ZEALAND

FINALIST, SINGLE

CWFS-McCANN
AUCKLAND

CLIENT Caverject
CREATIVE DIRECTOR Sue Worthington/Kate Saarinen
COPYWRITER Sue Worthington
ART DIRECTOR Kate Saarinen
PHOTOGRAPHER Roger Corona
OTHER Warren Yee/Robert Munro

PANAMA

FINALIST, SINGLE

MARQUEZ BATES
PAITILLA

CLIENT Mylanta
CREATIVE DIRECTOR Bolivar Marquez
COPYWRITER Bolivar Marquez
ART DIRECTOR Katya Medina
PHOTOGRAPHER Ilumitec

INDUSTRIAL & AGRICULTURAL

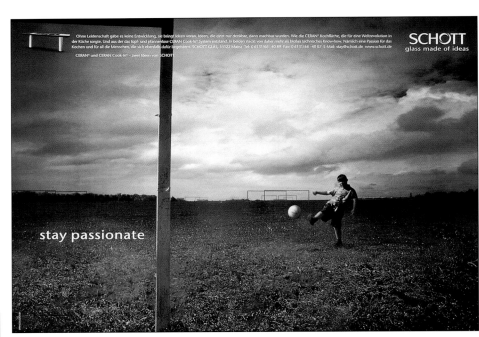

GERMANY

FINALIST, CAMPAIGN

SPRINGER & JACOBY WERBUNG GMBH
HAMBURG

CLIENT Schott Glass
CREATIVE DIRECTOR Arndt Dallmann/Guido Heffels
COPYWRITER Till Eckel
ART DIRECTOR Paul Snowden
PHOTOGRAPHER John Offenbach/London

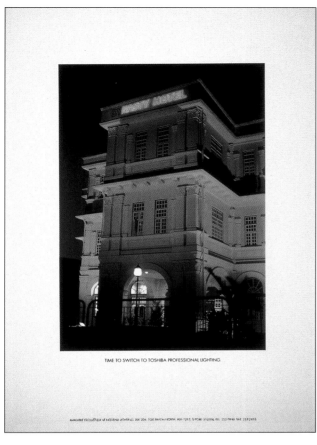

TIME TO SWITCH TO TOSHIBA PROFESSIONAL LIGHTING.

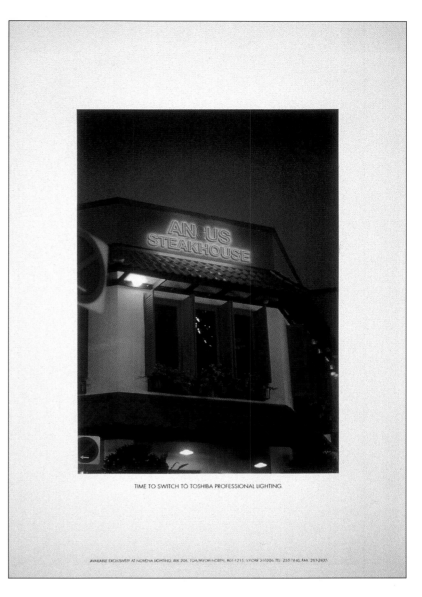

TIME TO SWITCH TO TOSHIBA PROFESSIONAL LIGHTING.

SINGAPORE

GOLD WORLDMEDAL, CAMPAIGN
TBWA SINGAPORE
SINGAPORE

CLIENT Novena Lighting
CREATIVE DIRECTOR Michael Fromowitz
COPYWRITER Justin Lim
ART DIRECTOR Gregory Yeo
PHOTOGRAPHER Eric Seow

Der erste Sportsfreund mit GDI-Motor.

Der neue GDI Galant Kombi.

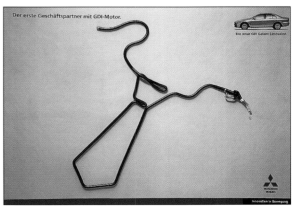

Der erste Geschäftspartner mit GDI-Motor.

Die neue GDI Galant Limousine.

GERMANY

BRONZE WORLDMEDAL, CAMPAIGN
ASATSU
TREBUR

CLIENT Mitsubishi Space Star
CREATIVE DIRECTOR Christof Jorg
COPYWRITER Andreas Jurkowitsch
ART DIRECTOR Christof Jorg
PHOTOGRAPHER Thomas Balzer/Andre Schoppe

Ich kleide meine Fenster wie mich selbst! cosiflor

Man ist ja wählerisch

Ich kleide meine Fenster wie mich selbst! cosiflor

Man ist ja wählerisch

GERMANY

SILVER WORLDMEDAL, CAMPAIGN

WACHTER & WACHTER MUNCHEN
MUNCHEN

CLIENT Blocker Falt Stores
CREATIVE DIRECTOR Ulrich Schmitz
COPYWRITER Johanna Rumohr
ART DIRECTOR Axel Burgler
PHOTOGRAPHER Thomas Spiebl/Munich

OTHER

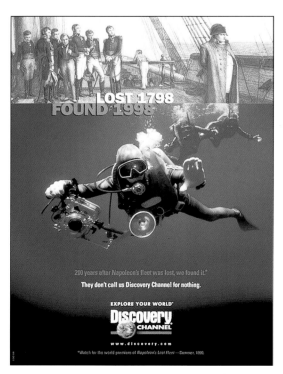

USA

FINALIST, SINGLE

DISCOVERY NETWORKS
BETHESDA, MD

CLIENT Discovery Channel
CREATIVE DIRECTOR John Hite
COPYWRITER Tim Masters/
Steve Lance/
Unconventional Wisdom

CHILE

FINALIST, SINGLE

ZEGERS DDB
SANTIAGO

CLIENT Renner
CREATIVE DIRECTOR Jorge Leiva
COPYWRITER Claudio Lagos
ART DIRECTOR Jorge Espinoza
PHOTOGRAPHER Zegers DDB

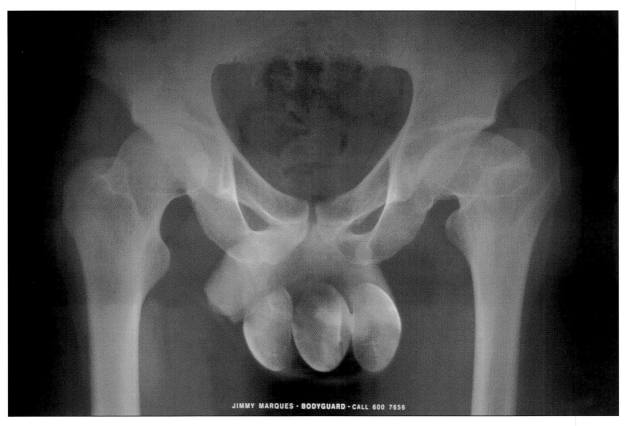

JIMMY MARQUES · BODYGUARD · CALL 600 7656

URUGUAY

SILVER WORLDMEDAL, SINGLE
ADN PUBLICIDAD
MONTEVIDEO

CLIENT Equipo
CREATIVE DIRECTOR Jaime Cueto
COPYWRITER Pablo Sorondo
ART DIRECTOR Esteban Sacco
PHOTOGRAPHER JEP Studio

Daimler-Benz Aerospace

Internationale Luft- und Raumfahrtausstellung.
Die Daimler-Benz Aerospace: vom 18. bis 24. Mai auf dem Flughafen Schönefeld.

GERMANY

BRONZE WORLDMEDAL, CAMPAIGN
JUNG VON MATT AN DER ISAR
MUNCHEN

CLIENT Daimler Chrysler Aerospace
CREATIVE DIRECTOR Oliver Voss
COPYWRITER Norman Storl/Till Hohmann
ART DIRECTOR Tobias Eichinger
PHOTOGRAPHER Adrian Burke

Daimler-Benz Aerospace

Internationale Luft- und Raumfahrtausstellung.
Die Daimler-Benz Aerospace: vom 18. bis 24. Mai auf dem Flughafen Schönefeld.

BEST ART DIRECTION

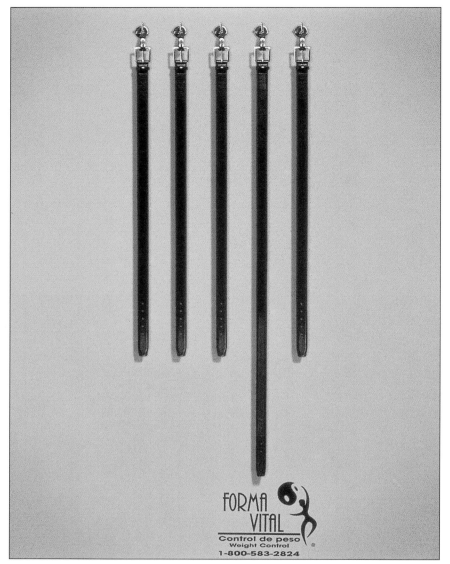

FORMA VITAL
Control de peso
Weight Control
1-800-583-2824

USA

SILVER WORLDMEDAL, SINGLE
DIESTE & PARTNERS
DALLAS, TX

CLIENT   Forma Vital
CREATIVE DIRECTOR   Aldo Quevedo/Javier Guemes
COPYWRITER   Javier Guemes/Inaky Escudero
ART DIRECTOR   Chris Sendra/Patty Martinez

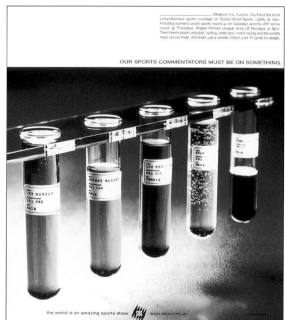

AUSTRALIA

FINALIST, CAMPAIGN
BAM SSB
EAST SYDNEY

CLIENT   SBS Television
CREATIVE DIRECTOR   Darryn Devlin
COPYWRITER   R. Martin-Murphy/B. Jones/L. Jelliffe/
I. Einfeld
ART DIRECTOR   D. Devlin/D. Heytman/L. Jelliffe
PHOTOGRAPHER   Julian Watt/Sydney

DER SPIEGEL

SPIEGEL-readers know more.

GERMANY
BRONZE WORLDMEDAL, SINGLE
SPRINGER & JACOBY WERBUNG GMBH
HAMBURG
CLIENT Spiegel Magazine
CREATIVE DIRECTOR
Kurt-Georg Dieckert/
Stefan Schmidt
COPYWRITER Thomas Chudalla
ART DIRECTOR
Wolf-Peter Camphausen
PHOTOGRAPHER Thomas Strogalski

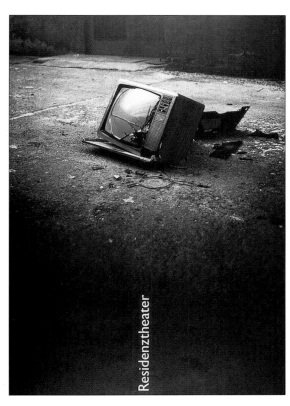

Residenztheater

GERMANY
FINALIST, SINGLE
JUNG VON MATT AN DER ISAR
MUNCHEN
CLIENT Jung von Matt an der Isar
ADVERTISING AGENCY Bayrisches Staatstheater
CREATIVE DIRECTOR Oliver Voss
ART DIRECTOR Tobias Eichinger

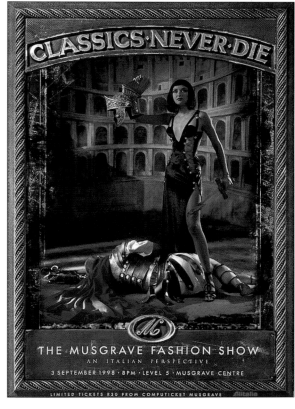

CLASSICS·NEVER·DIE

THE·MUSGRAVE FASHION SHOW
AN ITALIAN PERSPECTIVE
3 SEPTEMBER 1998 · 8PM · LEVEL 5 · MUSGRAVE CENTRE
LIMITED TICKETS R30 FROM COMPUTICKET MUSGRAVE

SOUTH AFRICA
FINALIST, SINGLE
LINDSAY SMITHERS BOND
DURBAN
CLIENT Lindsay Smithers Bond
CREATIVE DIRECTOR Michael Bond
COPYWRITER Lynton Heath
ART DIRECTOR David Gaylard/Scott Robertson
PHOTOGRAPHER Patrick McGee/Durban
ILLUSTRATOR Birgitta Gaylard
OTHER D. Gaylard/S. Robertson (Typographers)

BEST ART DIRECTION 151

JAPAN
GOLD WORLDMEDAL, CAMPAIGN
DENTSU, INC.
TOKYO
CLIENT   Dentsu Institute For Human Studies
CREATIVE DIRECTOR   Katsumi Yutani
COPYWRITER   Akira Kikuchi
ART DIRECTOR   S.Sakaguchi/K.Hatano/
E. Oishi/N.Nishioka
PHOTOGRAPHER   Naohiro Tsukada

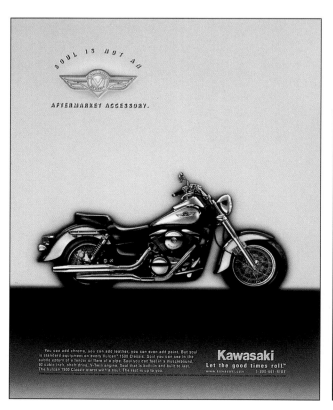

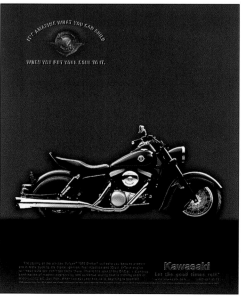

USA
FINALIST, CAMPAIGN
BOZELL WORLDWIDE
COSTA MESA, CA
CLIENT   Kawasaki Motorsports
CREATIVE DIRECTOR   Ken Sakoda
COPYWRITER   Chris Brown
ART DIRECTOR   John Zegowitz
PHOTOGRAPHER   William Hawkes

おーい、ドキドキしてるかい？

ヨッ！ワクワクしてるかい？

JAPAN

FINALIST, CAMPAIGN

DENTSU, INC.
TOKYO

CLIENT Shogakan Encyclopedia
CREATIVE DIRECTOR Mitsuhiro Wada
COPYWRITER Eita Nakajima
ART DIRECTOR Kazumi Murat/
Mikio Takeda/Kaoru Yamaguchi

SONY

A Happy New Ear.

JAPAN

FINALIST, CAMPAIGN

INTERVISION INC.
TOKYO

CLIENT Sony
CREATIVE DIRECTOR Toshiro Fumizono
COPYWRITER Kohtaro Shimada
ART DIRECTOR Yutaka Murakoshi
PHOTOGRAPHER Kazuyasu Hagane/Tokyo

SONY

A Happy New Ear.

Handcrafted, individually tuned crankbaits featuring thru-wire construction, tangle-free double strength **SLAMMER** Mustad™ hooks and unbreakable lexan lips. Talk about tension in the workplace. Call 414-695-0370 for a free catalog.

USA

BRONZE WORLDMEDAL, SINGLE
CRAMER-KRASSELT
MILWAUKEE, WI

CLIENT Slammer
CREATIVE DIRECTOR Neil Casey
COPYWRITER Dan Ames
ART DIRECTOR Matt Herrmann
PHOTOGRAPHER Dave Gilo/
Milwaukee

CANADA

FINALIST, CAMPAIGN
PALM PUBLICITE MARKETING
MONTREAL

CLIENT Volkswagen-New Beetle
CREATIVE DIRECTOR Paulette Arsenault
COPYWRITER Normand Boisvert/M-Andre Rivard
ART DIRECTOR Yvon Paquette/J-Luc Bouvy
PHOTOGRAPHER Ron Strong
ILLUSTRATOR Mettle
OTHER Trans-Optique/HSP Graphics (Printer)

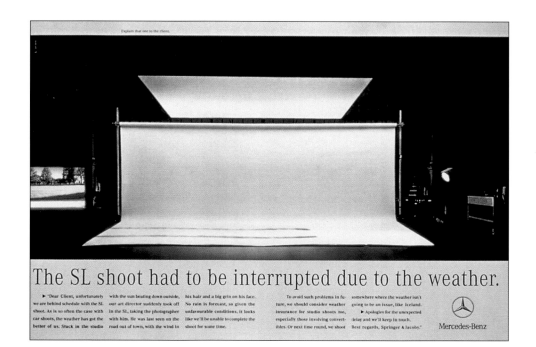

The SL shoot had to be interrupted due to the weather.

GERMANY

FINALIST, SINGLE

SPRINGER & JACOBY WERBUNG GMBH

HAMBURG

CLIENT   Mercedes-Benz Deutschland/SL
CREATIVE DIRECTOR   Alexander Schill/ A. Thomsen
COPYWRITER   E. Jung/W.-P. Camphausen
ART DIRECTOR   W.-P. Camphausen
PHOTOGRAPHER   I. Hansen

Are you in the right framework?

INDIA

FINALIST, CAMPAIGN

REDIFFUSION - DYAR

MUMBAI

CLIENT   Diner's Club Card
CREATIVE DIRECTOR   Adrian Mendoza
COPYWRITER   Adrian Mendoza
ART DIRECTOR   Mangesh Rane
PHOTOGRAPHER   Mahesh Hiremash/Mumbai

Drink in this ad, very very slowly.

BEST ILLUSTRATION

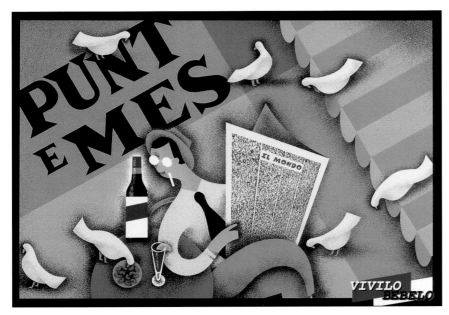

ARGENTINA

FINALIST, SINGLE
DE LUCA PUBLICIDAD
BUENOS AIRES

CLIENT Punt e Mes
CREATIVE DIRECTOR Omar Di Nardo
COPYWRITER Mauricio Olivera
ART DIRECTOR Eduardo Arnau
ILLUSTRATOR El Nino Rodriguez/Buenos Aires

JAPAN

FINALIST, SINGLE
MASAHARU OGAWA DESIGN OFFICE
CHOU-KU, SAPPORO

CLIENT The Design Exhibition Of Hokkaido
CREATIVE DIRECTOR Masaharu Ogawa
ART DIRECTOR Masaharu Ogawa
ILLUSTRATOR Masaharu Ogawa
OTHER Masaharu Ogawa (Designer)

USA

FINALIST, SINGLE
TBWA/CHIAT/DAY
SAN FRANCISCO, CA

CLIENT Levi's® Silvertab®
CREATIVE DIRECTOR Lee Clow/Peter Angelos/Rob Smiley
COPYWRITER Scott Duchon
ART DIRECTOR Jennifer Boyd
ILLUSTRATOR Graham Roundthwaite

JAPAN

SILVER WORLDMEDAL, CAMPAIGN

ASATSU-DK INC.

TOKYO

CLIENT The Sanwa Bank Limited
COPYWRITER Nakaigawa Isao
ART DIRECTOR Masuda Hideaki/Saito Yoshihiro
ILLUSTRATOR Carlotta
OTHER Nishioka Atsushi (Designer)

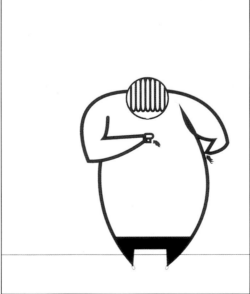

GERMANY

BRONZE WORLDMEDAL,
CAMPAIGN

**.START
ADVERTISING
GMBH**

MUNICH

CLIENT
MTV Networks
GmbH

CREATIVE DIRECTOR
Gregor Woltje

COPYWRITER
Chris Boje

ART DIRECTOR
Benny Lommel

ILLUSTRATOR
Francois Chalet/
Munich

GERMANY

GOLD WORLDMEDAL, CAMPAIGN

SCHOLZ & FRIENDS BERLIN
BERLIN

CLIENT   Frankfurter Allgemeine Zeitung
CREATIVE DIRECTOR   Sebastian Turner
ART DIRECTOR   Petra Reichenbach
PHOTOGRAPHER   Alfred Seiland

HONG KONG

BRONZE WORLDMEDAL, CAMPAIGN

OGILVY & MATHER ADVERTISING
HONG KONG

CLIENT   Conrad International
CREATIVE DIRECTOR   Neil French
COPYWRITER   Troy Sullivan
ART DIRECTOR   Alex Wilcox
PHOTOGRAPHER   Francois Gillet
OTHER   Sarah Hale/Kara Cartin

GERMANY

SILVER WORLDMEDAL, CAMPAIGN

JVM WERBEAGENTUR GMBH
HAMBURG

CLIENT   Audi TT
CREATIVE DIRECTOR   Hermann Waterkamp
COPYWRITER   Doerte Spengler
ART DIRECTOR   Holger Bultmann
PHOTOGRAPHER   Blinkk

USA

FINALIST, SINGLE

ARNELL GROUP BRAND CONSULTING
NEW YORK, NY

CLIENT   Rena Lange Women's Apparel
CREATIVE DIRECTOR   Peter Arnell
ART DIRECTOR   Steven Hankinson
PHOTOGRAPHER   Peter Arnell/NY
OTHER   B. Lederberg (Account Executive)/
Y. Yamazaki/V. Leong/
J. Goldberg Production Managers

AUSTRIA

FINALIST, CAMPAIGN

HORST STASNY
THALHEIM BEI WELS

CLIENT   Artist's Portrait
ADVERTISING AGENCY   Sigi Mayer/Linz
CREATIVE DIRECTOR   Sigi Mayer
COPYWRITER   Christoph Wagner
ART DIRECTOR   Sigi Mayer
PHOTOGRAPHER   Horst Stasny/
Thalheim, Wels

BEST USE OF MEDIUM

GRAND AWARD

BEST POSTER

BRAZIL

GRAND AWARD BEST POSTER

PUBLICIS-NORTON

SAO PAULO

CLIENT Rowenta
CREATIVE DIRECTOR Gilberto Dos Reis
COPYWRITER Wanderley Doro
ART DIRECTOR Jack Ronc
PHOTOGRAPHER Freitas/Sao Paulo

Novo
Rowenta
Professional.

BEST MAGAZINE ADVERTISEMENT

AUSTRALIA

SILVER WORLDMEDAL, SINGLE
SAATCHI & SAATCHI
SYDNEY

CLIENT   Toyota 3811Hiace
CREATIVE DIRECTOR   Michael Newman
COPYWRITER   Scot Waterhouse
ART Director   Steve Carlin
PHOTOGRAPHER   Jon Higgs
OTHER   Michelle Greenhalgh (Account Supervisor)

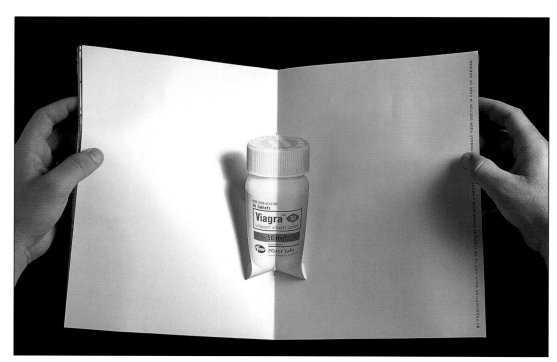

ARGENTINA

BRONZE WORLDMEDAL, SINGLE
GREY ARGENTINA S.A.
BUENOS AIRES

CLIENT   Viagra
CREATIVE DIRECTOR   Carlos Perez/
Martin Vinacur
COPYWRITER   Gustavo Otto Soria
ART DIRECTOR   Gabriel Huici
PHOTOGRAPHER   Sergio Assabi

USA

FINALIST, SINGLE
DIESTE & PARTNERS
DALLAS, TX

CLIENT   Tabasco
CREATIVE DIRECTOR   Aldo Quevedo
COPYWRITER   Javier Guemes
ART DIRECTOR   Chris Sendra

BEST PRE-PRINTED MAGAZINE INSERT

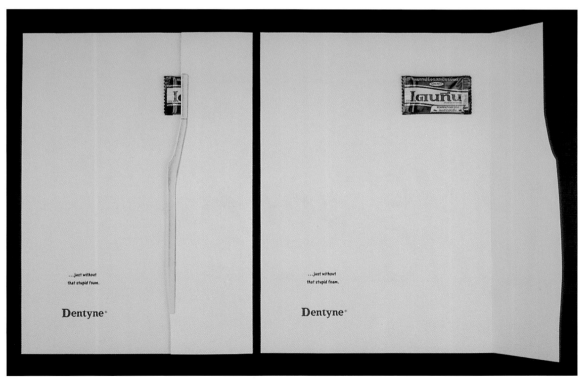

THAILAND

BRONZE WORLDMEDAL, SINGLE
BATES THAILAND
BANGKOK

CLIENT   Warner-Lambert Dentyne
CREATIVE DIRECTOR   Alex Beuchel
COPYWRITER   Kingrak Ingkawat/
Alex Beuchel
ART DIRECTOR   Alex Beuchel
PHOTOGRAPHER   Eric Chocat/Bangkok

BEST POSTER

HONG KONG

FINALIST, SINGLE

DENTSU YOUNG & RUBICAM BRAND
HONG KONG

CLIENT Sony
CREATIVE DIRECTOR Tony Yeung
COPYWRITER Timothy Lau
ART DIRECTOR Bary Mok
PHOTOGRAPHER Lester Lee

USA

FINALIST, SINGLE

FX NETWORKS
NEWPORT BEACH, CA

CREATIVE DIRECTOR Gavin Harvey
ART DIRECTOR Sally Daws
ADVERTISING AGENCY
Simon Design/Jason Simon
OTHER Kim Adelman (Producer)

GERMANY

FINALIST, SINGLE

N. W. AYER COMMUNICATIONS GMBH
FRANKFURT

CLIENT Goethe Institut
CREATIVE DIRECTOR Olli Hesse
COPYWRITER Olli Hesse
ART DIRECTOR Andreas Redlich
ILLUSTRATOR I. Glamann/D. Muno

SPAIN

FINALIST, SINGLE

YOUNG & RUBICAM S.A.
MADRID

CLIENT Lufthansa Airline
CREATIVE DIRECTOR
Jose Maria Pujol/ German Silva/
Manolo Moreno M.
COPYWRITER Jose Maria Pujol/
German Silva/Manolo Moreno M.
ART DIRECTOR Ramon Ruiz de la Prada
PHOTOGRAPHER Alfonso Zubiaga

SEE PAGE 136

JAPAN

BRONZE WORLDMEDAL, CAMPAIGN

PACKAGING CREATE INC.

OSAKA

CLIENT   Inter Medium Institute Graduate School
ART DIRECTOR   Akio Okumura
OTHER   Aki Inoue/Sotatsu Tokuoka (Designer)

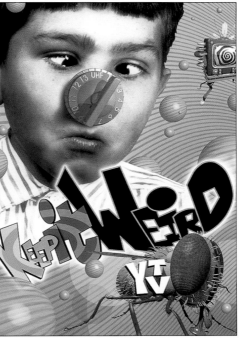

CANADA

FINALIST, CAMPAIGN

YTV CANADA, INC.

TORONTO, ONTARIO

CLIENT   YTV Canada, Inc.
ADVERTISING AGENCY   Amoeba Corp./
Toronto
CREATIVE DIRECTOR   Mike Kelar/
Dolores Keating Mallen
ART DIRECTOR   Mike Richardson/
Nicolas Kadima
ILLUSTRATOR   Steve McArdle

BEST BILLBOARD

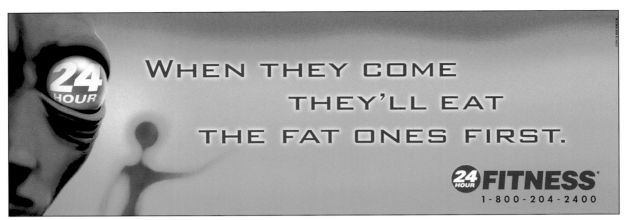

WHEN THEY COME
THEY'LL EAT
THE FAT ONES FIRST.

24 HOUR FITNESS
1-800-204-2400

USA

FINALIST, SINGLE

GREY INTERNATIONAL, SAN FRANCISCO
SAN FRANCISCO, CA

CLIENT 24 Hour Fitness

CREATIVE DIRECTOR
Alan Randolph

COPYWRITER
Saurabh Sharma

ART DIRECTOR
Julian Schmidt

Time to go?
REAL ESTATE ON SATURDAYS
Berliner Zeitung

New flat?
REAL ESTATE ON SATURDAYS
Berliner Zeitung

GERMANY

FINALIST, CAMPAIGN

SCHOLZ & FRIENDS BERLIN
BERLIN

CLIENT Berliner Zeitung
CREATIVE DIRECTOR Moi Soltek/Sebastian Turner
COPYWRITER Robert Krause
ART DIRECTOR Raphael Puttmann
PHOTOGRAPHER Matthias Koslik

BEST TRANSIT

ARGENTINA

FINALIST, SINGLE

LAUTREC NAZCA SAATCHI & SAATCHI
BUENOS AIRES

CLIENT Argentine Transplant Foundation
CREATIVE DIRECTOR Pablo Del Campo (CCD)/
Esteban Pigni
COPYWRITER Guillermo Castaneda
ART DIRECTOR Sebastian Garin

SEE PAGE 168

CIVIC / SOCIAL EDUCATION

USA

GOLD WORLDMEDAL, SINGLE
**D'ARCY MASIUS
BENTON & BOWLES**
NEW YORK, NY

CLIENT
United Way Of New York
CREATIVE DIRECTOR
Cathy Aromando
COPYWRITER Betty Green
ART DIRECTOR Jackie Leak
PHOTOGRAPHER
Christopher Baker

GERMANY

BRONZE WORLDMEDAL, SINGLE
JVM WERBEAGENTUR GMBH
HAMBURG

CLIENT Noah, Menschen Fuer Tiere E.V.
CREATIVE DIRECTOR
Hermann Waterkamp/Frank Dovidat
COPYWRITER Jan Kesting
ART DIRECTOR Goetz Ulmer

ARGENTINA
SILVER WORLDMEDAL, SINGLE
**LAUTREC NAZCA
SAATCHI & SAATCHI**
BUENOS AIRES

CLIENT Argentine
Transplant Foundation
CREATIVE DIRECTOR
Pablo Del Campo/
Esteban Pigni
COPYWRITER
Guillermo Castaneda
ART DIRECTOR
Sebastian Garin

PORTUGAL

FINALIST, SINGLE
BBDO PORTUGAL
LISBON

CLIENT CAIS - Homeless Assistance Magazine
CREATIVE DIRECTOR Jorge Teixeira
COPYWRITER Gaspar
ART DIRECTOR Karina Cid
PHOTOGRAPHER Rodrigo Cabral/Nuno Soares/Lisboa

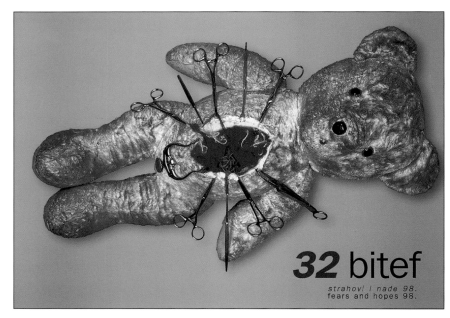

YUGOSLAVIA
FINALIST, SINGLE
I&F McCANN - ERICKSON BELGRADE
BELGRADE

CREATIVE DIRECTOR Srdan Saper
COPYWRITER Sahja Rudic
ART DIRECTOR Sahja Rudic
PHOTOGRAPHER Talent

AUSTRIA
FINALIST, SINGLE
DEMNER, MERLICEK & BERGMANN
VIENNA

CLIENT   Initiative "Sauberes Wien"/
Initiative for a Clean City"
CREATIVE DIRECTOR   Ernst Baechtold
COPYWRITER   Jan Froscher
ART DIRECTOR   Ernst Baechtold/Alexander Kellas
PHOTOGRAPHER   Udo Titz
ILLUSTRATOR   Antonia Demmer (Graphics)

SOUTH AFRICA
FINALIST, SINGLE
HERDBUOYS McCANN-ERICKSON
JOHANNESBURG
CLIENT   Road Safety Initiative
CREATIVE DIRECTOR   Jono Swanepoel/
Steve Richards
COPYWRITER   Louis Maass/Jono Swanepoel
ART DIRECTOR   Jono Swanepoel
PHOTOGRAPHER   Ignus Gerber

COLOMBIA
FINALIST, SINGLE
J.WALTER THOMPSON COLOMBIA
BOGOTA

CREATIVE DIRECTOR   David Rodriquez
COPYWRITER   David Rodriguez
ART DIRECTOR   Alejandro Benavides

DON'T LET PREGN
(Call 0860

Pregnancy isn't easy. It's exciting, it's thrilling, it's miraculous, but not easy. And relationships suffer because he doesn't understand why you're behaving differently and you don't understand

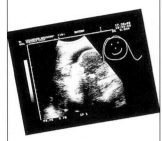

why he isn't! The key word is "understand" and that is what Childbirth Education is all about - a clearer understanding of what is happening so that you can anticipate the birth and the first few weeks of your baby's new life with confidence in yourself and each other. So start classes today. Call 0860 18 18 18.

This community message is brought to you

CHILDBIRTH EDUCATORS' RESOURCE GROUP
A good pregnancy is a learning curve.

SAATCHI & SAATCHI 29959/L

ANCY SPLIT YOU UP.
18 18 18)

During pregnancy, your partner's body undergoes huge hormonal changes. The amount of blood circulating in her body increases by a third. She's hot and sweaty one minute, cold and clammy

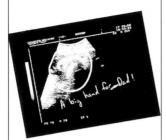

the next. She feels physically and emotionally drained most of the time and, not surprisingly, your relationship takes strain. Naturally, the more you understand, the better you will cope, so sign on now for Childbirth Education classes. After all, it's your pregnancy too, so get involved.

by the Pampers Mum and Baby Programme.

CHILDBIRTH EDUCATORS' RESOURCE GROUP
A good pregnancy is a learning curve.

SAATCHI & SAATCHI 29959/R

SOUTH AFRICA
FINALIST, SINGLE
SAATCHI & SAATCHI
JOHANNESBURG
CLIENT Childbirth Education Resource Group
CREATIVE DIRECTOR Wyn Crane
COPYWRITER Wyn Crane
ART DIRECTOR Wyn Crane
OTHER Beith Digital

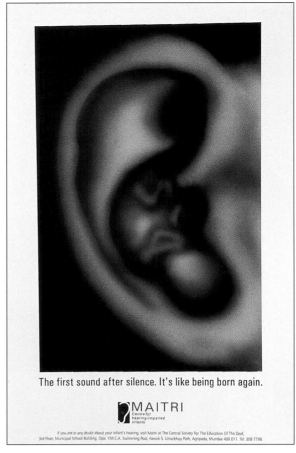

The first sound after silence. It's like being born again.

INDIA
FINALIST, SINGLE
SSC&B LINTAS
MUMBAI
CLIENT Maitri
COPYWRITER Amar Deb
ART DIRECTOR Shantanu Gholkar
OTHER Ajay Chandwani

GERMANY
FINALIST, SINGLE
JVM WERBEAGENTUR GMBH
HAMBURG
CLIENT Noah, Menschen Fuer Tiere E.V.
CREATIVE DIRECTOR
Hermann Waterkamp/ Frank Davidat
COPYWRITER Jan Kesting
ART DIRECTOR Goetz Ulmer
ILLUSTRATOR Roland Warzecha

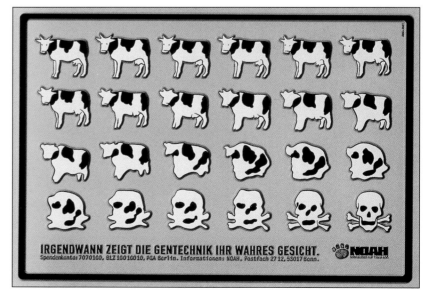

OF COURSE! WE CAN MOVE ON.
We gather our mind together for better Future

KOREA

GOLD WORLDMEDAL, CAMPAIGN
CHEIL COMMUNICATIONS
SEOUL

CLIENT   Ministry of Culture & Tourism
CREATIVE DIRECTOR   Sang Min Nam
COPYWRITER   Hong Tak Kim
ART DIRECTOR   Byung Won Choi/Ji Wang Hong
PHOTOGRAPHER   Sang Mo Koo

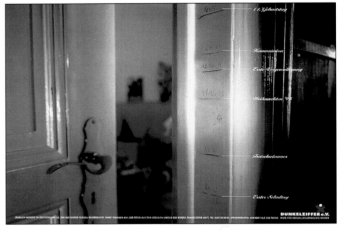

GERMANY
BRONZE WORLDMEDAL, CAMPAIGN
JVM WERBEAGENTUR GMBH
HAMBURG
CLIENT   Dunkelziffer E.V.
CREATIVE DIRECTOR   Hermann Waterkamp
COPYWRITER   Thorsten Meier
ART DIRECTOR   Roland Hess
PHOTOGRAPHER   Reinhard Hunger

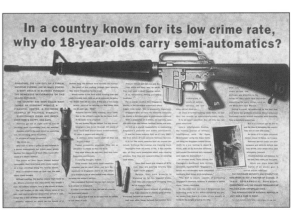

SINGAPORE
FINALIST, CAMPAIGN
DENTSU, YOUNG & RUBICAM
SINGAPORE

CLIENT   National Education
CREATIVE DIRECTOR   Patrick Low
COPYWRITER   Yu Sheng It
COPYWRITER   Mark Fong
ART DIRECTOR   Patrick Low

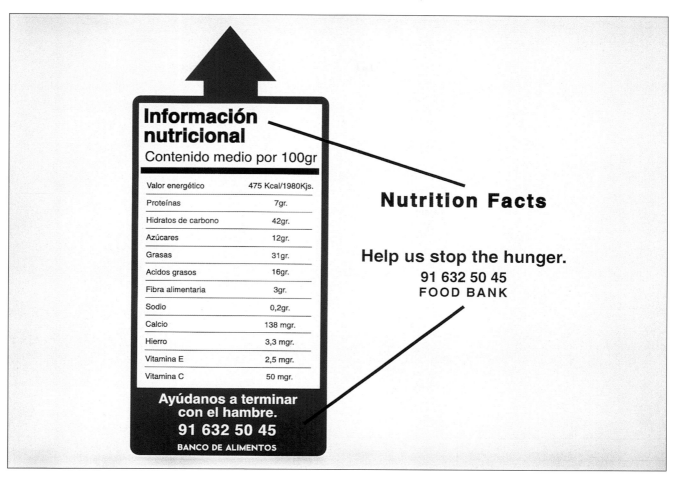

SPAIN
SILVER WORLDMEDAL, CAMPAIGN
RUIZ NICOLI
MADRID
CLIENT Food Bank
CREATIVE DIRECTOR
Ana Hidalgo
COPYWRITER David Marina/
Paco Ruiz Nicoli
ART DIRECTOR David Marina

Coming out? Come on in.

HORIZONS

773.929.HELP

USA
FINALIST, CAMPAIGN
LEO BURNETT
CHICAGO, IL
CLIENT Horizons
CREATIVE DIRECTOR Steffan Postaer/
Mark Faulkner
COPYWRITER Steffan Postaer/
Mark Faulkner
ART DIRECTOR Dustin Smith

Gosh darn it, just be the best darn Homosexual you can be then.

HORIZONS

CHICAGO'S LESBIAN & GAY COMMUNITY CENTER

773.929.HELP

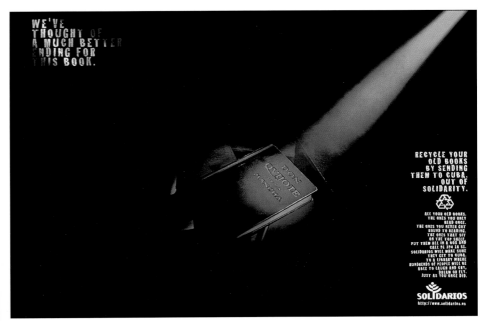

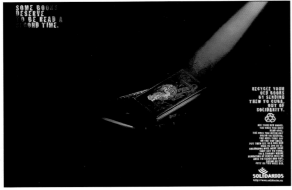

SPAIN

FINALIST, CAMPAIGN
McCANN-ERICKSON
MADRID

CLIENT   Solidarios/N.G.O.

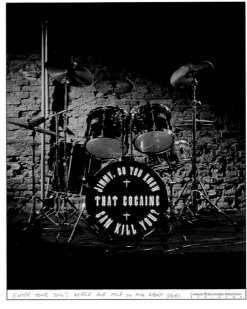

ARGENTINA

FINALIST, CAMPAIGN
VERDINO BATES FERNANDO FERNANDEZ
BUENOS AIRES

CLIENT   Consejo Publicitario Argentino
CREATIVE DIRECTOR   Fernando Fernandez
COPYWRITER   Sebastian Alfie
ART DIRECTOR   Carlos Brana
PHOTOGRAPHER   Hernan Churba
OTHER   Carlos Hermansson (Account Director)

AUSTRALIA

GOLD WORLDMEDAL, SINGLE

RACHEL HARRINGTON & HELEN SHORTIS

EAST SYDNEY

CLIENT   World Wide Fund For Nature
ADVERTISING AGENCY   Ogilvy & Mather/ Sydney
COPYWRITER   Rachel Harrington
ART DIRECTOR   Helen Shortis
PHOTOGRAPHER   Billy Wrencher

ARGENTINA

FINALIST, SINGLE

AD-HONOREM

BUENOS AIRES

CLIENT   Green Peace
CREATIVE DIRECTOR   Guillermo Caro
COPYWRITER   Guillermo Caro
ART DIRECTOR   Guillermo Caro
PHOTOGRAPHER   Focus/Caro

RUSSIA

FINALIST, SINGLE

BEGEMOT ADVERTISING AGENCY

MOSCOW

CREATIVE DIRECTOR   Pavel Poliautsev
COPYWRITER   Alexey Sinkin
ART DIRECTOR   Sergey Diatcheudo
ILLUSTRATOR   Alexey Sinkin

BRAZIL

FINALIST, SINGLE

F/NAZCA SAATCHI & SAATCHI
SAO PAULO

CLIENT Environmental Issues
CREATIVE DIRECTOR Fabio Fernandes
COPYWRITER Wilson Mateos
ART DIRECTOR Marco Aurelio Monteiro
PHOTOGRAPHER Rodrigo Ribeiro

PORTUGAL

FINALIST, SINGLE

McCANN-ERICKSON PORTUGAL
LISBOA

CLIENT Observatorio do ambiente
CREATIVE DIRECTOR McCann-Erickson
COPYWRITER McCann-Erickson
ART DIRECTOR McCann-Erickson
PHOTOGRAPHER Estudios Cidade/
Casa de Imagem

OBSERVATÓRIO DO AMBIENTE WARNING: Quitting Breathing Now
Greatly Reduces Serious Risks to Your Health.

HEALTH /HYGIENE

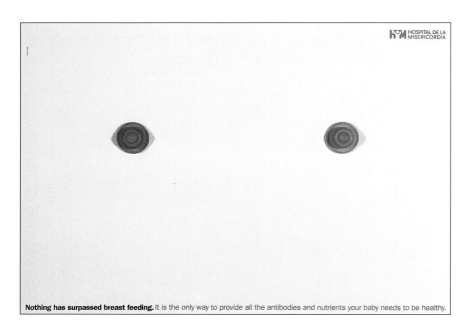

Nothing has surpassed breast feeding. It is the only way to provide all the antibodies and nutrients your baby needs to be healthy.

COLOMBIA

FINALIST, SINGLE

LOWE & PARTNERS /SSPM S.A.
BOGOTA

CLIENT Hospital de la Misericordia
CREATIVE DIRECTOR H. Polar/M. Sokolof/L Correa
COPYWRITER Eduardo Vargas
ART DIRECTOR Ivan Onatra

SINGAPORE

GOLD WORLDMEDAL, SINGLE
**BARTLE BOGLE HEGARTY LTD
ASIA PACIFIC**
SINGAPORE

CLIENT Singapore Cancer Society
COPYWRITER Robert Gaxiola
ART DIRECTOR Pearlyn Tan
PHOTOGRAPHER Teo Studio/Singapore
ILLUSTRATOR Phenomenon

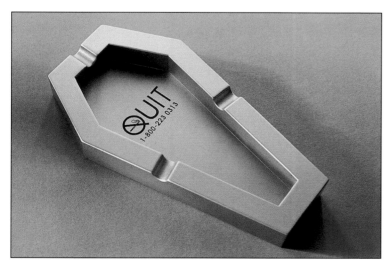

SINGAPORE

FINALIST, SINGLE
D'ARCY MASIUS BENTON & BOWLES
SINGAPORE

CLIENT Ministry of Health
COPYWRITER Perry Goh
ART DIRECTOR Perry Goh
PHOTOGRAPHER Dong/Singapore
OTHER Epcot Design Engineering (Model-Maker)

BRAZIL

FINALIST, SINGLE
DPZ PROPAGANDA
SAO PAULO

CLIENT GAPA
CREATIVE DIRECTOR Francesc Petit/Carlos Silverio
COPYWRITER Rui Branquinho
ART DIRECTOR Guime
PHOTOGRAPHER arquivo DPZ

ENVIRONMENTAL ISSUES • HEALTH / HYGIENE   177

WARNING: SMOKING CAUSES IMPOTENCE

USA

SILVER WORLDMEDAL, SINGLE
ASHER & PARTNERS
LOS ANGELES, CA
CREATIVE DIRECTOR Bruce Dundore
COPYWRITER Jeff Bossin
ART DIRECTOR Nancy Steinman
PHOTOGRAPHER Myron Beck/Los Angeles
OTHER ACD - John Krueger

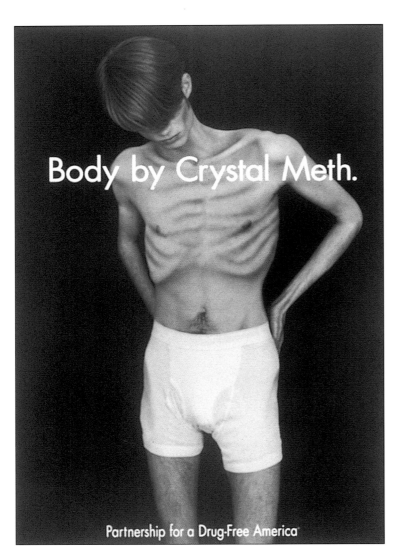

USA

BRONZE WORLDMEDAL, SINGLE
CRAMER-KRASSELT
CHICAGO, IL

CLIENT Partnership For A Drug Free America
CREATIVE DIRECTOR Marshall Ross
COPYWRITER Larry Lipson
ART DIRECTOR Lisa Howard
PHOTOGRAPHER Verser Engelhard

WITH THE AIDS. DON'T TAKE ANY CHANCES. USE CONDOM.

Fundacion Esperanza 2000   to prevent aids and drug adiction

If you want to know my problems, read my lips.

FUNDACION GANTZ
FUNDATION FOR CLEFT AND LIP PALATE CHILDREN

CHILE
FINALIST, SINGLE
NORTHCOTE OGILVY & MATHER
SANTIAGO

CLIENT Fundacion Gantz
CREATIVE DIRECTOR Matias Robeson
COPYWRITER Alejandro Arriagada
ART DIRECTOR Rene Zuniga/Jorge Schmitt
PHOTOGRAPHER Veronica Quense

ARGENTINA
FINALIST, SINGLE
OGILVY & MATHER ARGENTINA
BUENOS AIRES

CLIENT Fundacion Esperanza 2000
CREATIVE DIRECTOR Guillermo Caro/Daniel Comar
COPYWRITER Daniel Comar
ART DIRECTOR Guillermo Caro
PHOTOGRAPHER Charlie Mainardi/Buenos Aires
OTHER Maria Chanourdie (media)

THE HORRIFIC THING ABOUT IT IS, JUST A FEW DAYS AGO IT LOOKED LIKE A BEAUTY SPOT.

THE UK CENTRE FOR disfigurement

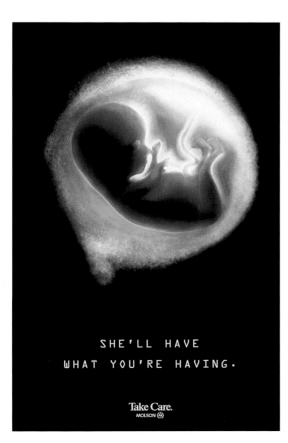

SHE'LL HAVE WHAT YOU'RE HAVING.

Take Care.
MOLSON

CANADA
FINALIST, SINGLE
MACLAREN McCANN
TORONTO, ONTARIO

CLIENT Molson Corporate -
Responsible Drinking
CREATIVE DIRECTOR Rick Davis
COPYWRITER Troy McClure
ART DIRECTOR Monique Kelley
PHOTOGRAPHER Stock
OTHER Barbara MacPherson
(Producer)

ENGLAND
FINALIST, SINGLE
WALLIS TOMLINSON
BIRMINGHAM

CLIENT Haemangiomanas
CREATIVE DIRECTOR Geoff Tomlinson
COPYWRITER Nick Galanides
ART DIRECTOR Martin Parkes
OTHER Obscura - Retouching

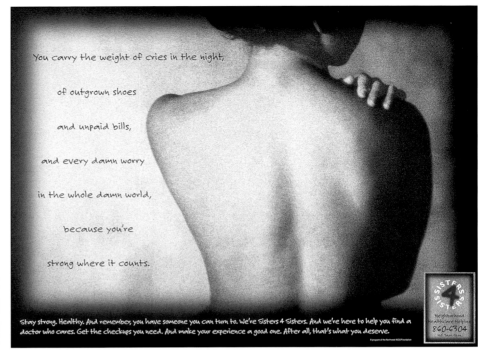

You carry the weight of cries in the night,

of outgrown shoes

and unpaid bills,

and every damn worry

in the whole damn world,

because you're

strong where it counts.

Stay strong. Healthy. And remember, you have someone you can turn to. We're Sisters 4 Sisters. And we're here to help you find a doctor who cares. Get the checkups you need. And make your experience a good one. After all, that's what you deserve.

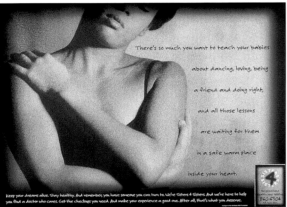

There's so much you want to teach your babies

about dancing, loving, being

a friend and doing right,

and all those lessons

are waiting for them

in a safe warm place

inside your heart.

Keep your dreams alive. Stay healthy. And remember, you have someone you can turn to. We're Sisters 4 Sisters. And we're here to help you find a doctor who cares. Get the checkups you need. And make your experience a good one. After all, that's what you deserve.

USA

FINALIST, CAMPAIGN

BOZELL WORLDWIDE/SEATTLE
SEATTLE, WA

CLIENT   Northwest AIDS Foundation
CREATIVE DIRECTOR   Mary Knight
COPYWRITER   Martha Craig
ART DIRECTOR   Shelly Baker
PHOTOGRAPHER   Rosanne Olson/Seattle

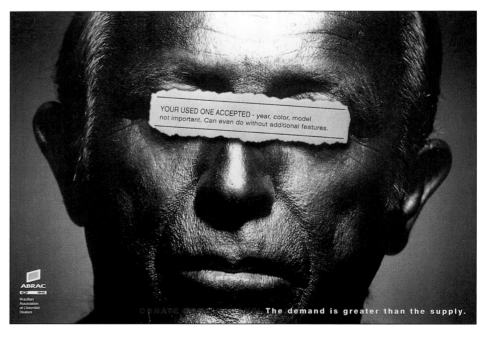

YOUR USED ONE ACCEPTED - year, color, model not important. Can even do without additional features.

The demand is greater than the supply.

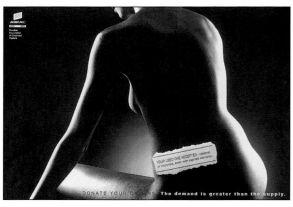

DONATE YOUR ORGANS. The demand is greater than the supply.

BRAZIL

FINALIST, CAMPAIGN

SALLES/DMB&B PUBLICIDADE LTDA.
SAO PAULO

CLIENT   Organ Donation
CREATIVE DIRECTOR   J. Palhares
COPYWRITER   Decio Gentil
ART DIRECTOR   Ilson Igreja
PHOTOGRAPHER   Richard Kohout
OTHER   Neio Amorim Leite (Graphic Producer)

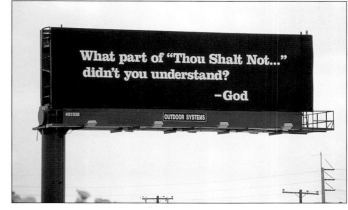

USA

SILVER WORLDMEDAL, CAMPAIGN

THE SMITH AGENCY
FORT LAUDERDALE, FL

CREATIVE DIRECTOR Charlie Robb
COPYWRITER Charlie Robb
ART DIRECTOR Daniel Borst

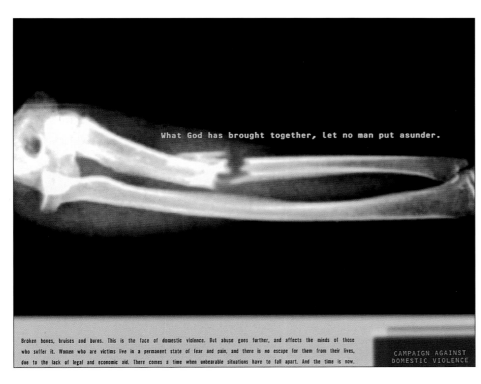

SPAIN

FINALIST, SINGLE

CONTRAPUNTO
MADRID

CLIENT Campaign Against Violence To Women
CREATIVE DIRECTOR Carlos Sanz de Andino
COPYWRITER Nacho Padilla
ART DIRECTOR Javier Perez

AUSTRIA

BRONZE WORLDMEDAL, CAMPAIGN
LOWE GGK
VIENNA

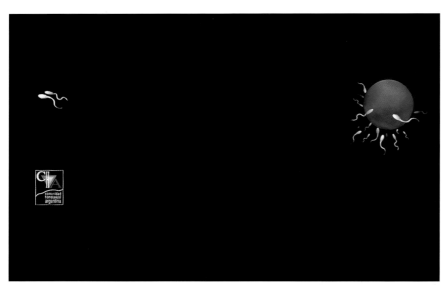

ARGENTINA

FINALIST, SINGLE
EJE PUBLICITARIA S.A.
BUENOS AIRES

CLIENT CHA
CREATIVE DIRECTOR Julian Bassotto
COPYWRITER Walter Vazquez
ART DIRECTOR Julian Bassotto

SOUTH AFRICA

FINALIST, SINGLE
SAATCHI & SAATCHI
CAPE TOWN

CLIENT Bell's Whisky Gay & Lesbian
Film Festival
CREATIVE DIRECTOR Eric Frank
COPYWRITER Mark Legward
ART DIRECTOR Duncan Wares
PHOTOGRAPHER Juan Espi/Cape Town

THE 5TH SOUTH AFRICAN GAY & LESBIAN
FILM FESTIVAL 1998

Extra Special Times. Extra Special Scotch.

SOUTH AFRICA

FINALIST, SINGLE

HERDBUOYS McCANN-ERICKSON
JOHANNESBURG

CLIENT   St Thomas Anglican Church
CREATIVE DIRECTOR   Steve Richards/
Jono Swanepoel
COPYWRITER   Louis Maass
ART DIRECTOR   Alison Stansfield
PHOTOGRAPHER   Juan Espi/Cape Town

PSA-PERSONAL DEVELOPMENT

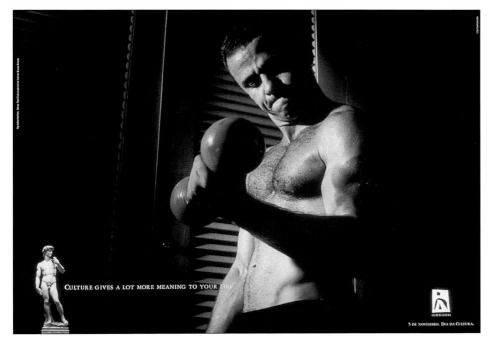

BRAZIL

FINALIST, CAMPAIGN
CONTEMPORANE
RIO DE JANEIRO

CLIENT   Culture Club
CREATIVE DIRECTOR   Jose Guilherme Vereza/
Mauro Matos
COPYWRITER   Victor Sant'Anna
ART DIRECTOR   Pedro Utzeri
PHOTOGRAPHER   Marcia Ramalho

USA

FINALIST, SINGLE
CAMPBELL - EWALD ADVERTISING
WARREN, MI

CLIENT Michigan Seat Belt
CREATIVE DIRECTOR Jim Gorman/Joe Puhy/
Brad Neeley
COPYWRITER Mark Renush
ART DIRECTOR Richard North
OTHER William Ludwig (Vice Chairman, CCO)

USA

FINALIST, CAMPAIGN
EQUALS THREE COMMUNICATIONS
BETHESDA, MD

CREATIVE DIRECTOR Meghan O'Connell
COPYWRITER David Page/Lisa Hagan
ART DIRECTOR Ron Ordanza
PHOTOGRAPHER Jim Douglass

KOREA

FINALIST, SINGLE
CHEIL COMMUNICATIONS
SEOUL

CLIENT Samsung Life Insurance
CREATIVE DIRECTOR Hae Young Lee
COPYWRITER Jae Wook Nam
ART DIRECTOR Eun Jang Lee

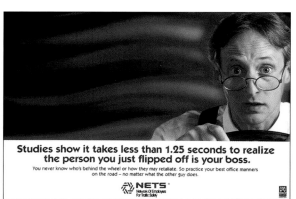

AUSTRALIA
SILVER WORLDMEDAL, SINGLE
MOJO PARTNERS
EAST SYDNEY

CLIENT Red Cross Organ Donation
CREATIVE DIRECTOR Gaby Bush
COPYWRITER Simon Langley/Richard Morgan
ART DIRECTOR Simon Langley/Richard Morgan
PHOTOGRAPHER Romp & Schee Photography

SPAIN
FINALIST, SINGLE
BASSAT OGILVY & MATHER
BARCELONA

CLIENT Fundaicon Vicente Ferrer
CREATIVE DIRECTOR Felipe Crespo/Beat Keller
COPYWRITER Felipe Crespo
ART DIRECTOR Beat Keller/Juan Carlos Cabrera
OTHER Ignacio Rufin (Account Director)

USA
FINALIST, SINGLE
CRAMER-KRASSELT
CHICAGO, IL
CLIENT College Football Hall Of Fame
CREATIVE DIRECTOR Marshall Ross
COPYWRITER Bob Volkman
ART DIRECTOR Ted Jenkins

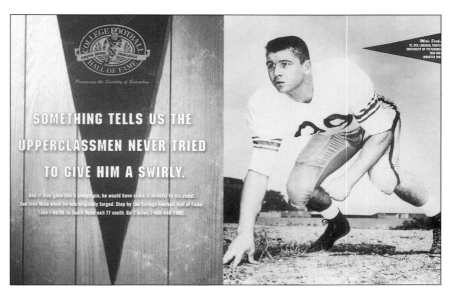

SINGAPORE

BRONZE WORLDMEDAL, SINGLE
LOWE & PARTNERS/MONSOON
SINGAPORE

CLIENT Doctors Without Borders
CREATIVE DIRECTOR Ng Khee Jin
COPYWRITER Rachel Goh
ART DIRECTOR Candy Kang
PHOTOGRAPHER Douglas Goh/Pictureman

USA

FINALIST, SINGLE
BATES USA MIDWEST
INDIANAPOLIS, IN

CLIENT Humane Society Of Indianapolis
CREATIVE DIRECTOR Marcia Stone
COPYWRITER Tom Aschauer
ART DIRECTOR Heidi Bobb/Pam Linsley

PORTUGAL

FINALIST, SINGLE
BATES PORTUGAL
LISBOA

CLIENT AMI - Medical Aid
International
CREATIVE DIRECTOR Pedro Ferreira/
Judite Mota
COPYWRITER Nuno Silva
ART DIRECTOR Luis Moreira
PHOTOGRAPHER Getty Image

CANADA

FINALIST, SINGLE
BBDO CANADA
TORONTO

CLIENT National Advertising
Benevolent Society
CREATIVE DIRECTOR
Michael McLaughlin
COPYWRITER Michael Clowater
ART DIRECTOR Les Soos
PHOTOGRAPHER Les Soos

SPAIN

FINALIST, SINGLE
CUATROMAS
MADRID

CLIENT Shangay Magazine
CREATIVE DIRECTOR Breno Cotta
COPYWRITER Breno Cotta
ART DIRECTOR Myriam Maneiro/
Lara Hernandez
PHOTOGRAPHER Angel Almena
ILLUSTRATOR Javier Eimar

USA

FINALIST, SINGLE
D'ARCY MASIUS BENTON & BOWLES
NEW YORK, NY

CLIENT Singapore Humane Society
CREATIVE DIRECTOR Curt Detweiler
COPYWRITER Curt Detweiler/Perry Goh/Allan Tay
ART DIRECTOR Perry Goh/Curt Detweiler
ILLUSTRATOR Perry Goh/Singapore
OTHER Curt Detweiler (Typographer)

USA

FINALIST, SINGLE
FJCANDN
SALT LAKE CITY, UT

CLIENT Catholic Community Services
CREATIVE DIRECTOR Dave Newbold
COPYWRITER Bryant Marcum
ART DIRECTOR Matt Manfull
PHOTOGRAPHER Tyler Gourley/
Salt Lake City/UT

THE NETHERLANDS

FINALIST, SINGLE
**NOORDERVLIET &
WINNINGHOFF/LB**
AMSTERDAM

CLIENT The Dutch Red Cross
CREATIVE DIRECTOR F. Brand/M. van Sonbeek
COPYWRITER A. van den Berg
ART DIRECTOR P. Hart

CANADA

BRONZE WORLDMEDAL, CAMPAIGN
PUBLICIS SMW
TORONTO

CLIENT UNICEF
CREATIVE DIRECTOR David Rosenberg/
Gerald Schoenhoff
COPYWRITER Trish Kavanagh
ART DIRECTOR Rosalinda Graziano
PHOTOGRAPHER George Simhoni/Toronto
OTHER Propeller Head (Model-Maker)

NEW ZEALAND

FINALIST, SINGLE
FOOTE, CONE & BELDING LTD.
AUCKLAND

CLIENT Royal New Zealand Coastguard
CREATIVE DIRECTOR Rob Sherlock
COPYWRITER Murry Watt
ART DIRECTOR Uwe Engbers
PHOTOGRAPHER Doug Cole/Auckland
OTHER Geof McDonald/Helen Scott
(Account Executives)

CANADA

FINALIST, SINGLE
YOUNG & RUBICAM TORONTO
TORONTO

CLIENT Make-A-Wish Foundation
CREATIVE DIRECTOR David Adams/
John Farquhar
COPYWRITER Simon Creet
ART DIRECTOR Dan Tanenbaum
PHOTOGRAPHER Rafael Goldchain/
Toronto

A vacation means so much more when your full-time job is fighting for your life.

We can't give Ryan what he really needs, so we give him what he really wants.

CANADA

GOLD WORLDMEDAL, CAMPAIGN

YOUNG & RUBICAM TORONTO
TORONTO, ONTARIO

CLIENT   Make-A-Wish Foundation
CREATIVE DIRECTOR   John Farquhar
CREATIVE DIRECTOR   David Adams
COPYWRITER   Simon Creet
ART DIRECTOR   Dan Tanenbaum
PHOTOGRAPHER   Rafael Goldchain/Toronto

USA
FINALIST, CAMPAIGN
THOMPSON & COMPANY
MEMPHIS, TN
CLIENT   Salvation Army
CREATIVE DIRECTOR
Trace Hallowell
COPYWRITER   Cliff Watson
ART DIRECTOR   Rick Baptist
ILLUSTRATOR   Marty Eastes/
Memphis

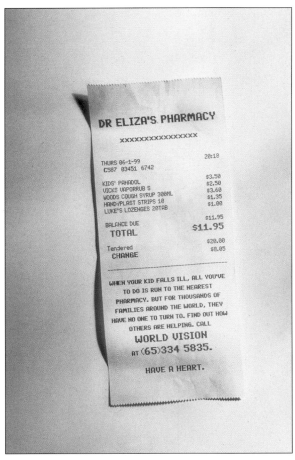

SINGAPORE

SILVER WORLDMEDAL, CAMPAIGN
LOWE & PARTNERS/MONSOON
SINGAPORE

CLIENT   World Vision International
CREATIVE DIRECTOR   Ng Khee Jin
COPYWRITER   Vijayan Ganesh
ART DIRECTOR   Lim Chye Ling
PHOTOGRAPHER   Alex Kaikeong
OTHER   Colourscan (Colour Separation)

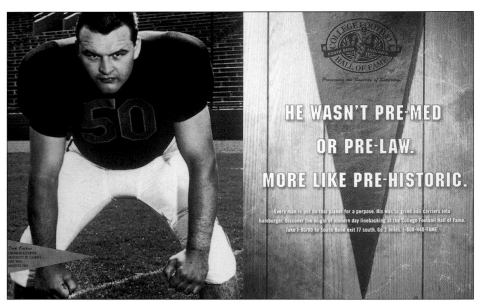

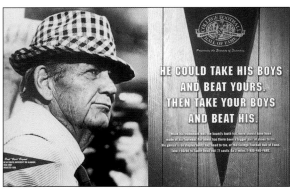

USA

FINALIST, CAMPAIGN
CRAMER-KRASSELT
CHICAGO, IL

CLIENT   College Football Hall of Fame
CREATIVE DIRECTOR   Marshall Ross
COPYWRITER   Bob Volkman
ART DIRECTOR   Ted Jenkins

YUGOSLAVIA

SILVER WORLDMEDAL, SINGLE

FOCUS COMMUNICATIONS

BELGRADE

CLIENT Radio B92
CREATIVE DIRECTOR Igor Avzner
COPYWRITER Ivana Cakic
ART DIRECTOR Marica Kuznhecov
PHOTOGRAPHER Nenad Kojadinovic/Belgrade

HONG KONG

FINALIST, SINGLE

**DENTSU INC.,
HONG KONG BRANCH**

QUARRY BAY

CREATIVE DIRECTOR David Chow/
Albert Wong
COPYWRITER Cora Chan
ART DIRECTOR Albert Wong
ILLUSTRATOR Gavin Lee

SPAIN

GOLD WORLDMEDAL, CAMPAIGN
SAATCHI & SAATCHI
MADRID

CLIENT Manos Unidas
CREATIVE DIRECTOR Cesar Garcia (Executive C.D.)
COPYWRITER Mercedes Ruiz
ART DIRECTOR Mar Frutos
PHOTOGRAPHER Rafael Abia
OTHER A. de Reguero (Account Dir)/
C. Rodriguez (Account exec)

JAPAN

FINALIST, SINGLE
TAKASHI AKIYAMA
TOKYO

ART DIRECTOR Takashi Akiyama
ILLUSTRATOR Takashi Akiyama

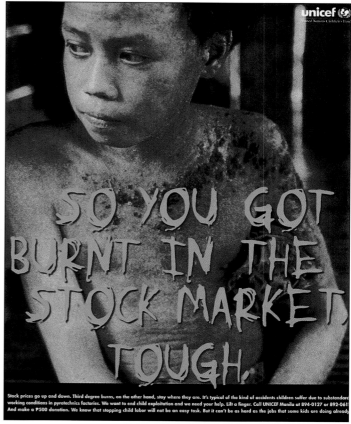

PHILIPPINES

BRONZE WORLDMEDAL, CAMPAIGN
OGILVY & MATHER PHILIPPINES
MAKATI

CLIENT UNICEF
CREATIVE DIRECTOR David Guerrero/Jun Carangan/Tom Trinidad
COPYWRITER Tom Trinidad/David Guerrero
ART DIRECTOR Nicky Montenegro/Jun Carangan
PHOTOGRAPHER Joseph Fortin/Joan Bondoc/Manila

USA

FINALIST, SINGLE
HAGGMAN ADVERTISING
MANCHESTER, MA

CLIENT Raising The Bar
CREATIVE DIRECTOR Eric Haggman
COPYWRITER Eric Haggman
ART DIRECTOR Katie Emery

The New York Festivals
The World's Best Work

NEWSPAPER ADVERTISING

NEWSPAPER ADVERTISING

GRAND AWARD

BEST NEWSPAPER ADVERTISEMENT

AUSTRALIA
GRAND AWARD BEST NEWSPAPER
ADVERTISEMENT
SAATCHI & SAATCHI
SYDNEY
CLIENT
No Frills Funerals
and Cremations
CREATIVE DIRECTOR
Michael Newman
COPYWRITER
Jay Furby
ART DIRECTOR
Steve Carlin
PHOTOGRAPHER
Gary Richardson
OTHER Mark Payne
(Account Supervisor)

This is what's left after an $8,000 cremation.

This is what's left after a $2,000 cremation.

When you're gone, you're gone.   **No Frills** FUNERALS & CREMATIONS   For information call 9247 6895.

This is what you're buried under in a $25,000 funeral.

This is what you're buried under in a $2,000 funeral.

When you're gone, you're gone.  For information call 9247 6895.

APPAREL & ACCESSORIES

SINGAPORE

FINALIST, SINGLE
FCB SINGAPORE
SINGAPORE

CLIENT Adidas
CREATIVE DIRECTOR Chris Kyme
COPYWRITER Chris Kyme
ART DIRECTOR Dali Meskam

SINGAPORE

FINALIST, SINGLE
FCB SINGAPORE
SINGAPORE

CLIENT Adidas
CREATIVE DIRECTOR Chris Kyme
COPYWRITER Chris Kyme
ART DIRECTOR Dali Meskam

SEE PAGE 199

CHILE

FINALIST, SINGLE
AMMIRATI PURIS LINTAS CHILE
SANTIAGO

CLIENT Power
CREATIVE DIRECTOR Quincy
COPYWRITER Pancho Gonzalez
ART DIRECTOR Mario Coloma
ILLUSTRATOR S-Files

USA

FINALIST, SINGLE
HMS PARTNERS
COLUMBUS, OH

CLIENT UnderWearhouse
CREATIVE DIRECTOR
Stephen Fechtor
COPYWRITER
Mark Borcherding
ART DIRECTOR Rocco Volpe
PHOTOGRAPHER Will Shivley
OTHER Dan Miceli
(Production Manager)

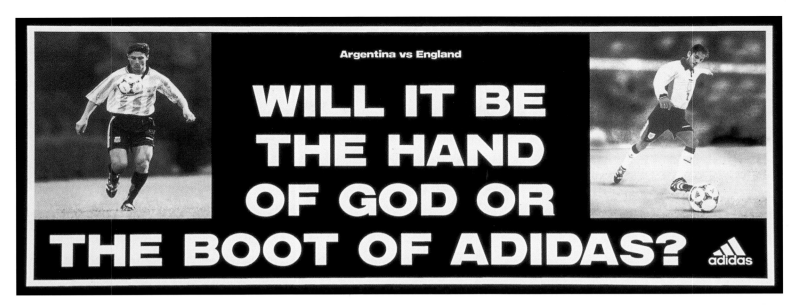

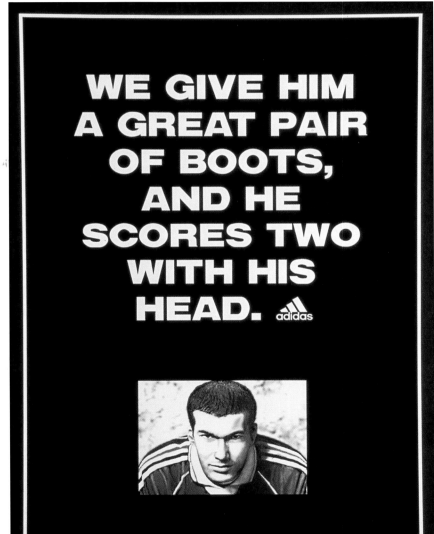

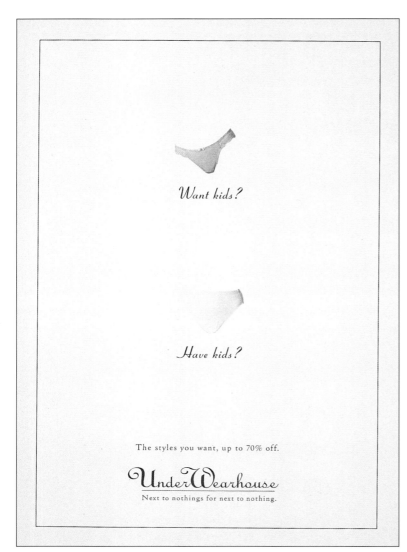

Want kids?

Have kids?

The styles you want, up to 70% off.

UnderWearhouse
Next to nothings for next to nothing.

The cable repairman is coming over.

He's cute.

Underwear for every occasion, up to 70% off.

UnderWearhouse
Next to nothings for next to nothing.

USA

SILVER WORLDMEDAL, CAMPAIGN

HMS PARTNERS
COLUMBUS, OH

CLIENT   UnderWearhouse
CREATIVE DIRECTOR   Stephen Fechtor
COPYWRITER   Mark Borcherding
ART DIRECTOR   Rocco Volpe
PHOTOGRAPHER   Will Shivley
OTHER   Dan Miceli (Production Manager)

FRANCE

FINALIST, CAMPAIGN

BOZELL PARIS/BOZELL NEW YORK
NEUILLY SUR SEINE

CLIENT   Ray-Ban
CREATIVE DIRECTOR   Eric Allouche
COPYWRITER   Eric Allouche
ART DIRECTOR   Sylvain Rollet
PHOTOGRAPHER   Enrique Badulescu

THE NEW SKYLINE NISSAN

No estaba muerto... andaba de parranda.

El nuevo Volky '98

Euroclass

Marginal Ave. Kennedy, Km 3.5 Teléfono 782-4C39

Drivers wanted.

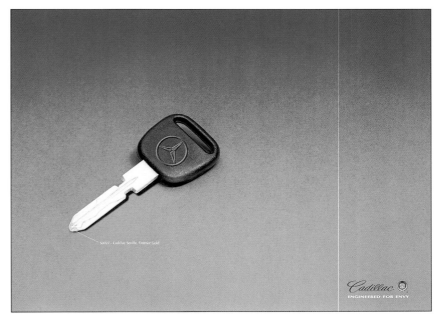

Cadillac
ENGINEERED FOR ENVY

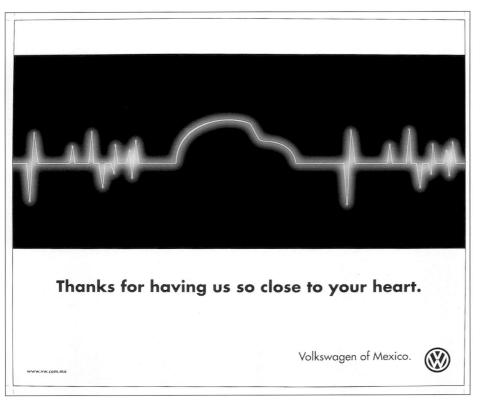

Thanks for having us so close to your heart.

www.vw.com.mx   Volkswagen of Mexico. **VW**

MEXICO
FINALIST, SINGLE
GIBERT DDB
MEXICO CITY
CLIENT Volkswagen
CREATIVE DIRECTOR Raul Cardos/
Federico Casillas
COPYWRITER Gustavo Duenas/Sandra Flores
ART DIRECTOR Armando Zubieta/
Jose Alfredo Perez

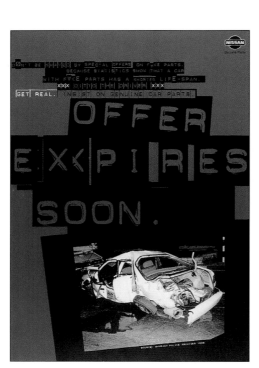

UNITED ARAB EMIRATES
FINALIST, CAMPAIGN
TEAM/YOUNG & RUBICAM , DUBAI
DUBAI
CLIENT Nissan
CREATIVE DIRECTOR Karen Chambers
COPYWRITER Shahir Ahmed
ART DIRECTOR Shahir Ahmed/Sameer Ahmed
OTHER Carlo Dei Tedeschi (Account Handler)

ISRAEL

SILVER WORLDMEDAL, SINGLE

BAUMANN BER RIVNAY

TEL-AVIV

CLIENT   Albar Managment,
Financing Leasing

CREATIVE DIRECTOR
Shony Rivnay

COPYWRITER   Oren Kari

ART DIRECTOR
Shay Moscona

PHOTOGRAPHER
Ernst Meron

OTHER   Miri Salhov
(Production Manager)

SWITZERLAND

BRONZE WORLDMEDAL, CAMPAIGN

PUBLICIS, FARNER, AEBI, STREBEL

ZURICH

CLIENT   Die Mobiliar Insurance
CREATIVE DIRECTOR   Jean Etienne Aebi
COPYWRITER   Matthias Freuler
ART DIRECTOR   Rene Sennhauser
PHOTOGRAPHER   Henrik Halvarsson

BEVERAGES

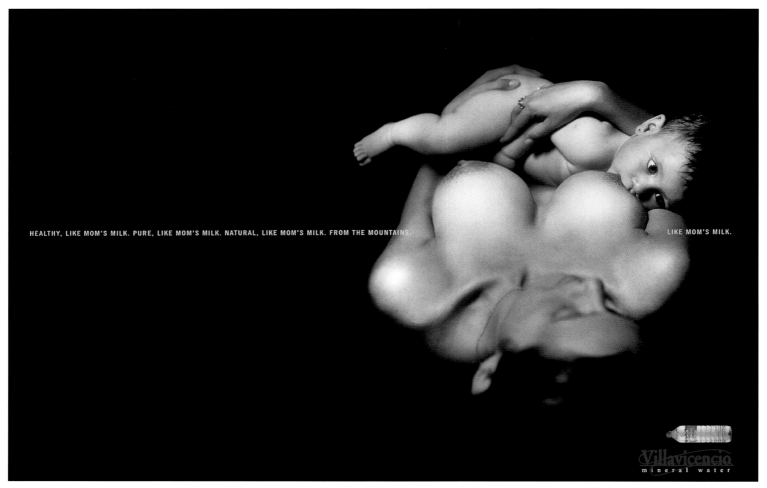

HEALTHY, LIKE MOM'S MILK. PURE, LIKE MOM'S MILK. NATURAL, LIKE MOM'S MILK. FROM THE MOUNTAINS. LIKE MOM'S MILK.

ARGENTINA
GOLD WORLDMEDAL, SINGLE
LAUTREC NAZCA SAATCHI & SAATCHI
BUENOS AIRES

CLIENT Villavicencio Mineral Water
CREATIVE DIRECTOR Juan Cravero/Esteban Pigni
COPYWRITER Esteban Pigni
ART DIRECTOR Toto Marelli
PHOTOGRAPHER Freddy Fabris/Buenos Aires
ILLUSTRATOR Victor Bustos/Buenos Aires

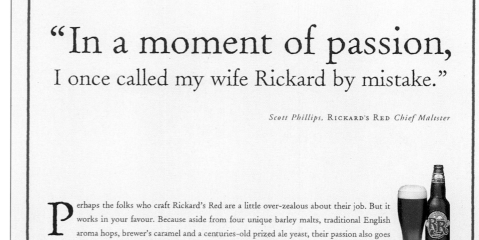

"In a moment of passion,
I once called my wife Rickard by mistake."

Scott Phillips, RICKARD'S RED *Chief Maltster*

Perhaps the folks who craft Rickard's Red are a little over-zealous about their job. But it works in your favour. Because aside from four unique barley malts, traditional English aroma hops, brewer's caramel and a centuries-old prized ale yeast, their passion also goes into the beer. And that's an ingredient you won't see on the label. TASTE THE LOVE.

CANADA
FINALIST, SINGLE
BBDO CANADA
TORONTO, ONTARIO
CLIENT Rickard's Red Beer
CREATIVE DIRECTOR Michael McLaughlin
COPYWRITER Katie Barni
ART DIRECTOR David Houghton
OTHER SGL Studios (Typography)

THE NETHERLANDS
SILVER WORLDMEDAL, SINGLE
DMB&B/WORLDWIDE COMMUNICATIONS
AMSTERDAM
CLIENT Bavaria Malt
COPYWRITER Edward Bardoul
ART DIRECTOR Jaap Sinke
PHOTOGRAPHER Paul Ruigrok/Amsterdam
OTHER Robert Pachovski (Modelmaker)

JAPAN
FINALIST, SINGLE
DENTSU, INC.
TOKYO

CLIENT Milk
CREATIVE DIRECTOR Kazuo Arai
COPYWRITER Yuka Tsukada
ART DIRECTOR Kazunari Eguchi/Yuji Suzuki
PHOTOGRAPHER Hatsuhiko Okada

INDIA
FINALIST, SINGLE
CHAITRA LEO BURNETT P.L.
MUMBAI
CLIENT Heinz India Pvt Ltd
CREATIVE DIRECTOR K.Y. Sridhar
COPYWRITER Agnello Dias
ART DIRECTOR Yayati Godbole
PHOTOGRAPHER Sanjeev Angang/Mumbai

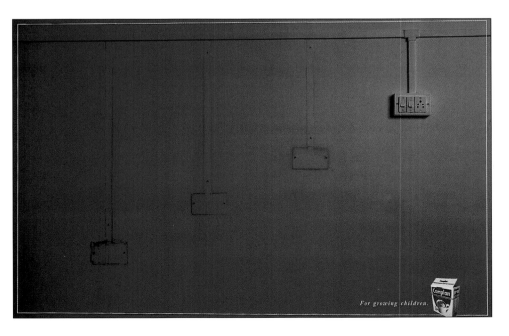

Good girls
go to bed
at 8 P.M.
For they got
to be
home before 12 A.M.
to sleep.

AN AMAZING
RUM

MEXICO

BRONZE WORLDMEDAL, SINGLE
CLEMENTE CAMARA Y ASOCIADOS SA DE CV
MEXICO
CLIENT Casa Pedro Domecq S.A de C.V./
Ron Baraima Citrus
CREATIVE DIRECTOR Eduardo Perez
COPYWRITER Salavdor Mejia/Edgar Hernandez
ART DIRECTOR Ricardo Anaya
PHOTOGRAPHER Enrique Covarrubias/Mexico D.F.

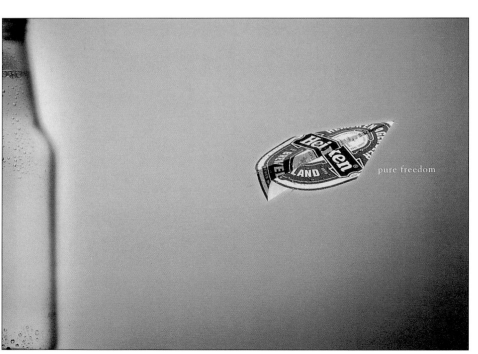

HONG KONG

FINALIST, CAMPAIGN
GREY ADVERTISING LTD.
QUARRY BAY
CLIENT Heineken Beer
CREATIVE DIRECTOR Sandy Higgins/Victor Kwan/
Richard Tunbridge
COPYWRITER Richard Tunbridge
ART DIRECTOR Victor Kwan/HK
PHOTOGRAPHER Jen Helim/HK
ILLUSTRATOR Rual Davadilla/HK
OTHER Johnny Mok/Andrew Au-Yeung

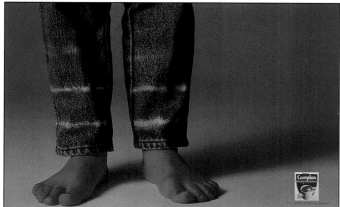

INDIA

BRONZE WORLDMEDAL, CAMPAIGN
CHAITRA LEO BURNETT P.L.
MUMBAI

CLIENT Heinz India Pvt Ltd.
CREATIVE DIRECTOR K.V. Sridhar
COPYWRITER Agnello Dias/Gokul Krishnan
ART DIRECTOR Yayati Godbole/B. Ramnathkar
PHOTOGRAPHER Sanjeev Angane/Mumbai

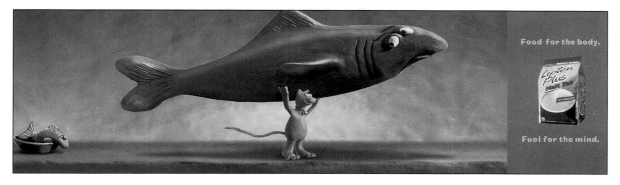

SINGAPORE
F.NALIST, CAMPAIGN
J. WALTER THOMPSON
SINGAPORE

CLIENT Unilever
COPYWRITER Cozette Hendricks
ART DIRECTOR Joel Chin
PHOTOGRAPHER Gin/Singapore
OTHER Alva Oh (Digital Imager)

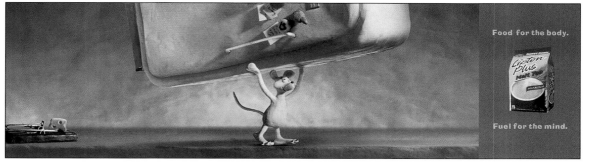

SWEDEN

FINALIST, CAMPAIGN

HOLLINGWORTH/MEHROTRA
STOCKHOLM

COPYWRITER Hans Malm
ART DIRECTOR Max Munch
PHOTOGRAPHER Calle Stoltz
OTHER Sunit Mehrotra (Account Director)

EMPLOYMENT / RECRUITMENT / REAL ESTATE OFFICES

GERMANY

FINALIST, SINGLE

SCHOLZ & FRIENDS GMBH
HAMBURG

CLIENT Faith, Professional Personal
Protection
CREATIVE DIRECTOR Richard
Jung/Christian Storck
COPYWRITER Bernd Huesmann
ART DIRECTOR Arwed Berendts
Other Feodor von Wedel

USA

FINALIST, CAMPAIGN

AUSTIN KNIGHT INC.
CHICAGO, IL

CLIENT Quickturn
CREATIVE DIRECTOR Tim Spry
COPYWRITER Hugh Gurin
ART DIRECTOR Ian Kawata

ART NOT AVAILABLE

ALTA FIDELIDAD

Technics

CHILE

GOLD WORLDMEDAL, SINGLE
AMMIRATI PURIS LINTAS
SANTIAGO
CLIENT Mellafe Y Salas/
Technics
CREATIVE DIRECTOR
Enrique Garcia
COPYWRITER
Enrique Garcia
ART DIRECTOR Leo Farfan
PHOTOGRAPHER
Proveedores Fotograficos
ILLUSTRATOR S-Files

Introducing Power Mac G3. The fastest personal computer on earth. Think different.

UNITED ARAB EMIRATES

BRONZE WORLDMEDAL, SINGLE
TEAM/YOUNG & RUBICAM , DUBAI
DUBAI

CLIENT Apple Power MacG3
CREATIVE DIRECTOR Karen Chambers
COPYWRITER Shahir Ahmed
ART DIRECTOR Sameer Ahmed
PHOTOGRAPHER Tejal Patni
ILLUSTRATOR Anil Palekar/Jojo Bihag

light ears?
light years...

62g : The World's Lightest PCS Phone! · Choice of four fashionable colors · Select from two LCD screen background colors

Cion

KOREA

SILVER WORLDMEDAL, SINGLE

LG AD INC.
SEOUL

CLIENT LG Information & Communication
CREATIVE DIRECTOR Chyu-Suk-Byen/Chang-Ho Kim
COPYWRITER Hee-Jeong Na
ART DIRECTOR Sung-Dong Choi
PHOTOGRAPHER Sang-Hoon Park
ILLUSTRATOR Ik-Kyu Lee
OTHER Designer Sang-Kuk Lee

אפשר לבנות עלינו.

סלקום מתאימה את עצמה לכל עסק.
גם לעסק שלך.

Cellcom סלקום

חייג עכשיו: 053-052-1-800 או 053+ מהסלקום

ISRAEL

BAUMANN BER RIVNAY

FINALIST, SINGLE
TEL-AVIV

CLIENT Cellcom
CREATIVE DIRECTOR Shony Rivnay
COPYWRITER Oren Kari
ART DIRECTOR Eytan Goldberg
PHOTOGRAPHER Oded Klein
OTHER Miri Salhov (Production Manager)

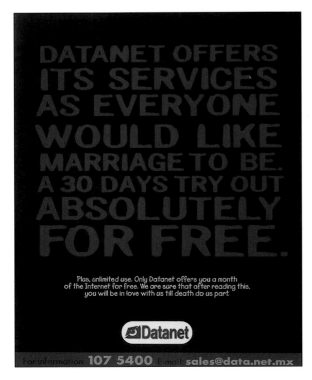

DATANET OFFERS ITS SERVICES AS EVERYONE WOULD LIKE MARRIAGE TO BE. A 30 DAYS TRY OUT ABSOLUTELY FOR FREE.

Plus, unlimited use. Only Datanet offers you a month of the Internet for free. We are sure that after reading this, you will be in love with us till death do us part.

Datanet

For information 107 5400. E-mail: sales@data.net.mx

MEXICO

FINALIST, SINGLE

BBDO/MEXICO
MEXICO CITY

CLIENT Datanet
CREATIVE DIRECTOR Hector Fernandez
COPYWRITER Ricardo Cardenas
ART DIRECTOR Blanca Maldonado
PHOTOGRAPHER Enrique Covarrubias

ENTERTAINMENT & RECREATION

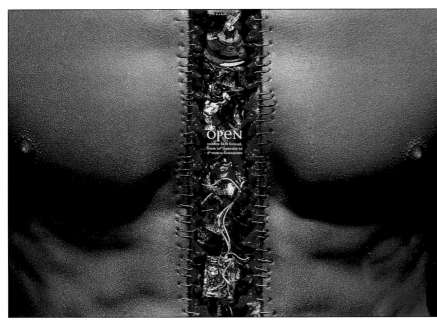

PORTUGAL

SILVER WORLDMEDAL, SINGLE

TBWA/EPG
LISBON

CLIENT Fantas Porto
CREATIVE DIRECTOR A.Homem De Mello/
S.Carvalho
COPYWRITER Albano Homem De Mello
ART DIRECTOR Sergio Carvalho
PHOTOGRAPHER Jorg Bregulla

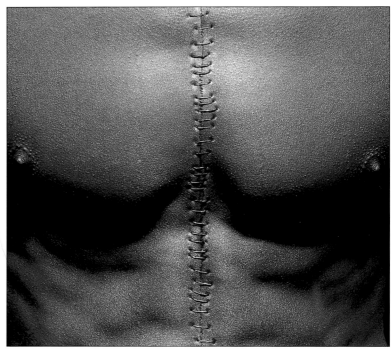

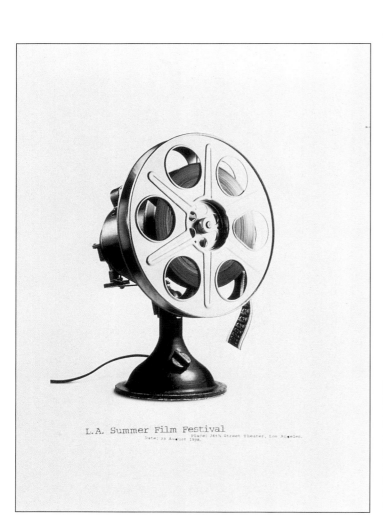

SINGAPORE

BRONZE WORLDMEDAL, SINGLE

DENTSU, YOUNG & RUBICAM
SINGAPORE

CLIENT L.A. Summer Film Festival
CREATIVE DIRECTOR Patrick Low
COPYWRITER Robert Gaxiola
ART DIRECTOR Jeanie Tan
PHOTOGRAPHER Teo Studio/Singapore
OTHER Felix Wong

FINALIST, SINGLE
GREY ARGENTINA S.A.
BUENOS AIRES

CLIENT   Warner Bros/Classic Films Week
CREATIVE DIRECTOR   Carlos Perez/Fernando Militerno
COPYWRITER   Carolina Morano/Matias Corbelle
ART DIRECTOR   Fernando Militerno/Lara Hernandez
PHOTOGRAPHER   Millennium

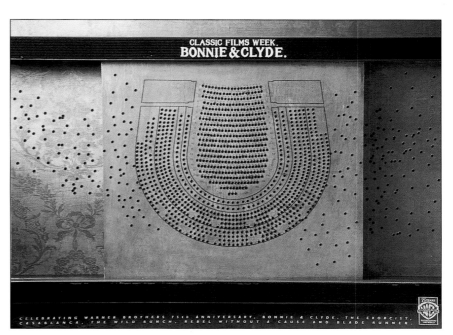

USA

FINALIST, CAMPAIGN
HARRIS DRURY COHEN
FORT LAUDERDALE, FL

CLIENT   Florida Panthers
CREATIVE DIRECTOR   Michael Cannon
COPYWRITER   Michael Cannon
ART DIRECTOR   Aimee Saroff/Mark Limbach

USA

FINALIST, CAMPAIGN
NKH&W INC.
KANSAS CITY, MO

CLIENT   The Pony Express Museum
CREATIVE DIRECTOR   John Harrington
COPYWRITER   Danny Bryan
ART DIRECTOR   John Stewart

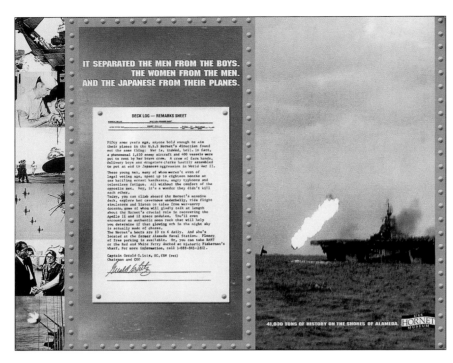

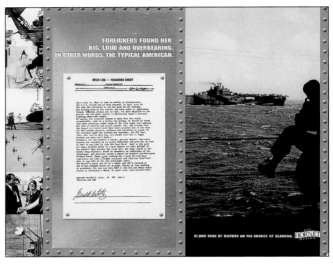

USA

FINALIST, CAMPAIGN

J.W.T. WEST
SAN FRANCISCO, CA

CLIENT   The Hornet Museum
CREATIVE DIRECTOR   Larry Tolpin
COPYWRITER   Bob Hall
ART DIRECTOR   Greg Rowan

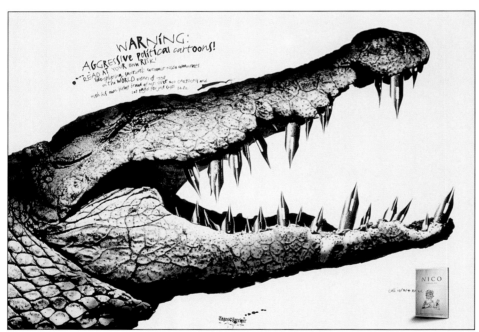

SWITZERLAND

FINALIST, CAMPAIGN

McCANN-ERICKSON
ZURICH

CLIENT   Nico Yearbook 2
CREATIVE DIRECTOR   Edi Andrist
COPYWRITER   Claude Catsky
ART DIRECTOR   Nicolas Vontobel
PHOTOGRAPHER   Felix Schregenberger/
Zurich

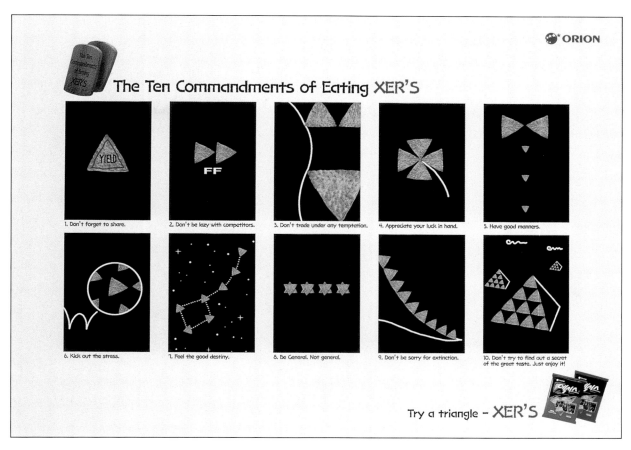

KOREA
SILVER WORLDMEDAL, SINGLE
CHEIL COMMUNICATIONS
SEOUL
CLIENT Orion Frito Lay
CREATIVE DIRECTOR Seung Yong Ji
COPYWRITER Ji Hyun Jo
ART DIRECTOR Dae Young Lee

JAPAN
BRONZE WORLDMEDAL, SINGLE
DENTSU, INC.
TOKYO

CLIENT Ajinomoto Co., Inc.
CREATIVE DIRECTOR
Kenichi Yatani/Etsufumi Umeda
COPYWRITER Yuriko Goto
ART DIRECTOR Taihei Okura/
Nobuhiko Sato
PHOTOGRAPHER
Masamitsu Morisawa

SPAIN

BRONZE WORLDMEDAL, SINGLE

YOUNG & RUBICAM S.A.
MADRID

CLIENT La Olla Caliente Erotic Restaurant
CREATIVE DIRECTOR Jose Maria Pujol
COPYWRITER Anselmo Ramos
ART DIRECTOR Cassio Moron
PHOTOGRAPHER Inaki Preisler

UNITED ARAB EMIRATES

FINALIST, SINGLE

IKON ADVERTISING & MARKETING
SHARJAH

CLIENT Al Kabeer
CREATIVE DIRECTOR Nityanand Singbal/
Kiran Mirchandani
COPYWRITER Kiran Mirchandani
ART DIRECTOR Nityanand Singbal

HOLLAND

FINALIST, CAMPAIGN

R. WALTJEN
ALKMAAR

CLIENT Restaurant Summers
COPYWRITER Joost van Praag Sigaar
ART DIRECTOR Raymond Waltjen
ILLUSTRATOR R.Waltjen/J.van Praag Sigaar/
G.Kuijper

URUGUAY

GOLD WORLDMEDAL, SINGLE
GINKGO SAATCHI & SAATCHI
MONTEVIDEO

CLIENT Maico del Uruguay
CREATIVE DIRECTOR G.Roman/J.Carlos Rodriguez/L.Gomez
COPYWRITER G.Roman/J.Carlos Rodriguez/L.Gomez
ART DIRECTOR Gonzalo Lopez/Marcelo Furrer
OTHER Retouching Lucas Caravia

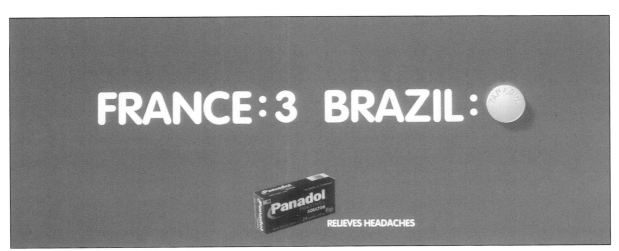

CHILE

BRONZE WORLDMEDAL, SINGLE
NORTHCOTE OGILVY & MATHER
SANTIAGO

CLIENT Panadol/
SmithKline Beecham
CREATIVE DIRECTOR
Matias Robeson
COPYWRITER
Alejandro Arriagada
ART DIRECTOR Rene Zuniga/
Jorge Schmitt

Los piojos pasarán a mejor vida

CHILE

FINALIST, SINGLE
AMMIRATI PURIS LINTAS CHILE
SANTIAGO

CLIENT Launol
CREATIVE DIRECTOR Quincy
COPYWRITER Pancho Gonzalez
ART DIRECTOR Eduardo De La Fuente
PHOTOGRAPHER Pablo Araneda
ILLUSTRATOR S-Files

Métaselo
en la cabeza

COSTA RICA

FINALIST, SINGLE
**JOTABEQU
ADVERTISING**
SAN JOSE

CLIENT Preservatios
Preventor
CREATIVE DIRECTOR
Fernando Sandi
COPYWRITER
Fernando Sandi
ART DIRECTOR
Victor Pardo
PHOTOGRAPHER
Ana Munoz

HOUSEHOLD CARE

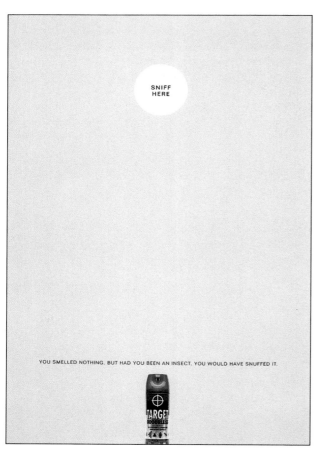

SNIFF
HERE

YOU SMELLED NOTHING, BUT HAD YOU BEEN AN INSECT, YOU WOULD HAVE SNUFFED IT.

SOUTH AFRICA

FINALIST, SINGLE
HERDBUOYS McCANN-ERICKSON
JOHANNESBURG

CLIENT Target Odourless
CREATIVE DIRECTOR Jone Swanepoel/
Steve Richards
COPYWRITER Jono Swanepoel/Louis Maass
ART DIRECTOR Jono Swanepoel
PHOTOGRAPHER Ignus Gerber

Some Families Won't Get A Chance
To Celebrate Chinese New Year.

All it takes is one cockroach to take the Combat bait. It crawls back to its
nest and dies. The family then feeds on the dead cockroach. They all die.
Imagine. One cockroach to kill up to 40 others. This calls for a celebration.

GETS THE COCKROACH YOU SEE
TO KILL THOSE YOU DON'T SEE

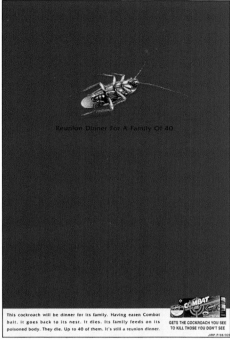

Reunion Dinner For A Family Of 40

This cockroach will be dinner for its family. Having eaten Combat
bait, it goes back to its nest. It dies. Its family feeds on its
poisoned body. They die. Up to 40 of them. It's still a reunion dinner.

GETS THE COCKROACH YOU SEE
TO KILL THOSE YOU DON'T SEE

MALAYSIA

FINALIST, CAMPAIGN
**DENTSU YOUNG & RUBICAM -
MALAYSIA**
KUALA LUMPUR

CLIENT Combat Roach Bait
CREATIVE DIRECTOR Dharma Somasundram
COPYWRITER Ree Chua
ART DIRECTOR Lydia Lim
PHOTOGRAPHER Looi Wing Fai/
Ikhlan Fotografic

HOUSEHOLD FURNISHISHINGS

The Sanyo air conditioner knows how to
sex make sex more pleasant in sex the
time of the year when sex all we think
about sex is having sex.

As temperature rises and summer approaches, human beings go through a mood which we could scientifically define as "ultra horny". Fact is, light clothing makes us feel like we want to make love with virtually anyone or anything (although the latter is not advisable). And Sanyo air conditioners can actually help us enjoy more. They are more intelligent, that means they can regulate the room temperature according to the intensity of the heat. E.g. when the couple are in the stage of caressing, it sets at 20°. It decreases when they pull each other's clothes with their teeth, and when moaning and yelling begin (in the best of cases) the temperature decreases even further. This way, you (or should I say both you) are not going to perspire or feel uncomfortable at any moment to the point of wondering if it would have been better to just watch TV or play Scrabble. And there is another good thing. It comes in different power grades (we are talking about air conditioners, you silly). They also have other functions like "sleep" which makes sex and sleeping (what everybody wants to do after sex) even more comfortable. But you better read about that in the instructions manual. Although, to take full advantage, we may also suggest that you read the Kamasutra. The last thing we can tell you is that Sanyo air conditioners have a remote control. How to use it, my dear friend, is entirely up to your imagination. **SANYO**

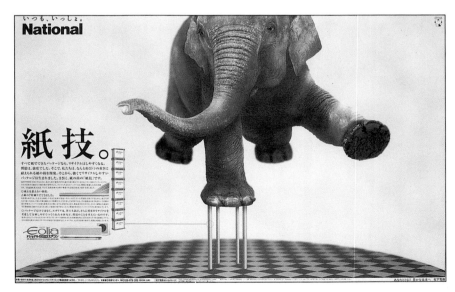

ARGENTINA

FINALIST, SINGLE
AGULLA Y BACCETTI
BUENOS AIRES

CLIENT Sanyo
CREATIVE DIRECTOR Ramiro Agulla/Carlos Baccetti/
S.Wilhelm/M.Anselmo/L.Raposo
COPYWRITER Fabio Mazia/Sebastian Wilhelm
ART DIRECTOR Marcelo Vergara/Maximiliano Anselmo

JAPAN

FINALIST, SINGLE
DENTSU INC. KANSAI
OSAKA

CLIENT Paper Packaging Of Air Conditioners
CREATIVE DIRECTOR Tutomu Takada/Taira Shimazu
COPYWRITER Toshiyuki Inaba/Terumi Isomura
ART DIRECTOR Masahisa Wada/Toshio Kurihara
PHOTOGRAPHER Hisao Hayashi
OTHER J.Tada/N.Maeda/S.Kimura (Designers)

ARGENTINA
SILVER WORLDMEDAL, SINGLE
GREY ARGENTINA S.A.
BUENOS AIRES
CLIENT BGH Silent Air
CREATIVE DIRECTOR
Carlos Perez/
Fernando Militerno
COPYWRITER
Carolina Morano
ART DIRECTOR
Fernando Militerno
PHOTOGRAPHER Millennium

JAPAN
BRONZE WORLDMEDAL, CAMPAIGN
HAKUHODO INCORPORATED
TOKYO
CLIENT Matsushita Electric Industrial Co./
National Wine Cellar
CREATIVE DIRECTOR Kazunori Tsuyama/
Noboru Yamauchi
COPYWRITER Tetsuo Nishii/Noboru Yamauchi
ART DIRECTOR Noriyuki Ogai/Shozo Yorioka
PHOTOGRAPHER Noboru Aoki/Tokyo
OTHER Kiyomi Yoneda/Minako Matsuo

USA

GOLD WORLDMEDAL, SINGLE
YOUNG & RUBICAM
GUAYNABO, PR

CLIENT Red Cross
CREATIVE DIRECTOR Sylvia Soler
ART DIRECTOR Sacha Moser

Make sure you give it to a better cause. Blood services 758 3405. ✚ Cruz Roja Americana

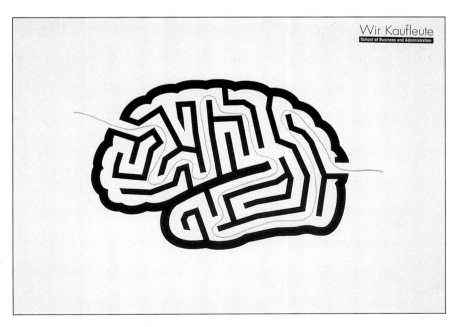

SWITZERLAND

FINALIST, SINGLE
ADVICO YOUNG + RUBICAM
ZURICH GOCKHAUSEN

CLIENT Swiss Commercial
Business School
CREATIVE DIRECTOR Francisco Rodon
COPYWRITER Francisco Rodon
ART DIRECTOR Vanessa Rodriguez/
Francisco Rodon

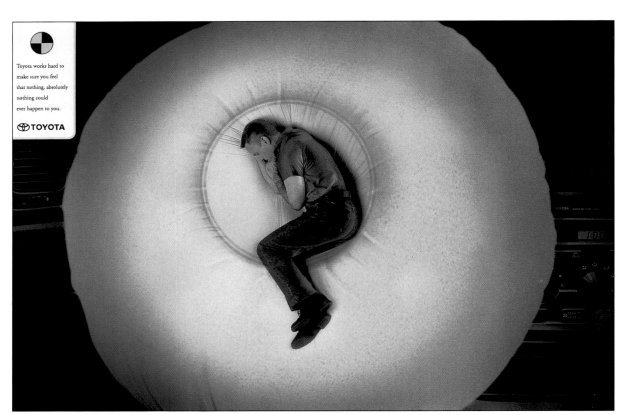

Toyota works hard to make sure you feel that nothing, absolutely nothing could ever happen to you.

TOYOTA

ARGENTINA
SILVER WORLDMEDAL, SINGLE
**LAUTREC NAZCA
SAATCHI & SAATCHI**
BUENOS AIRES

CLIENT Toyota
CREATIVE DIRECTOR
Juan Cravero
COPYWRITER
Sebastian Castaneda
ART DIRECTOR
Maureen Hufnagel
PHOTOGRAPHER
Ackerman/Buenos Aires
ILLUSTRATOR
Pablo Romanos/
Buenos Aires

LG Whenever you need us ⋯

We put people first. LG

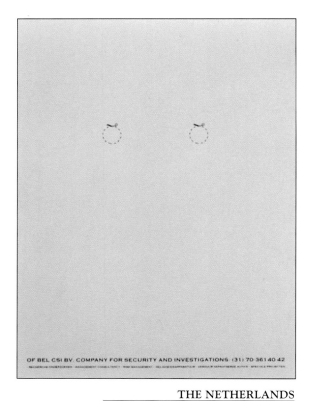

OF BEL CSI BV. COMPANY FOR SECURITY AND INVESTIGATIONS (31) 70 361 40 42

KOREA
BRONZE WORLDMEDAL, SINGLE
LG AD INC.
SEOUL

CREATIVE DIRECTOR
Dong-Wan Jo
COPYWRITER
Hyung-Jong Lee
ART DIRECTOR
Hae-Won Chong
ILLUSTRATOR Method/
Seoul

THE NETHERLANDS
FINALIST, SINGLE
TBWA/CAMPAIGN COMPANY
AMSTERDAM

CLIENT Investigations And Research
COPYWRITER Poppe van Pelt
ART DIRECTOR Diederick Hillenius

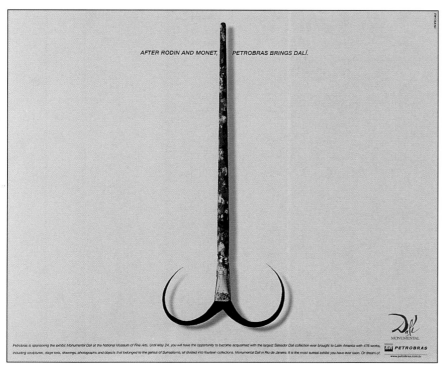

AFTER RODIN AND MONET, PETROBRAS BRINGS DALÍ.

BRAZIL
FINALIST, SINGLE
PROPEG COMUNICACAO SOCIAL
E MERCADOLOGICA
SAO PAULO

CLIENT Petrobras
CREATIVE DIRECTOR Eduardo Silva Correa
COPYWRITER Francisco D'elia Lucchini
ART DIRECTOR Eduardo Lisker
PHOTOGRAPHER Ed Mesquita/Rio de Janeiro
ILLUSTRATOR Joao Rodrigues/Rio de Janeiro

USA
FINALIST, SINGLE
D'ARCY MASIUS BENTON & BOWLES
NEW YORK, NY

CLIENT Underwater World
CREATIVE DIRECTOR Curt Detweiler
COPYWRITER Curt Detweiler
ART DIRECTOR Curt Detweiler/Shannan Tham
PHOTOGRAPHER Roy Zhang/Singapore
ILLUSTRATOR Phenomenon/Singapore
OTHER Curt Detweiler (Typographer)

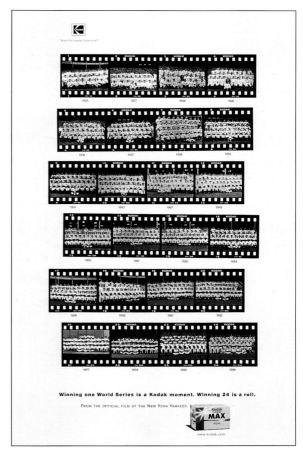

PHILIPPINES
FINALIST, SINGLE
OGILVY & MATHER PHILIPPINES
MAKATI
CLIENT Kodak Film
CREATIVE DIRECTOR David Apicella/
David Page
COPYWRITER Marc Lucas
ART DIRECTOR Ann Phares
PHOTOGRAPHER Steve Candrall/
New York

IT'S NOT THE SAME WITHOUT THE ANIMALS ADOPT AN ANIMAL AT THE JOHANNESBURG ZOO - (011) 6462000

IT'S NOT THE SAME WITHOUT THE ANIMALS
ADOPT AN ANIMAL AT THE JOHANNESBURG ZOO - (011) 6462000

SOUTH AFRICA

GOLD WORLDMEDAL, CAMPAIGN
THE JUPITER DRAWING ROOM
RIVONIA

CLIENT Johannesburg Zoo
CREATIVE DIRECTOR Graham Warsop
COPYWRITER Vaughn Townsend
ART DIRECTOR Mariana O'Kelly

SPAIN

FINALIST, SINGLE
CP COMUNICACION
MADRID

CLIENT
CANAL+ Private Television Channel
CREATIVE DIRECTOR Gonzalo Figari
COPYWRITER Gonzalo Figari
ART DIRECTOR
Chema Bernard/Ruben Perez
PHOTOGRAPHER
Still Life/Madrid

SEE PAGE 46

INDUSTRIAL

JAPAN
BRONZE WORLDMEDAL, SINGLE
DENTSU, INC.
TOKYO
CLIENT Hitachi. Ltd.
CREATIVE DIRECTOR
Koji Yanagishima
COPYWRITER Hitoshi Sato/
Masato Okada
ART DIRECTOR M.Fujit-
omi/S.Takanashi/
T.Fukaya
PHOTOGRAPHER
Kazuhiro Takahashi

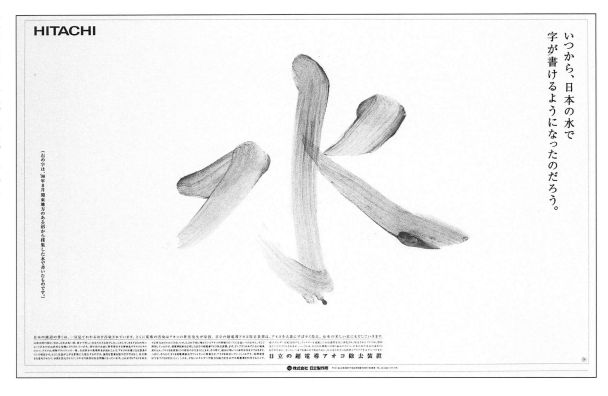

MEDIA PROMOTION

SPAIN
FINALIST, SINGLE
CP COMUNICACION
MADRID
CLIENT CANAL+ Private Television Channel
CREATIVE DIRECTOR Gonzalo Figari
COPYWRITER Gonzalo Figari/Alberto Payo
ART DIRECTOR Chema Bernard
PHOTOGRAPHER Still Life/Madrid
SEE PAGE 100

AUSTRIA
FINALIST, SINGLE
DEMNER, MERLICEK & BERGMANN
VIENNA
CLIENT NEWS
CREATIVE DIRECTOR Mariusz Jan Demner
COPYWRITER Gerda Schebesta
ART DIRECTOR Tomek Luczynski
OTHER Stephanie Lackner (Graphics)/
Laura Latanza

Sexo Virtual
Jueves, 6 de Abril 20:30h en el Canal Odisea.

SPAIN
SILVER WORLDMEDAL, SINGLE
VITRUVIO/LEO BURNETT
MADRID
CLIENT Via Digital

PAVAROTTI AND FRIENDS.

Pavarotti with Jon Bon Jovi, Celine Dion, Stevie Wonder, Spice Girls, Eros Ramazzotti, Vanessa Williams and a children's chorus. A show directed by Spike Lee. Tonight at 11 pm on Rede Record.

REDE RECORD

BRONZE WORLDMEDAL

BRAZIL
STANDARD OGILVY & MATHER
SAO PAULO

CLIENT Rede Record
CREATIVE DIRECTOR Camila Franco
COPYWRITER Renato Konrath/Fabio Victoria
ART DIRECTOR Virgilio Neves

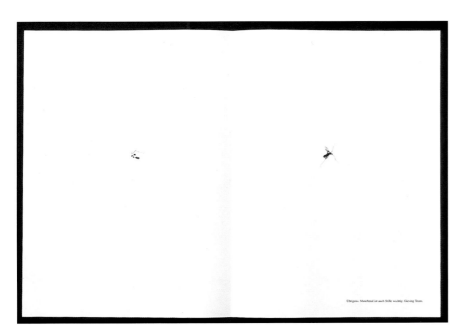

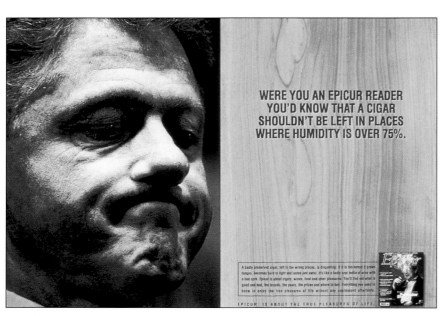

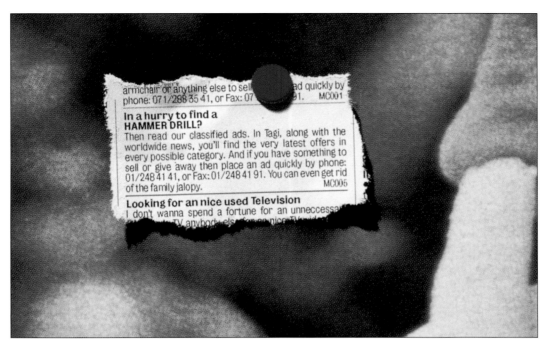

SWITZERLAND

GOLD WORLDMEDAL, CAMPAIGN
McCANN-ERICKSON
ZURICH

CLIENT   TA Media AG
CREATIVE DIRECTOR   Edi Andrist
COPYWRITER   Claude Catsky
ART DIRECTOR   Daniel Comte/
Nicolas Vontobel

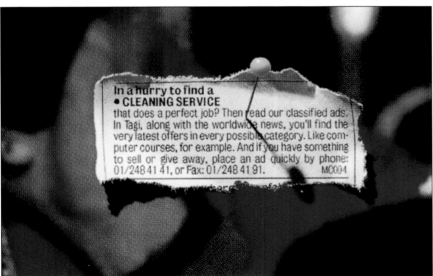

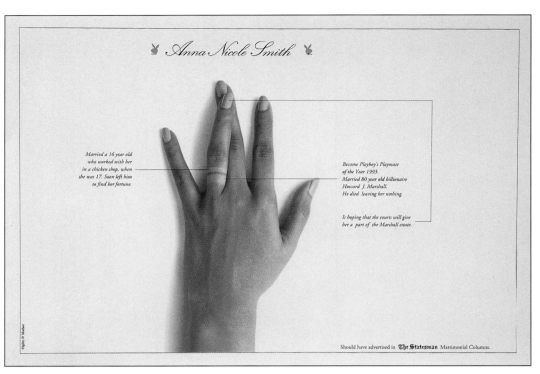

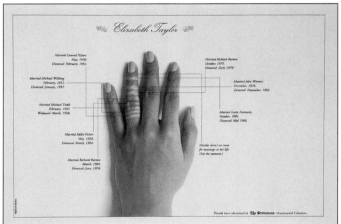

INDIA

SILVER WORLDMEDAL, CAMPAIGN
OGILVY & MATHER LTD.
BOMBAY

CLIENT   Statesman - Matrimonial Columns
CREATIVE DIRECTOR   Piyush Pandey
COPYWRITER   Bobby Pawar
ART DIRECTOR   Sonal Dabral/Sagar Mahabaleshwarkar
PHOTOGRAPHER   Sydney D'Souza

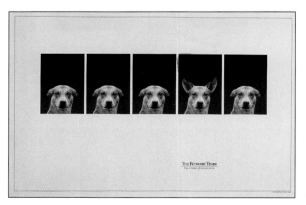

INDIA

FINALIST, CAMPAIGN
ENTERPRISE NEXUS COMMUNICATIONS PVT. LTD.
MUMBAI

CLIENT   The Economic Times
CREATIVE DIRECTOR   Mohammed Khan
COPYWRITER   Abhijit Avasthi
ART DIRECTOR   Raj Kamble
ILLUSTRATOR   Shiram Mandale

OFFICE SUPPLIES / EQUIPMENT

INDIA
BRONZE WORLDMEDAL, SINGLE
OGILVY & MATHER LTD.
BOMBAY
CLIENT Hindustan Pencils/Apsara Eraser
CREATIVE DIRECTOR Piyush Pandey
ART DIRECTOR Sonal Dabral/Radhika Vissanji

NEWSPAPER: PERSONAL CARE

POLAND
FINALIST, SINGLE
AMMIRATI PURIS LINTAS WARSAW
WARSAW
CREATIVE DIRECTOR Chris Matyszczyk
COPYWRITER Agnieszka Galas
ART DIRECTOR Chris Mrozek
PHOTOGRAPHER Marcin Tyszka

INDIA
FINALIST, SINGLE
CHAITRA LEO BURNETT P.L.
MUMBAI
CLIENT Shop-2
CREATIVE DIRECTOR K.V.Sridhar
COPYWRITER Agnello Dias
ART DIRECTOR B.Ramnathkar
PHOTOGRAPHER Tejal Patni

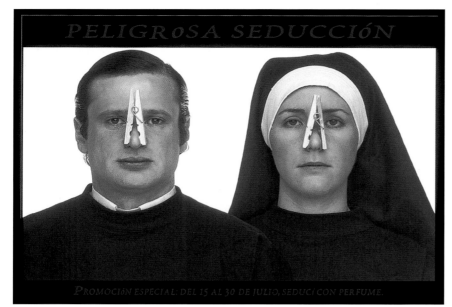

ARGENTINA

FINALIST, SINGLE

PUBLICIS CAPURRO
CAPITAL FEDERAL

CLIENT Fiesta Del Perfume
CREATIVE DIRECTOR Gabriel Tosar
COPYWRITER Ricardo Spatola
ART DIRECTOR Laura Serra

JAPAN

FINALIST, CAMPAIGN

SHISEIDO CO., LTD.
TOKYO

CLIENT New Year's Greeting Poster
CREATIVE DIRECTOR Masao Oota
COPYWRITER Teturo Kanegae
ART DIRECTOR Katuhiko Shibuya
PHOTOGRAPHER Ellchiro Sakata

RETAIL STORES OTHER

MEXICO

FINALIST, SINGLE

TERAN TBWA, S.A. DE C.V.
MEXICO

CLIENT El Palacio de Hierro
CREATIVE DIRECTOR Ana Ma.Olabuenaga/Gonzalo Munoz
COPYWRITER Vivian Gleich
ART DIRECTOR Gabriela Fenton
PHOTOGRAPHER Michel Nafziger/New York
OTHER Gerardo Manero

PORTUGAL

BRONZE WORLDMEDAL, SINGLE

YOUNG & RUBICAM, PORTUGAL

LISBON

CREATIVE DIRECTOR Jorge Leixeiea
COPYWRITER Jorge Leixeiea
ART DIRECTOR Lourenco Tomaz
ILLUSTRATOR Lourenco Tomaz

TRANSPORTATION, TRAVEL & SERVICES

Travel, they used to say, frees the mind.
It still can. So relax. Think your thoughts.
And leave everything else to us.
Swissair. We care.

swissair

SWITZERLAND

FINALIST, CAMPAIGN

ADVICO YOUNG + RUBICAM

ZURICH GOCKHAUSEN

CLIENT Swissair
CREATIVE DIRECTOR Francisco Rodon
COPYWRITER Andrew White
ART DIRECTOR Francisco Rodon
PHOTOGRAPHER Torkil Gudnason

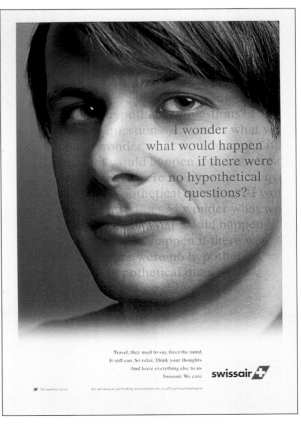

Travel, they used to say, frees the mind.
It still can. So relax. Think your thoughts.
And leave everything else to us.
Swissair. We care.

swissair

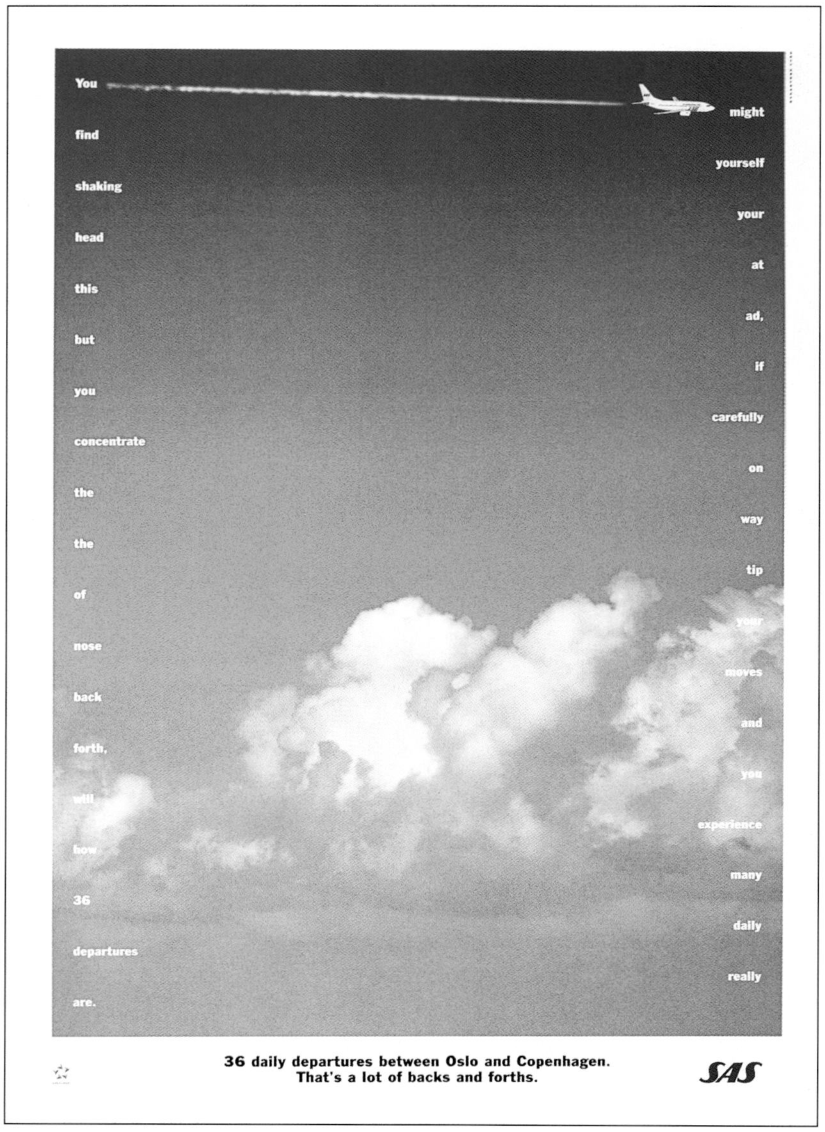
You might find yourself shaking your head at this ad, but if you concentrate carefully on the way the tip of the your nose moves back and forth, you will experience how many daily 36 departures really are.
36 daily departures between Oslo and Copenhagen.
That's a lot of backs and forths.
SAS

DENMARK

SILVER WORLDMEDAL, SINGLE

GREY COPENHAGEN

COPENHAGEN

CLIENT SAS

COPYWRITER Niels Thomsen

ART DIRECTOR Mikkel Jangaard

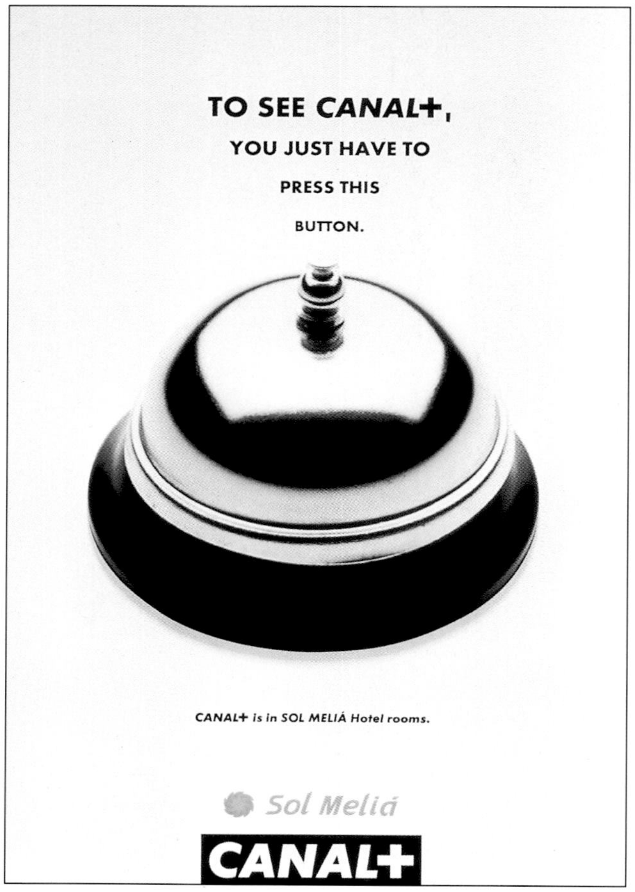
TO SEE CANAL+,
YOU JUST HAVE TO
PRESS THIS
BUTTON.
CANAL+ is in SOL MELIÁ Hotel rooms.
Sol Meliá
CANAL+

SPAIN

BRONZE WORLDMEDAL, SINGLE

CP COMUNICACION

MADRID

CLIENT CANAL+ Private Television Channel

CREATIVE DIRECTOR Gonzalo Figari

COPYWRITER Gonzalo Figari/Alberto Payo

ART DIRECTOR Ruben Perez

PHOTOGRAPHER Still Life/Madrid

FULL PAGE

SOUTH AFRICA
GOLD WORLDMEDAL, SINGLE
THE JUPITER DRAWING ROOM
RIVONIA

CLIENT Nike
CREATIVE DIRECTOR Graham Warsop
COPYWRITER Lawrence Seftel
ART DIRECTOR Vanessa Pearson

Competitors in the gruelling "Comrades" road race run 90km from Durban to Pietermaritzburg.

The 11,000 words of copy conjure up the emotion of participation in the race through the eyes of a first time competitor.

MULTIPLE PAGE

BEST COPY

USA
FINALIST, SINGLE
DMB&B
TROY, MI
CLIENT Cadillac Eldorado
CREATIVE DIRECTOR Gary Horton
COPYWRITER Jeff Eaker
ART DIRECTOR Renee Mashione

ARGENTINA
FINALIST, CAMPAIGN
LAUTREC NAZCA SAATCHI & SAATCHI
BUENOS AIRES
CLIENT Web Site
CREATIVE DIRECTOR Juan Cravero/Esteban Pigni
COPYWRITER Chavo D'Emilio
ART DIRECTOR Toto Marelli
PHOTOGRAPHER Freddy Fabris/Buenos Aires
ILLUSTRATOR Pablo Romanos/Buenos Aires

SOUTH AFRICA

SILVER WORLDMEDAL,
CAMPAIGN

SAATCHI & SAATCHI
CAPE TOWN

CREATIVE DIRECTOR
Eric Frank
COPYWRITER
Mark Mason/
Mark Legward/
Andrew Durkan
ART DIRECTOR
Mark Mason
ILLUSTRATOR
Mark Mason

Readers who phoned the number on the ad receive this message.
"Hi stranger, what's your name? You can call me Candy, but let's skip the foreplay 'cause I'm so wet I want you now. Take that big cock out and put it between my legs. Ooh yeah, now pump me big boy. Come on, stick it all in, ooh, harder, lover, yes make me come, ooh don't stop just fuck me!

If this was more than just a phone call, ask yourself if you'd have had the sense to wear a condom."

Readers who phoned the number on the ad received this message.
"Hi, this is Pamela A. Unfortunately I can no longer offer my services , as I have just received the results of my most recent HIV test.

So, if you want good, clean, sex, I'm living proof that you should always wear a condom. Thank you."

ARGENTINA

BRONZE WORLDMEDAL, SINGLE

**FAILLACE & ASOCIADOS
COMUNICACION**
BUENOS AIRES

CLIENT Pick-Up Isuzu
CREATIVE DIRECTOR Flavio Damian
COPYWRITER Martin Bonadeo
ART DIRECTOR Damian Constante

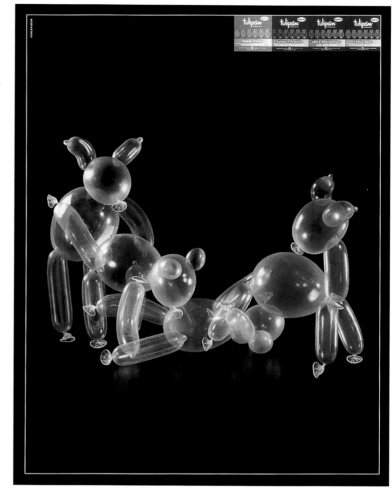

ARGENTINA
SILVER WORLDMEDAL, SINGLE
YOUNG & RUBICAM
BUENOS AIRES
CLIENT Tulipan
CREATIVE DIRECTOR Pablo Del Campo/Chanel Basualdo
COPYWRITER S.Lucero/D.Livachoff
ART DIRECTOR Chanel Basualdo
PHOTOGRAPHER Daniel Maestri

The New Renault Twingo Automatic. **Left foot optional.**

ARGENTINA
BRONZE WORLDMEDAL, SINGLE
AGULLA Y BACCETTI
BUENOS AIRES
CREATIVE DIRECTOR S.Wilhelm/M.Anselmo/
L. Raposo/R. Agulla/C. Baccetti
COPYWRITER Maximiliano Itzkoff
ART DIRECTOR Nicolas Kasakoff

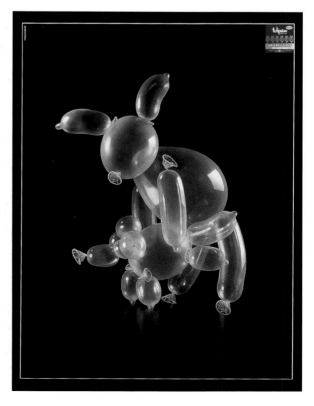

ARGENTINA
FINALIST, SINGLE
YOUNG & RUBICAM
BUENOS AIRES
CLIENT Tulipan
CREATIVE DIRECTOR
Pablo Del Campo/
Chanel Basualdo
COPYWRITER S.Lucero/
D.Livachoff
ART DIRECTOR
Chanel Basualdo
PHOTOGRAPHER
Daniel Maestri

AUSTRALIA
GOLD WORLDMEDAL, CAMPAIGN
SAATCHI & SAATCHI
SYDNEY
CLIENT No Frills Funerals and Cremations
CREATIVE DIRECTOR Michael Newman
COPYWRITER Jay Furby
ART DIRECTOR Steve Carlin
PHOTOGRAPHER Gary Richardson
OTHER Mark Payne (Account Supervisor)
SEE GRAND AWARD PAGE 196

PUBLIC SERVICE ADVERTISING
NEWSPAPER

GRAND AWARD

BEST NEWSPAPER PUBLIC SERVICE ADVERTISEMENT

SPAIN

BEST NEWSPAPER PUBLIC SERVICE ADVERTISEMENT
FCB/TAPSA
MADRID

CLIENT   Fundacion Cear
CREATIVE DIRECTOR   Julian Zuazo
COPYWRITER   Oriol Villar
ART DIRECTOR   Yuri Alemany
PHOTOGRAPHER   Eduardo Diaz/Madrid

CIVIC / SOCIAL EDUCATION

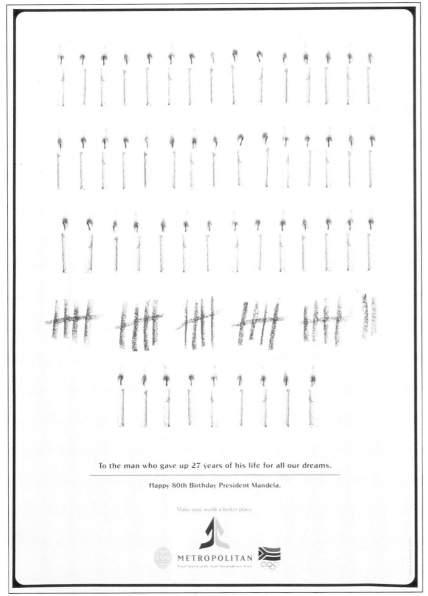

To the man who gave up 27 years of his life for all our dreams.

Happy 80th Birthday President Mandela.

Make your world a better place

METROPOLITAN

SOUTH AFRICA

GOLD WORLDMEDAL. SINGLE
SAATCHI & SAATCHI
CAPE TOWN

CLIENT   Metropolitan
CREATIVE DIRECTOR   Eric Frank
COPYWRITER   Andrew Durakn
ART DIRECTOR   Duncan Wares
PHOTOGRAPHER   Mike Carelse
ILLUSTRATOR   Duncan Wares

USA

FINALIST. SINGLE
BADILLO NAZCA S&S
GUAYNABO, PR

CLIENT   Safe Sex
CREATIVE DIRECTOR   Malcolm Walker
COPYWRITER   Ricardo Marti
ART DIRECTOR   Malcolm Walker
PHOTOGRAPHER   Junior
ILLUSTRATOR   Jose Daniel Gonzalez

SEX WITHOUT A CONDOM.

ALWAYS INSIST YOUR CLIENTS USE A CONDOM. GET FREE ONES BY CALLING 250-3029.

SINGAPORE

SILVER WORLDMEDAL. SINGLE

OGILVY & MATHER SINGAPORE

SINGAPORE

CLIENT   Abortion Convention
CREATIVE DIRECTOR   Neil French
COPYWRITER   Justin Lim
ART DIRECTOR   Gregory Yeo/Eugene Cheong

1. A teenage girl is pregnant. Her husband is not the father of the child. Under these circumstances, would you recommend an abortion?

2. A family has three children. The first child is blind, the second is deaf and the third has Tuberculosis. The mother also has TB. Suddenly, she discovers she is pregnant again. In view of their predicament, would you suggest an abortion?

3. A preacher and his wife are living on the edge of poverty. They already have fourteen children. The mother is pregnant once again with their fifteenth child. Considering their hardship, would you advocate abortion?

If you said yes to abortion: you would have killed Jesus Christ in the first situation; Beethoven in the second; and John Wesley, the great Methodist evangelist, in the last instance. TO FIND OUT MORE ABOUT ABORTION, ATTEND THE ABORTION CONVENTION, TO BE HELD AT THE BOULEVARD HOTEL, SINGAPORE, ON 28 DECEMBER. CALL 229 2229 OR FAX 736 6388 FOR DETAILS OF REGISTRATION. **ABORTION CONVENTION 1998**

Uw pensioenaanvulling zou er wel eens
heel anders uit kunnen gaan zien.

THE NETHERLANDS

BRONZE WORLDMEDAL. SINGLE

TBWA/CAMPAIGN COMPANY

AMSTERDAM

CLIENT   Verbond van Verzekeraars
COPYWRITER   Poppe van Pelt
ART DIRECTOR   Diederick Hillenius
PHOTOGRAPHER   Carli Hermes

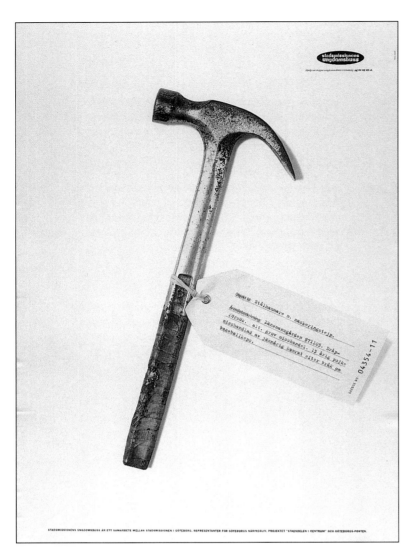

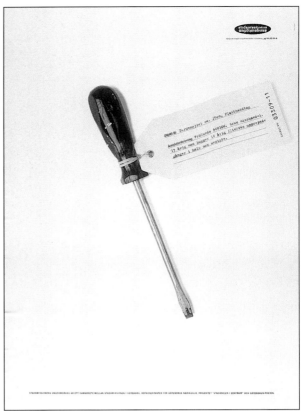

SWEDEN

BRONZE WORLDMEDAL, CAMPAIGN
TENNIS, ANYONE?
GOTHENBURG

CLIENT Stadsmissionen
COPYWRITER Daniel Rojnemark
ART DIRECTOR Fredrik Ganslandt
PHOTOGRAPHER Branko

ENGLAND

FINALIST. SINGLE
McCANN HEALTHCARE, MANCHESTER
CHESHIRE

CLIENT Marie Stopes International
COPYWRITER Neil Lancaster
ART DIRECTOR Dave Price
PHOTOGRAPHER Rob Walker

SEE PAGE 255

ENGLAND

FINALIST. SINGLE
**McCANN HEALTHCARE,
MANCHESTER**
CHESHIRE

CLIENT Marie Stopes
International
COPYWRITER Neil Lancaster
ART DIRECTOR Dave Price
PHOTOGRAPHER Jonathan Oakes

HONG KONG
FINALIST, CAMPAIGN
BOZELL WORLDWIDE
CAUSEWAY BAY, HONG KONG
CLIENT   Hong Kong Breastfeeding
Mother's Association
CREATIVE DIRECTOR   Poh Hwee Beng
COPYWRITER   K.Wong/A.Chen/
H.Yu/S. Leong
ART DIRECTOR   Phoebe Yeung/John Poon
ILLUSTRATOR   Phoebe Yeung/John Poon
OTHER   Cheng Kin Kong
(Computer Retouching)
Curry Leung (Print Production)

CHINA
FINALIST, CAMPAIGN
McCANN ERICKSON GUANGMING
SHANHAI
CLIENT   Social Education
CREATIVE DIRECTOR   Bing Chiu
COPYWRITER   Laurance Wang
ART DIRECTOR   Su Yin Tan/William Li
PHOTOGRAPHER   Hong Bing Cheng
OTHER   Ming Chan (Print Production)

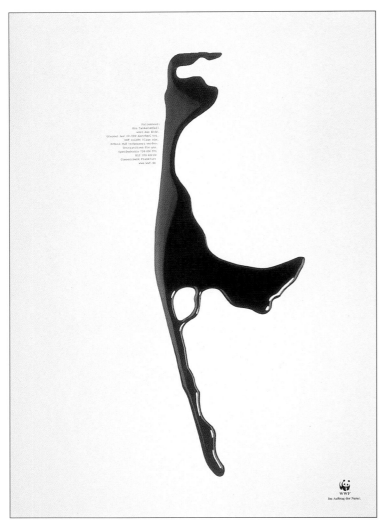

GERMANY

BRONZE WORLDMEDAL, SINGLE

OGILVY & MATHER FRANKFURT
FRANKFURT

CLIENT   Worldwide Fund For Nature
CREATIVE DIRECTOR   Johannes Krempl
COPYWRITER   Johannes Krempl
ART DIRECTOR   Patrick They
PHOTOGRAPHER   Jo Bacherl

AUSTRALIA
FINALIST, CAMPAIGN
**McCANN-ERICKSON
BRISBANE**
BRISBANE

CLIENT   Clean Air
CREATIVE DIRECTOR   Ian Jensen
COPYWRITER   Matt Hoyle
ART DIRECTOR   Andrew Ness
OTHER   Kim Murray

PHILIPPINES
FINALIST, SINGLE
AMA-DDB NEEDHAM PHILIPPINES
MANILA

CLIENT Department of Environment & Natural
CREATIVE DIRECTOR Roger Pe
COPYWRITER Roger Pe
ART DIRECTOR Roger Pe/Mike Gamalinda
PHOTOGRAPHER Giraffe-X
OTHER Cely Flores (Media Director)

HEALTH / HYGIENE

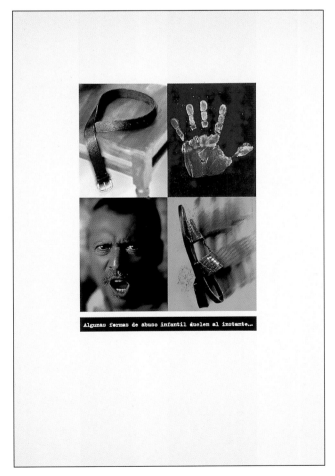

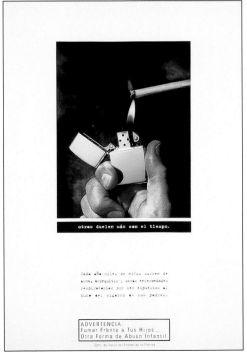

USA
FINALIST, SINGLE
DEL RIVERO MESSIANU
CORAL GABLES, FL

CLIENT Florida Anti-Tobacco

Pedro slept with ~~Maria, who was~~ ~~dating Fernando, who had slept with~~ ~~Verónica, who slept with Alexandre,~~ ~~who had slept with Zé, who slept with~~ ~~Helena, who had slept with João, who~~ ~~was dating Cristina and Diogo,~~ ~~Cristina slept with Afonso and Diogo~~ ~~slept with Margarida, who was dating~~ ~~Tomás, who had slept with Conceição,~~ ~~who slept with Nuno, who had slept~~ ~~with Antónia, who was dating Sérgio,~~ ~~who was also dating Marta, who had~~ ~~an affair with Gonçalo, who was mar-~~ ~~ried to Madalena, who was sleeping~~ ~~with Miguel, who slept with Joana,~~ ~~who is dating~~ you.

Be Protected. Every minute, five youngsters are infected with the HIV virus.
December 1st. World Aids Day.

PORTUGAL
SILVER WORLDMEDAL, SINGLE
YOUNG & RUBICAM, PORTUGAL
LISBON
CLIENT Portuguese Foundation the co against AIDS
CREATIVE DIRECTOR De Jaz Mena/ Cristiano Zanguoghi
COPYWRITER Teresa Pinto Leite
ART DIRECTOR Lorenco Tomes

ABCDEFG⊙
⊙JKLMNOPQ
RSTU⊙WXYZ

GET THESE 3 LETTERS OUT OF YOUR LIFE. USE CONDOMS.

BRAZIL
BRONZE WORLDMEDAL, SINGLE
DPZ PROPAGANDA
SAO PAULO
CLIENT GAPA-Grupo de Apoioa Prevencao a AIDS
CREATIVE DIRECTOR Francesc Petit/ Carlos Silverio
COPYWRITER Rui Branquinho
ART DIRECTOR Guime

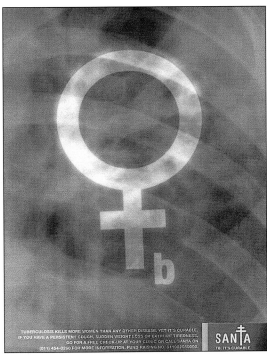

In the initial stage of a ~, the subject experiences a decline in general health and a stretching pain in the affected part of the body. This is followed by mucus secretion (→*flow*), at first semi-transparent and watery, later thicker and yellow in colour, which produces an unpleasant smell. In the case of a ~, the repeated wiping of mucus (→*suppuration*) frequently leads to ulceration of the affected organ.

And that is just the common cold.
Venereal infections are much more serious.

Always enjoy the protection of a condom.

HUNGARY
FINALIST, SINGLE
McCANN-ERICKSON BUDAPEST
BUDAPEST
CLIENT McCann-Erickson Budapest
CREATIVE DIRECTOR Robert Lorincz
COPYWRITER Robert Lorincz/
Gergely Baraczka
ART DIRECTOR Gabor Havasi
PHOTOGRAPHER Gabor Mate

He keeps track of MLB.

What about his PSA?

Sports. Men just love to talk stats and scores, don't they? If only it was the same with their health. Most men don't know their PSA number, or even what a PSA is. Most women don't either, so read on. A PSA is a simple blood test used to detect prostate cancer in its earliest, most curable stages.
   The fact is, prostate cancer is the second largest killer of men in the U.S. today.

Males over 50 are the most susceptible, with African-Americans at even greater risk. Help your guys stay in the game. Urge your father, husband, grandfather, brother, or any men you know over 50, to ask their doctor about taking a PSA test at their next physical. It's simple, painless, and it just might boost their "lifetime average."
   Tell them about it during the seventh inning stretch.

AMERICAN CANCER SOCIETY

LEARN MORE ABOUT PROSTATE CANCER, CALL 1-800-ACS-2345

USA
FINALIST, SINGLE
MERIDIAN ADVERTISING
TROY, MI
CLIENT American Cancer Society
CREATIVE DIRECTOR Kathi Presutti
COPYWRITER Greg Gersabeck
ART DIRECTOR Eric Maes
PHOTOGRAPHER Pete Crane/
Ambrosi/Troy

KEEP A LOOK OUT FOR BREAST CANCER. LOOK AFTER YOURSELF.

TUBERCULOSIS KILLS MORE WOMEN THAN ANY OTHER DISEASE, YET IT'S CURABLE. IF YOU HAVE A PERSISTENT COUGH, SUDDEN WEIGHT LOSS OR EXTREME TIREDNESS, GO FOR A FREE CHECK-UP AT YOUR CLINIC OR CALL SANTA ON (011) 454-0260 FOR MORE INFORMATION. FUND RAISING NO. 011002080000.

SANTA
TB. IT'S CURABLE.

SOUTH AFRICA
FINALIST, SINGLE
OGILVY & MATHER RIGHTFORD SEARLE-TRIPP & MAKIN
GAUTENG
CLIENT Women's Day
CREATIVE DIRECTOR Sheli Hersch
COPYWRITER James Wolfaardt
ART DIRECTOR Sergio Lauceva
ILLUSTRATOR Sergio Lacueva

PORTUGAL
FINALIST, SINGLE
YOUNG & RUBICAM, PORTUGAL
LISBON
CLIENT Socosmet
CREATIVE DIRECTOR Be Jaz Mena/
Cristiano Zanguoghi
COPYWRITER Teresa Pinto Leite
ART DIRECTOR Lourenco Tomes

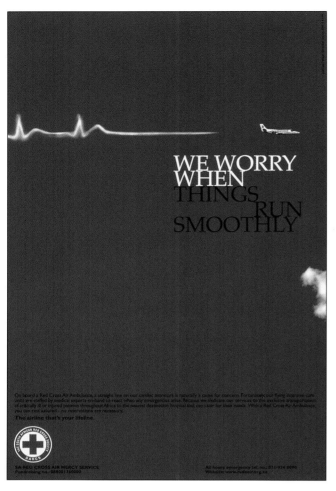

WE WORRY WHEN THINGS RUN SMOOTHLY

ONLY SICK PEOPLE FLY WITH US

SOUTH AFRICA
FINALIST, CAMPAIGN
ADDISON WANT STROEBEL GORIN JWT
ROGGEBAAI

CLIENT Red Cross Air Mercy Service
CREATIVE DIRECTOR Paul Sellars
COPYWRITER Melanie Horenz
ART DIRECTOR Kirk Gainsford
PHOTOGRAPHER Juan Espi/ Cape Town

Sharing needles may give you HIV. Call our Needle Exchange Program: 250-8829.

Most people who share needles end up in bed together.

USA
FINALIST, SINGLE
BADILLO NAZCA S&S
GUAYNABO, PR

CLIENT Iniciativa Comunitaria
CREATIVE DIRECTOR Malcolm Walker
COPYWRITER Marcus Grajales/Antonio Lopez
ART DIRECTOR Malcolm Walker
PHOTOGRAPHER Junior
ILLUSTRATOR Jose Daniel Gonzalez

USA

GOLD WORLDMEDAL, SINGLE
CRAMER-KRASSELT
MILWAUKEE, WI

CLIENT   Sojourner Truth House
CREATIVE DIRECTOR   Neil Casey
COPYWRITER   Pat Pritchard
ART DIRECTOR   Vince DeMarinis
PHOTOGRAPHER   Scott Lanza/Milwaukee
ILLUSTRATOR   Jay Harris/East Troy

BRAZIL

SILVER WORLDMEDAL, SINGLE
V&S COMUNICACOES LTDA.
RIO DE JANIERO/RJ

CLIENT   Viva Rio
CREATIVE DIRECTOR   Paulo Castro
COPYWRITER   Alvaro Rodrigues
ART DIRECTOR   Luis Claudio Savestroni
PHOTOGRAPHER   Humberto Medeiros
ILLUSTRATOR   Gustavo Toscano

Why men get a better **D**eal than women **I**s **C**ommon **K**nowledge.

Don't you think?

Because with a penis or a prick, a dick and balls your chance to improve dramatically. It's astonishing, but bigger muscles, a deeper voice and a hairy chest still pay better than education, experience and skill.

The notion that men and women stand the same chances in life is absolute nonsense. There is no equality between the sexes. Those who believe that, they case are wrong.

Because no matter how you look at it, men are better off. They earn more, they take more and enjoy a higher status. And it is easy to see who power, at we all know, whit rule from men.

The whole thing starts at school. Boys are brought to the fore at the expense of girls. And when the first jobs come around, young men get better pay than young women. Despite the fact that women today are better educated than men.

Then men start climbing the ladder, while women have kids and then realise there's a limit to how far they can get. An invisible barrier that bars women from rising fast the very top.

There's any number of examples. When men marry they advance at work, while women remain when they leave. The more men there are in a profession, the higher the salary level. The more women, the lower.

A financially independent woman gets by without a man. A financially independent man, on the other hand, is so well-off he doesn't have to work at all.

Very early in my life it was too late, Marguerite Duras, the French writer, once said. She referred to what was moving between her legs.

John Lennon put it more bluntly.

Woman is the nigger of the world, he said.

IT'S IN BREACH OF THE SWEDISH CONSTITUTION TO DISCRIMINATE ON THE BASIS OF GENDER WWW.TCO.SE

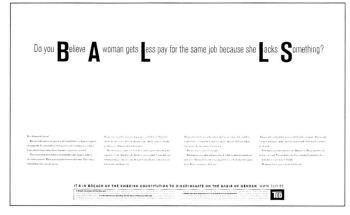

Do you **B**elieve **A** woman gets **L**ess pay for the same job because she **L**acks **S**omething?

IT'S IN BREACH OF THE SWEDISH CONSTITUTION TO DISCRIMINATE ON THE BASIS OF GENDER WWW.TCO.SE

SWEDEN

BRONZE WORLDMEDAL, CAMPAIGN

THE E COMPANY
STOCKHOLM

CLIENT TCO (The Swedish Confederation of Professional Employees)
CREATIVE DIRECTOR Lars Noren
COPYWRITER Lars Noren
ART DIRECTOR Jonas Bergstrom
OTHER Typographer Leif Arback

PERSONAL DEVELOPMENT

ARGENTINA

FINALIST, SINGLE

GREY ARGENTINA S.A.
BUENOS AIRES

CLIENT Grupo Clarin
CREATIVE DIRECTOR Carlos Perez/
Fernando Militerno
COPYWRITER Nicolas Pimentel
ART DIRECTOR Carolina Speilmann
PHOTOGRAPHER Paez

DENMARK
BRONZE WORLDMEDAL, SINGLE
BBDO DENMARK
COPENHAGEN
CLIENT   Radet For Storre Faerdselssikkerhed
CREATIVE DIRECTOR   Michael Chr. Knudsen
COPYWRITER   Tom Lundquist
ART DIRECTOR   Simon Wooller

Your boss has been hinting at bondage for years

We'll show you how.

We'll teach you first-aid in your office environment, simply call 011 403 4227.

SOUTH AFRICA
FINALIST, SINGLE
HERDBUOYS McCANN-ERICKSON
JOHANNESBURG
CLIENT St John"s - First Aid
CREATIVE DIRECTOR Jono Swanepoel/
Steve Richards
COPYWRITER Jono Swanepoel
ART DIRECTOR Jono Swanepoel
PHOTOGRAPHER Rory McLean
OTHER Suzanne Strydom (Typography)

PHILANTHROPIC APPEALS

BRAZIL
FINALIST, CAMPAIGN
EM3!
GOIANIA/GOIAS
CLIENT ADIAL
CREATIVE DIRECTOR
Alex Daher Da Cunha
COPYWRITER Alex Daher Da Cunha
ART DIRECTOR
Daniel Fernando Cortizo
PHOTOGRAPHER Rosary Esteves/
Goiania
OTHER Irom Rocha Lima (Producer)

It isn't a diet soda advertising, but has little calories.

FIGHT AGAINST HUNGER
Feed this idea.

INITIATIVE ADIAL   SUPPORT Jaime Câmara

Businessman, help to put an end in the North-east region in Brazil's hunger. Call: 295-4580 or 295-8739 and make your donation.

It's a starving man in brazil's north-east.

FIGHT AGAINST HUNGER
Feed this idea.

INITIATIVE ADIAL   SUPPORT Jaime Câmara

Businessman, help to put an end in the North-east region in Brazil's hunger. Call: 295-4580 or 295-8739 and make your donation.

ENGLAND

SILVER WORLDMEDAL, SINGLE
McCANN HEALTHCARE, MANCHESTER
CHESHIRE

CLIENT Marie Stopes International
COPYWRITER Neil Lancaster
ART DIRECTOR Dave Price
PHOTOGRAPHER Rob Walker

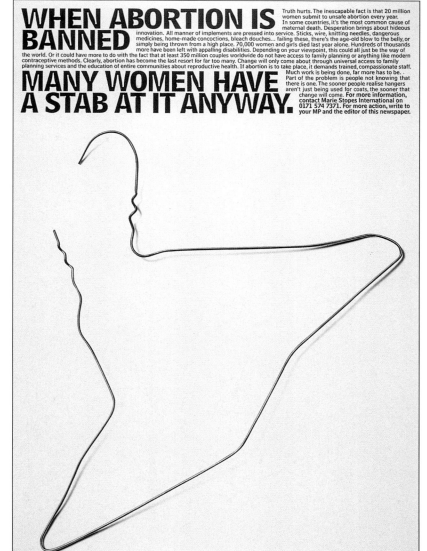

WHEN ABORTION IS BANNED

Truth hurts. The inescapable fact is that 20 million women submit to unsafe abortion every year. In some countries, it's the most common cause of maternal death. Desperation brings about hideous innovation. All manner of implements are pressed into service. Sticks, wire, knitting needles, dangerous medicines, home-made concoctions, bleach douches... failing these, there's the age-old blow to the belly, or simply being thrown from a high place. 70,000 women and girls died last year alone. Hundreds of thousands more have been left with appalling disabilities. Depending on your viewpoint, this could all just be the way of the world. Or it could have more to do with the fact that at least 350 million couples worldwide do not have access to family planning or anything like modern contraceptive methods. Clearly, abortion has become the last resort for far too many. Change will only come about through universal access to family planning services and the education of entire communities about reproductive health. If abortion is to take place, it demands trained, compassionate staff. Much work is being done, far more has to be. Part of the problem is people not knowing that there is one. The sooner people realise hangers aren't just being used for coats, the sooner that change will come. For more information, contact Marie Stopes International on 0171 574 7371. For more action, write to your MP and the editor of this newspaper.

MANY WOMEN HAVE A STAB AT IT ANYWAY.

MARIE STOPES
INTERNATIONAL
153-157 Cleveland Street, London W1P 5PG

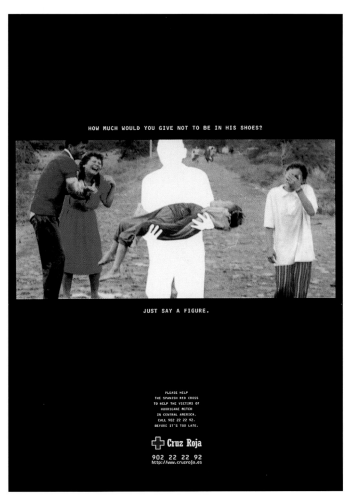

HOW MUCH WOULD YOU GIVE NOT TO BE IN HIS SHOES?

JUST SAY A FIGURE.

PLEASE HELP
THE SPANISH RED CROSS
TO HELP THE VICTIMS OF
HURRICANE MITCH
IN CENTRAL AMERICA.
CALL 902 22 22 92.
BEFORE IT'S TOO LATE.

Cruz Roja
902 22 22 92
http://www.cruzroja.es

SPAIN

BRONZE WORLDMEDAL, SINGLE
McCANN-ERICKSON
MADRID

CLIENT Cruz Roja/N.G.O.
CREATIVE DIRECTOR Nicolas Hollander/
Andres Martinez

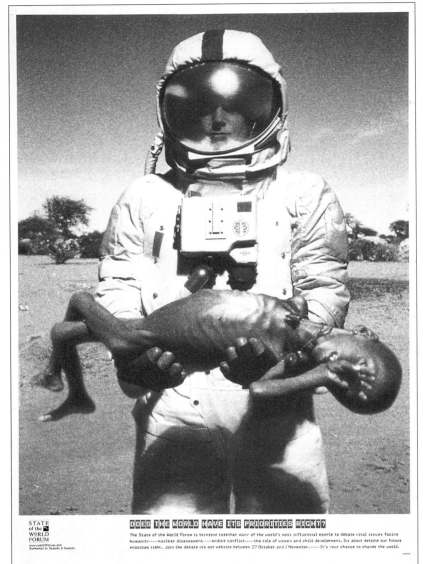

NEW ZEALAND

SILVER WORLDMEDAL, SINGLE

SAATCHI & SAATCHI WELLINGTON
WELLINGTON

CLIENT   State Of The World Forum
CREATIVE DIRECTOR   Gavin Bradley
COPYWRITER   John Plimmer
ART DIRECTOR   John Fisher/Oliver Maisey/Gavin Bradley
PHOTOGRAPHER   Benoit Fysembergh/Mark Lever/Auckland
ILLUSTRATOR   Andy Salisbury/Wellington
OTHER   Len Cheeseman/Hayden Doughty (Typographer)

SPAIN

GOLD WORLDMEDAL, CAMPAIGN

FCB/TAPSA
MADRID

CLIENT   Fundacion Cear
CREATIVE DIRECTOR   Julian Zuazo
COPYWRITER   Oriol Villar
ART DIRECTOR   Yuri Alemany
PHOTOGRAPHER   Eduardo Diaz/Madrid

SEE GRAND AWARD PAGE 240

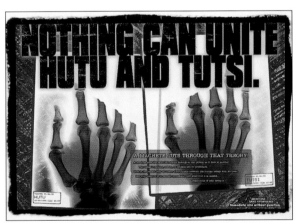

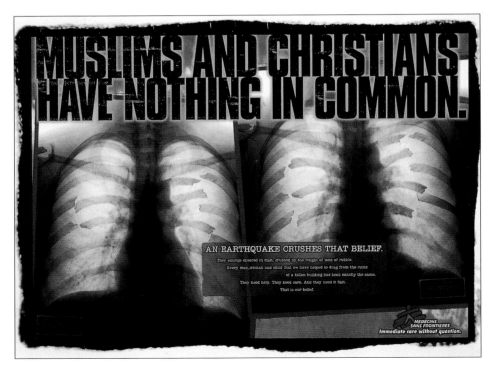

UAE

BRONZE WORLDMEDAL, CAMPAIGN

SAATCHI & SAATCHI
DUBAI

CLIENT   Medecin Sans Frontieres
CREATIVE DIRECTOR   Philip Rhoades
COPYWRITER   Philip Rhoades
ART DIRECTOR   David Taylor
OTHER   Abdel Rahman Ghandour (Client)

The New York Festivals

The World's Best Work

**PROMOTIONS MARKETING, DIRECT RESPONSE
SPECIALTY ADVERTISING, WEBSITES**

TRADE PROMOTION

JAPAN

SILVER WORLDMEDAL, SINGLE

OFFICE KAWAMOTO, INC.

OSAKA

CLIENT Kawashima Textile Manufactures Ltd.
CREATIVE DIRECTOR Junko Sera
COPYWRITER Shingo Endo
ART DIRECTOR Fumio Kawamoto
PHOTOGRAPHER Masanobu Fukuda/Osaka
DESIGNER/DESIGN Office Kawmoto Inc./Osaka

WHEN YOU SEE OUR COUNTRY
YOU'LL UNDERSTAND WHY NELSON MANDELA WAS WILLING
TO GIVE UP HIS LIFE FOR IT

SOUTH AFRICA

BRONZE WORLDMEDAL, SINGLE

**OGILVY & MATHER RIGHTFORD
SEARLE-TRIPP & MAKIN**

GAUTENG

CLIENT Satour
CREATIVE DIRECTOR Robyn Putter/
Peter Badenhorst
COPYWRITER Peter Badenhorst/
Jacques Massardo
ART DIRECTOR Greg Roberts

SOUTH AFRICA

FINALIST, CAMPAIGN

SAATCHI & SAATCHI

CAPE TOWN

CLIENT Metropolitan Employee Benefits
CREATIVE DIRECTOR Eric Frank
COPYWRITER Mark Legward/Mac Ntlokwana
ART DIRECTOR Mark Mason/Guy Parsonage
PHOTOGRAPHER Martin Hahn

SEE PAGE 266

SINGAPORE

FINALIST, CAMPAIGN

TEQUILA SINGAPORE

SINGAPORE

CLIENT LR Brand Cigarettes
CREATIVE DIRECTOR Shane Weaver
COPYWRITER Shane Weaver
ART DIRECTOR Steve Hewellyn

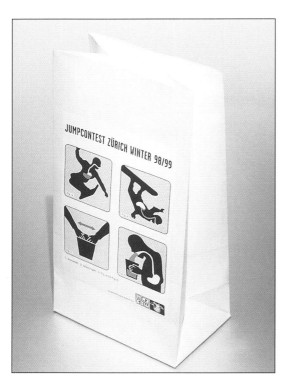

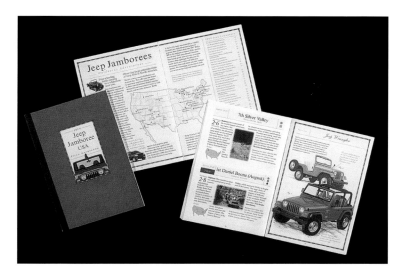

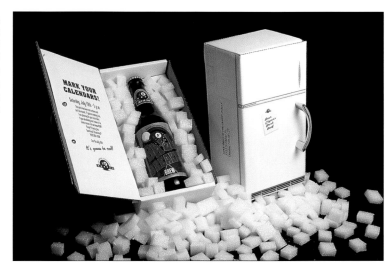

CHILE

FINALIST, CAMPAIGN
PIANO & PIANO
SANTIAGO

CREATIVE DIRECTOR
Luis Piano
ART DIRECTOR Daniela Piano/
Born in Mendoza/Argentina
PHOTOGRAPHER
Diego Bromberg/
Santiago/Chile
ILLUSTRATOR Daniela Piano/
Born in Mendoza/Argentina
DESIGNER/DESIGN
Piano & Piano/
Santiago/Chile
OTHER Impreta Italiana/
Cannoni Hnos/Chile

MIXED MEDIA PROMOTION CAMPAIGN

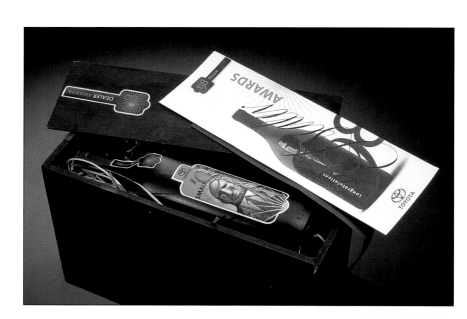

USA

FINALIST, CAMPAIGN
FCB DIRECT/NEW YORK
NEW YORK, NY

CLIENT AT&T
CREATIVE DIRECTOR John Olds/Heather Higgins
COPYWRITER Steve Klausner/Todd Filipps
ART DIRECTOR Mark Hriciga/Scott Cocchiere/
Jason Zangrilli
PHOTOGRAPHER Harry David Stewart/
Lori Adamsky Peak/New York

SOUTH AFRICA

FINALIST, CAMPAIGN
FCB IMPACT
SANDTON

CLIENT Vintage Year
CREATIVE DIRECTOR Mandy Croucamp
ART DIRECTOR Natalie Davidson
ILLUSTRATOR Peter Simpson
DESIGNER/DESIGN FCB Impact

DIRECT RESPONSE ADVERTISING

CONSUMER PRODUCTS & SERVICES

UAE
FINALIST, SINGLE
SAATCHI & SAATCHI
DUBAI
CLIENT DHL
CREATIVE DIRECTOR Kurt Blanckenburg
ART DIRECTOR Louise Miller

SELF PROMOTION

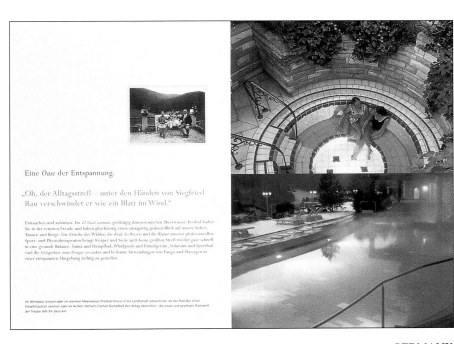

GERMANY
FINALIST, SINGLE
CLAUS KOCH CORPORATE COMMUNICATIONS
DUESSELDORF
CLIENT Hotel Traube Tonbach
CREATIVE DIRECTOR Claus Koch
COPYWRITER Sabine Schmitt/Traube Tonbach
ART DIRECTOR P. Mehl/J. Theurer/A.Lintel/C. Koch
PHOTOGRAPHER Marc Hillesheim/Archives
DESIGNER/DESIGN CKCC
OTHER Sabine Schmitt/Traube Tonbach

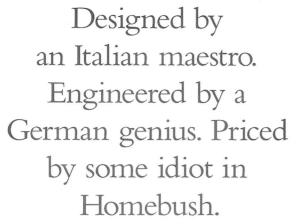

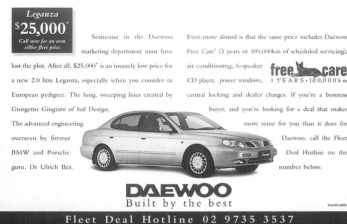

AUSTRALIA

FINALIST, SINGLE
BKM OGILVYONE
SYDNEY

CLIENT Daewood Fleet
CREATIVE DIRECTOR Peter Vierod
COPYWRITER Peter Vierod
ART DIRECTOR Peter Wennersten

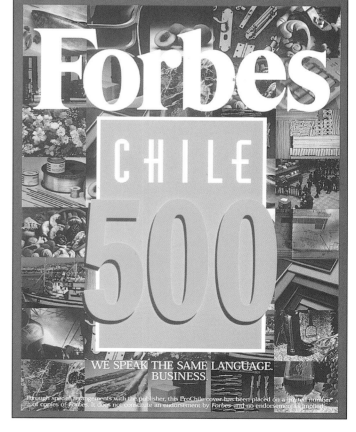

USA

FINALIST, SINGLE
CMG COMMUNICATIONS
NEW YORK, NY

CLIENT ProChile
CREATIVE DIRECTOR Dave Berger/
Mark D'Arcy
COPYWRITER Dave Wilson
ART DIRECTOR Talo Kawasaki

USA

SILVER WORLDMEDAL, CAMPAIGN
FCB DIRECT/NEW YORK
NEW YORK, NY

CLIENT
Citymeals-On-Wheels
CREATIVE DIRECTOR
Bob Cesiro/
Heather Higgins
COPYWRITER
Rebecca Reese
ART DIRECTOR
Mark Hriciga

AUSTRALIA

FINALIST, SINGLE
BAM SSB
EAST SYDNEY

CLIENT SBS/World Cup Soccer 1998
CREATIVE DIRECTOR Darryn Devlin
COPYWRITER Brendan Jones
ART DIRECTOR Mario Sanasi
PHOTOGRAPHER Jon Bader

DIRECT MAIL

FINANCIAL SERVICES

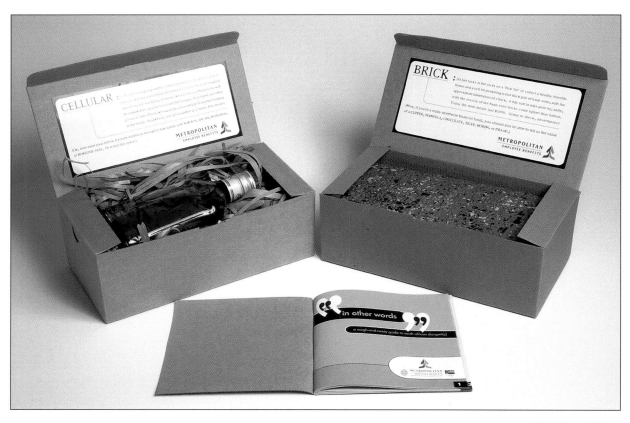

SOUTH AFRICA

SILVER WORLDMEDAL, CAMPAIGN

SAATCHI & SAATCHI
CAPE TOWN

CLIENT   Metropolitan/Employee Benefits
CREATIVE DIRECTOR   Eric Frank
COPYWRITER   Mark Legward/Mac Ntlokwana
ART DIRECTOR   Mark Mason/Guy Parsonage
PHOTOGRAPHER   Martin Hahn/Cape Town

CANADA

FINALIST, SINGLE

VBDI
TORONTO, ONTARIO

CLIENT   Bank of Montreal/
First Canadian Funds
CREATIVE DIRECTOR   Steve Murray
COPYWRITER   Colin Mitchell
ART DIRECTOR   George Shewchuk
PHOTOGRAPHER   Dave Sloan

GERMANY

GOLD WORLDMEDAL, SINGLE

OGILVYONE WORLDWIDE

FRANKFURT/M.

CLIENT   Bloomberg LP
CREATIVE DIRECTOR   Alexander Szugger
COPYWRITER   Alexander Szugger
ART DIRECTOR   Conny Moser

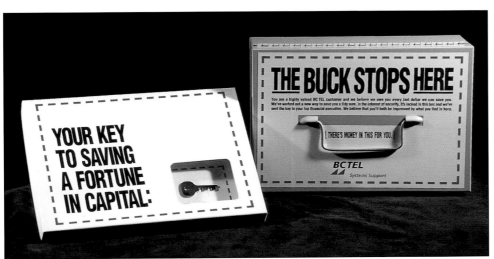

CANADA

FINALIST, SINGLE

NEW VISION STRATEGIC COMMUNICATIONS

VANCOUVER, BC

CLIENT   Technology Rollover
CREATIVE DIRECTOR   Don Veinish
COPYWRITER   Don Veinish
ART DIRECTOR   Robert Bowser
OTHER   Heather Carter (Account Director)

SPAIN

SILVER WORLDMEDAL, SINGLE
CP COMUNICACION
MADRID

CLIENT Iberia
CREATIVE DIRECTOR Ezequiel Trivino
COPYWRITER Alvaro Gonzalez
ART DIRECTOR David Lee
PHOTOGRAPHER Still Life/Madrid

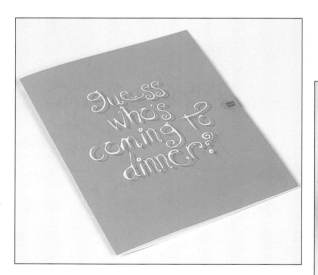

BRAZIL

BRONZE WORLDMEDAL, SINGLE
MASTER COMUNICACAO
CURITIBA, PR

CLIENT Confianca Bug killers
CREATIVE DIRECTOR Renato Cavalher
COPYWRITER Luiz Henrique Groff
ART DIRECTOR Renato Fernandez/Roberto Fernandez
PHOTOGRAPHER Regis Marcel Fernandez

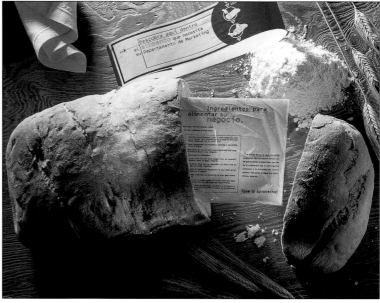

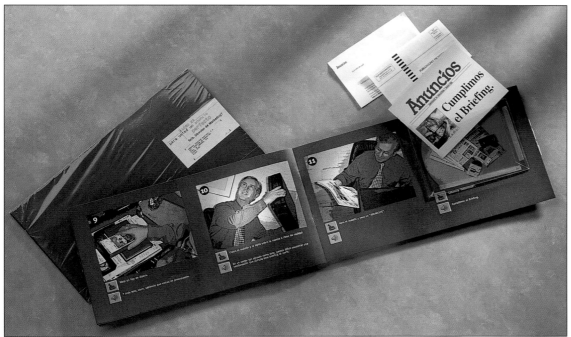

CHILE

FINALIST, SINGLE
DIMENSION MARKETING DIRECTO
SAN SEBASTIAN - CUIPUZCOA

CLIENT Anuncios
CREATIVE DIRECTOR
Guillermo Viglione/David Torrejon
COPYWRITER Oscar Bilbao
ART DIRECTOR Josse Luis Conde
DESIGNER/DESIGN
Dimension Mk. Directo
OTHER Mohemi Castell/
Santiago Hernandez/
Vidal Rodriguez/Corka Lopez

SPAIN

FINALIST, SINGLE
WUNDERMAN CATO JOHNSON
MADRID

CLIENT IBM
CREATIVE DIRECTOR Sonia Rodriguez/
Javier Gomez
COPYWRITER Rafael Diaz Gomez
ART DIRECTOR Antonio Fernandez
OTHER M. Martinez (Production)/
B. Cuadrado (Account Dir.)

SOUTH AFRICA

GOLD WORLDMEDAL, CAMPAIGN
FCB IMPACT
SANDTON

CLIENT Toyota Landcruiser 100
CREATIVE DIRECTOR Mandy Croucamp
COPYWRITER Stuart Stobbs
ART DIRECTOR Mandy Croucamp
OTHER Peter Lowe

SOUTH AFRICA

FINALIST, CAMPAIGN
FCB IMPACT
SANDTON

CLIENT Toyota Landcruiser Prado
CREATIVE DIRECTOR Mandy Croucamp
COPYWRITER Stuart Stobbs
ART DIRECTOR Peter Lowe
PHOTOGRAPHER Horst Klemm

SPAIN

FINALIST, SINGLE
WUNDERMAN CATO JOHNSON
MADRID

CLIENT Ford Focus
CREATIVE DIRECTOR Sonia Rodriguez/Javier Gomez
COPYWRITER Rafael Diaz
ART DIRECTOR Antonio Fernandez/Marta Lorrio

USA

SILVER WORLDMEDAL, CAMPAIGN

McCANN RELATIONSHIP MARKETING
NEW YORK, NY

CLIENT   GMC Envoy/Pontiac
CREATIVE DIRECTOR   Richard Eber
COPYWRITER   Gary Scheiner/Melissa Bank/Joe Sweet
ART DIRECTOR   Lisa Pfitzner/Darcy Eveleigh
PHOTOGRAPHER   Ivo von Renner
ILLUSTRATOR   Mike Regan
OTHER   W. Patterson (Management Sup.)/
K. K. Recenello (Production)

SWEDEN

FINALIST, SINGLE

FALTMAN & MALMEN
STOCKHOLM

CLIENT   Europeiska Reseforsakringar
COPYWRITER   Bo Tidelius
ART DIRECTOR   Fredrik Claesson
OTHER   Jarl Fernaeus/Fred Raaum

STORE/RETAIL PROMOTION

GERMANY

SILVER WORLDMEDAL, CAMPAIGN
WUNDERMAN CATO JOHNSON
FRANKFURT

CLIENT   Inside Her
CREATIVE DIRECTOR   Jorg Puphal
COPYWRITER   Claudia Herdt/Stella Friedrichs
ART DIRECTOR   Ute Deyerling/
Elke Mohlenbrock
OTHER   Edith Swiezy (Account Manager)

SPAIN

FINALIST, SINGLE
CP COMUNICACION
MADRID

CLIENT   Cepsa Diesel Fuel Heating
CREATIVE DIRECTOR   Alfonso Marian
COPYWRITER   Guillermo Garcia/Francisco Garcia
ART DIRECTOR   Lala Baldrich
PHOTOGRAPHER   Stll Life/Madrid

Marriage doesn't mean
your husband has to go to bed
with the same woman
every night.

Underwear for every occasion, up to 70% off.

UnderWearhouse
Next to nothings for next to nothing.

USA

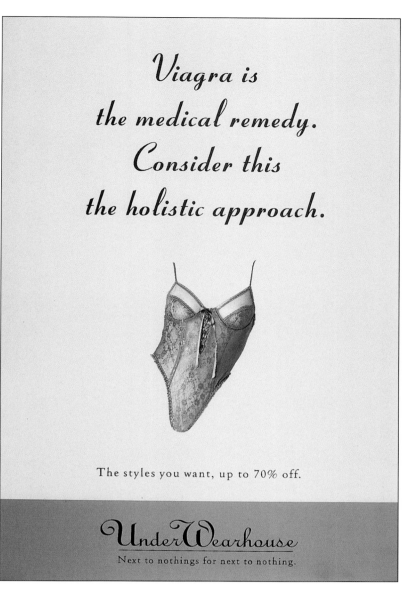

Viagra is
the medical remedy.
Consider this
the holistic approach.

The styles you want, up to 70% off.

UnderWearhouse
Next to nothings for next to nothing.

SELF PROMOTION

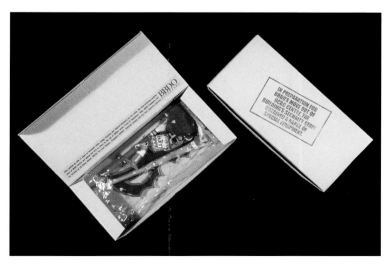

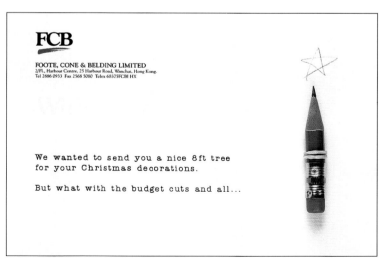

FCB

FOOTE, CONE & BELDING LIMITED
2/Fl., Harbour Centre, 25 Harbour Road, Wanchai, Hong Kong.
Tel 2886 0933 Fax 2568 5080 Telex 68375FCBI HX

We wanted to send you a nice 8ft tree
for your Christmas decorations.

But what with the budget cuts and all...

SINGAPORE

HONG KONG

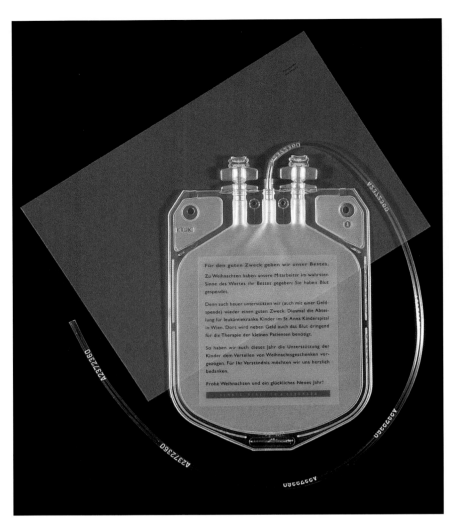

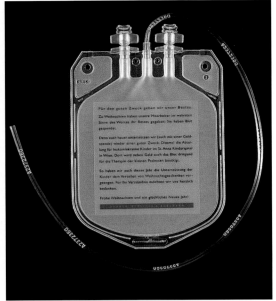

AUSTRIA

SILVER WORLDMEDAL, SINGLE
DEMNER, MERLICEK & BERGMANN
VIENNA

CREATIVE DIRECTOR   Mariusz Jan Demner/
Stephan Klein
COPYWRITER   Stephan Klein/Helge Haberzettl
ART DIRECTOR   Bernhard Grafl
GRAPHICS COMPANY   Sigrid Pfanzelter

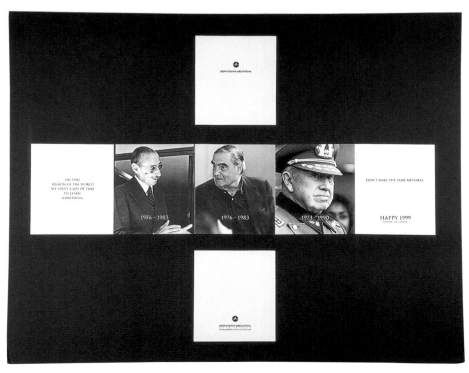

ARGENTINA

BRONZE WORLDMEDAL, SINGLE
DOWNTOWN
BUENOS AIRES

CLIENT   End of Year Greeting Card
CREATIVE DIRECTOR   Sergio Pollaccia
ART DIRECTOR   Claudio Basile

CHINA

FINALIST, SINGLE

GALLERY LTD
HONG KONG

CREATIVE DIRECTOR Mike Staniford
ART DIRECTOR Nichola Dearn
PHOTOGRAPHER Gerald Colley/Sydney
DESIGNER/DESIGN M.Staniford/N.Dearn

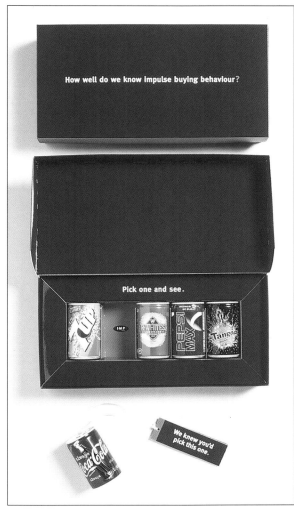

U K

FINALIST, SINGLE

IMP
LONDON

CREATIVE DIRECTOR Dave Harris
COPYWRITER Christian Clark
ART DIRECTOR Rod Clausen
OTHER Gavin Ferguson (Typography)

USA

FINALIST, SINGLE

JODY DOLE STUDIO
NEW YORK, NY

ADVERTISING AGENCY Addison Design
CREATIVE DIRECTOR David Kohler
ART DIRECTOR David Kohler
PHOTOGRAPHER Judy Dole
DESIGNER/DESIGN Addison/NY
OTHER L.P. Thebault (Printer)

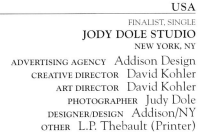

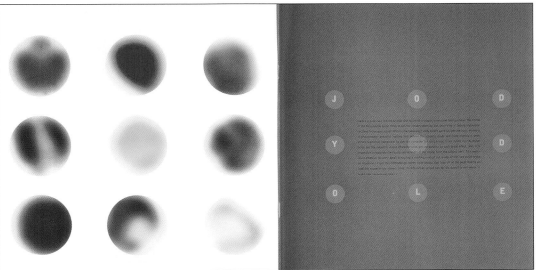

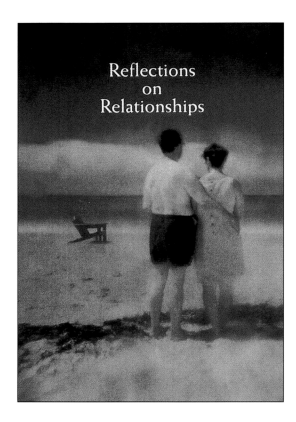

Harmony

thrives on

occasional discord.

relationships

Gary Wade

USA

FINALIST, SINGLE
McCANN RELATIONSHIP MARKETING
NEW YORK, NY

CREATIVE DIRECTOR Richard Eber
COPYWRITER Jenny Raybould
ART DIRECTOR Liz Wynn
PHOTOGRAPHER A. Kaplan/C. Maeder/
N. Rica Schiff/G. Wade/N.David Smith/NYC

GERMANY

FINALIST, SINGLE
PHARMA PERFORMANCE EURO RSCG
MUNICH

CLIENT Pharma Performance
CREATIVE DIRECTOR Karl Armer
COPYWRITER Karl Armer
ART DIRECTOR Stefan Oevermann

GERMANY

FINALIST, SINGLE
PUBLICIS BERLIN
BERLIN

CREATIVE DIRECTOR Christain Alberti
COPYWRITER Irina Gragoll/Esther Schneider
ART DIRECTOR Maike Koch

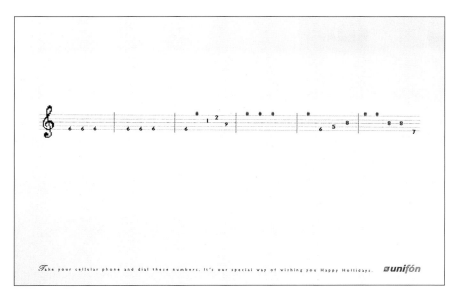

Take your cellular phone and dial these numbers. It's our special way of wishing you Happy Hollidays. *unifón*

ARGENTINA
FINALIST, SINGLE
SAVAGLIO TBWA
BUENOS AIRES

CLIENT   Unifon
CREATIVE DIRECTOR   Ernesto Savaglio
COPYWRITER   Diego Donato
ART DIRECTOR   Inaqui/Marcelo Virgilito/
Demiian Veled

GERMANY
FINALIST, SINGLE
STAWICKI
MUNCHEN

CLIENT   Erinnerungen An Die Gute Alte Zeit
CREATIVE DIRECTOR   Axel Schmalschlager
COPYWRITER   Udo Stabler
ART DIRECTOR   Claudia Becker

RUSSIA
FINALIST, CAMPAIGN
**MEDIA ARTS MARKETING
COMMUNICATIONS**
MOSCOW

CREATIVE DIRECTOR   Grigory Fedorov
COPYWRITER   A. Agatov/A. Bulanov
ART DIRECTOR   Vladimir Corshkov

TRADE & MANUFACTURING

GERMANY

FINALIST, SINGLE
RTS RIEGER TEAM
LEINFELDEN-ECHTERDINGEN

CLIENT Honeywell
CREATIVE DIRECTOR Giovanni Perna
COPYWRITER Michael Mayer/Joachim Kaufmann
ART DIRECTOR Tobias Urban/Annette Pientka

CHILE

FINALIST, SINGLE
THE SALES MACHINE CHILE
SANTIAGO

CLIENT Direct Marketing Advertising
CREATIVE DIRECTOR Pablo Sanchez
COPYWRITER Gonzalo Santibanez
ART DIRECTOR Marcelo Feliu
DESIGNER/DESIGN Tecno Print
OTHER Francisca Roman

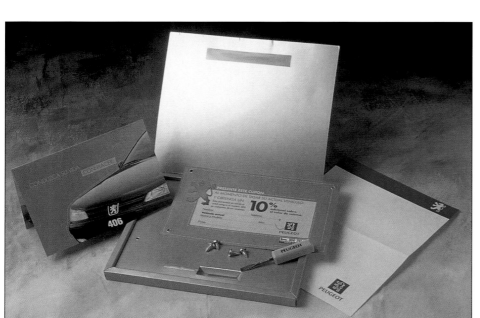

ARGENTINA
SILVER WORLDMEDAL, SINGLE
RATTO/BBDO S.A.
BUENOS AIRES
CLIENT NIKE S.A.
CREATIVE DIRECTOR
Juan Manuel Ricciarelli/
Joaquin Molla
COPYWRITER
Federico Cabral
ART DIRECTOR
Bruno Tortolano

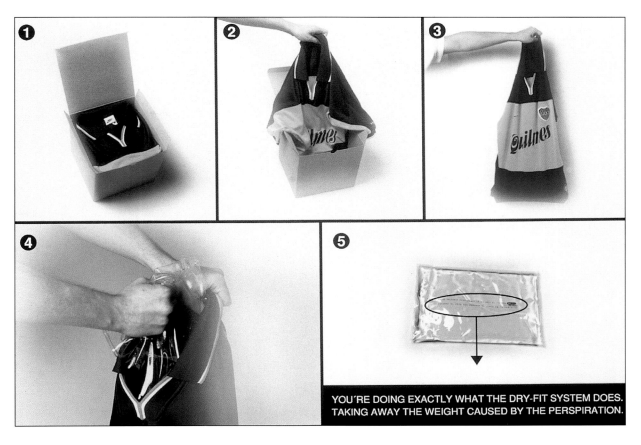

YOU´RE DOING EXACTLY WHAT THE DRY-FIT SYSTEM DOES.
TAKING AWAY THE WEIGHT CAUSED BY THE PERSPIRATION.

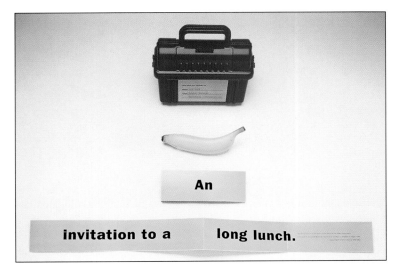

AUSTRALIA
FINALIST, SINGLE
AMMIRATI PURIS LINTAS DIRECT
NORTH SYDNEY
CLIENT ADMA Long Lunch
CREATIVE DIRECTOR Robin Sinclair
COPYWRITER Robin Sinclair
ART DIRECTOR Rob Stephenson
OTHER Julie Sanderson (AE)

HONG KONG
FINALIST, SINGLE
BOZELL WORLDWIDE
CAUSEWAY BAY, HONG KONG
CLIENT Kowloon Dairy Fresh Milk
CREATIVE DIRECTOR Fornita Wong/Poh
Hwee Beng
COPYWRITER Shea Kar Leong
ART DIRECTOR Eric Lai
OTHER Curry Leung (Print Production)

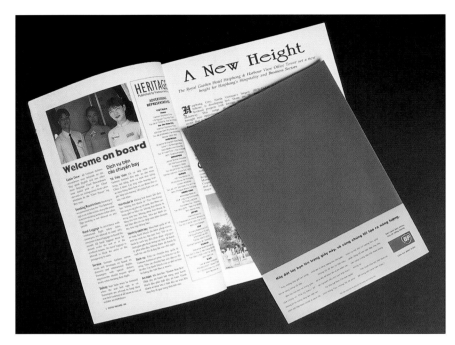

VIETNAM

BRONZE WORLDMEDAL, SINGLE

SAATCHI & SAATCHI VIETNAM
HO CHI MINH CITY

CLIENT British Petroleum
CREATIVE DIRECTOR Mike Sands
COPYWRITER Paul Vincent Ewen
ART DIRECTOR Mike Sands/Le Duc Thang
OTHER Hoang Thi Mai Huong/
To Linh Lan (Translation)

AUSTRALIA

FINALIST, SINGLE

BRISTOW & PRENTICE
ALBERT PARK, VICTORIA

CLIENT Royal Victorian Institute For The Blind
CREATIVE DIRECTOR Tony Van Lambaart
COPYWRITER Ben Lilley
ART DIRECTOR Paul Moriarty
PHOTOGRAPHER Image Bank
OTHER Loan Ho

U K

FINALIST, SINGLE

IMP
LONDON

CREATIVE DIRECTOR David Harris
COPYWRITER Ian Ford-Batey
ART DIRECTOR Hamish Dixon

SPECIALTY ADVERTISING

SALES PROMOTION-CONSUMER

GERMANY

FINALIST, SINGLE

.START ADVERTISING GMBH
MUNICH

CLIENT Car Hire
CREATIVE DIRECTOR Gregor Woltje
COPYWRITER Rob Filler
ART DIRECTOR Kai Kier

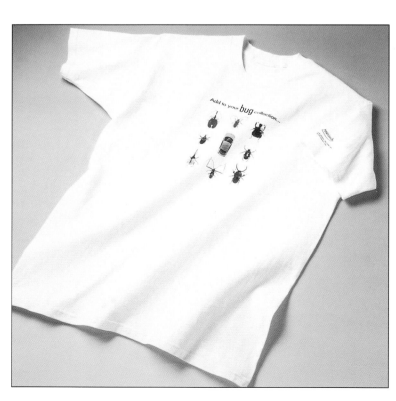

USA

FINALIST, SINGLE

FLAIR COMMUNICATIONS AGENCY
CHICAGO, IL

CLIENT Ameritech/Telecommunications
CREATIVE DIRECTOR Ann Wiegand
COPYWRITER Richard Conlon
ART DIRECTOR Ward Starrett
ILLUSTRATOR Ward Starrett

USA
BRONZE WORLDMEDAL, SINGLE
PHARMADESIGN INC.
WARREN, NJ
CLIENT Zeneca Pharmaceuticals
ILLUSTRATOR Beth Willert
DESIGNER/DESIGN Mathew Coe
OTHER Robin Ansel (Account Director)

USA
FINALIST, SINGLE
PHARMADESIGN INC.
WARREN, NJ
CLIENT Phone-Pouleric Rorer
ILLUSTRATOR Beth Willert
DESIGNER/DESIGN Mathew Coe
OTHER Robin Ansel (Account Director)

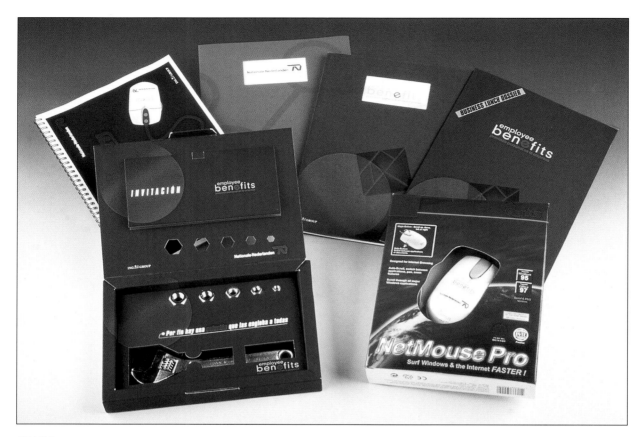

SPAIN

SILVER WORLDMEDAL, SINGLE
CP COMUNICACION
MADRID

CLIENT Nationale-Nederlanden
CREATIVE DIRECTOR Ezequiel Trivino
COPYWRITER Fernando de Miguel
ART DIRECTOR Gonzalo de Gregorio/
Luis Echvarria/Hector Valencia
PHOTOGRAPHER Still Life/Madrid

USA

BRONZE WORLDMEDAL, SINGLE
TBWA/CHIAT/DAY
SAN FRANCISCO, CA

CLIENT Levi's Hard Jeans
CREATIVE DIRECTOR Lee Clow/
Peter Angelos/Rob Smiley
DESIGNER/DESIGN Roz Romney

USA

FINALIST, SINGLE
EISNOR INTERACTIVE
NEW YORK, NY

CLIENT I-Traffic
CREATIVE DIRECTOR Jennifer Nash
COPYWRITER David Poole

ARGENTINA

FINALIST, SINGLE
MORANOBMC ADVERTISING
BUENOS AIRES

CLIENT EF-Christmas Card
CREATIVE DIRECTOR Adrian Morano
COPYWRITER Santiago Simionati
ART DIRECTOR Federico Macko
OTHER Esteban Morano

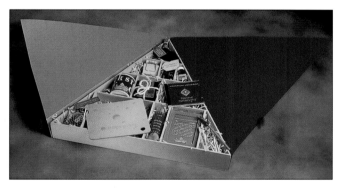

SOUTH AFRICA

FINALIST, SINGLE
FCB IMPACT
SANDTON

CLIENT Incredible Connection
CREATIVE DIRECTOR Mandy Croucamp
COPYWRITER Stuart Stobbs
ART DIRECTOR Lloyd Moore
ILLUSTRATOR Peter Simpson
DESIGNER/DESIGN Sue Dexter

USA

FINALIST, SINGLE

FLAIR COMMUNICATIONS AGENCY

CHICAGO, IL

CLIENT GPC/Tobacco
CREATIVE DIRECTOR Stan Hardwick
COPYWRITER Ken Monahan
ART DIRECTOR Liz Scoggins

CHILE

FINALIST, SINGLE

WCJ CHILE

SANTIAGO

CLIENT WCJ Chile
CREATIVE DIRECTOR Olaf Ulriksen/
Mario Salman/Carlos Corrales
COPYWRITER Olaf Ulriksen/Mario Salman/
Carlos Corrales
ART DIRECTOR Olaf Ulriksen/Mario Salman/
Carlos Corrales

HONG KONG

GOLD WORLDMEDAL, SINGLE
LEO BURNETT LTD.
HONG KONG

CLIENT SmarTone
CREATIVE DIRECTOR Ringo Chan
ART DIRECTOR Dennis Ou

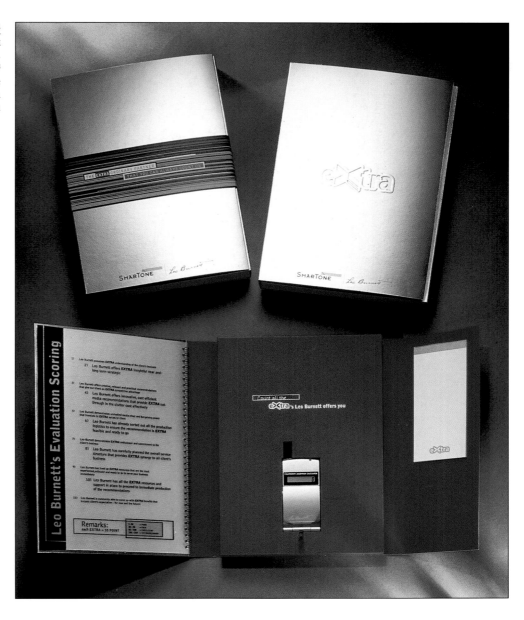

SINGAPORE

FINALIST, SINGLE
FCB SINGAPORE
SINGAPORE

CLIENT Snoopy Restaurants Singapore
ADVERTISING AGENCY Foote, Cone & Belding/Singapore
CREATIVE DIRECTOR Chris Kyme
COPYWRITER Lim Wei
ART DIRECTOR Chow Kok Keong

GERMANY

SILVER WORLDMEDAL, SINGLE

KNSK, BBDO

HAMBURG

CLIENT SPD

CREATIVE DIRECTOR

Ulrike Wegert/
Detlef Kruger

COPYWRITER

Ulrich Zunkeler

ART DIRECTOR

Andreas Geyer

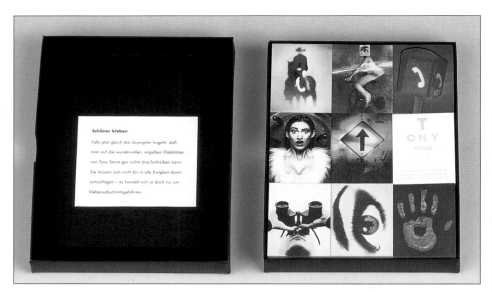

GERMANY

BRONZE WORLDMEDAL, SINGLE

HEYE + PARTNER GMBH

UNTERHACHING

CLIENT Tony Stone Stock Market

CREATIVE DIRECTOR Ralph Taubenberger/
Peter Hirrlinger

COPYWRITER Doris Haider

ART DIRECTOR Oliver Oelkers

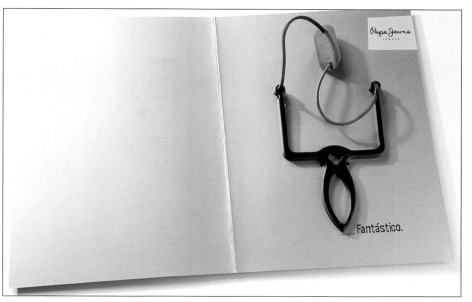

SPAIN
FINALIST, SINGLE
GREY TRACE
BARCELONA

CREATIVE DIRECTOR Pablo Torreblanca/Gerardo Silva
COPYWRITER Borja Abos
ART DIRECTOR Blanca Valverde

USA
FINALIST, SINGLE
THE ATLANTIC GROUP
NORWALK, CT

CREATIVE DIRECTOR Suzanne Haas/Greg Voornas
COPYWRITER Greg Voornas
ART DIRECTOR Brian Miller
ILLUSTRATOR CSA Archive

USA
FINALIST, SINGLE
MELANIE EVE BAROCAS PHOTOGRAPHER
GUILFORD, CT

CREATIVE DIRECTOR Melanie Eve Barocas
COPYWRITER Melanie Eve Barocas
ART DIRECTOR John Phillion
PHOTOGRAPHER Melanie Eve Barocas/Guilford, CT
OTHER Van Dyck Press

OTHER

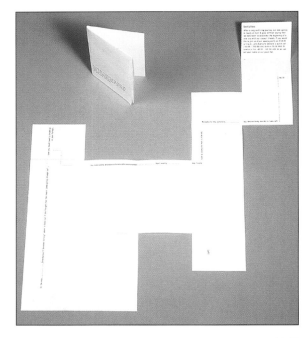

GERMANY
SILVER WORLDMEDAL, SINGLE
.START ADVERTISING GMBH
MUNICH

CREATIVE DIRECTOR Gregor Woltje
COPYWRITER Anna Maier
ART DIRECTOR Benny Lommel/Otilia Vakej

GERMANY
FINALIST, SINGLE
.START ADVERTISING GMBH
MUNICH

CREATIVE DIRECTOR Gregor Wotje
COPYWRITER Olli Dahl/
Thorsten Sannwald/Anna Maier
ART DIRECTOR Kai Kier/Frank Aldorf

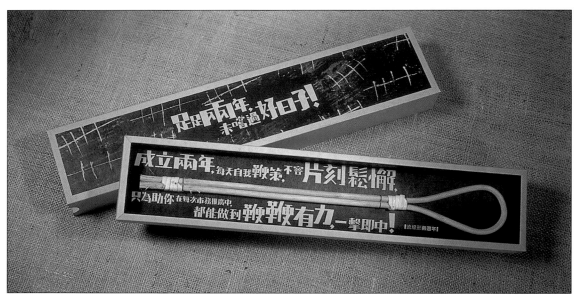

HONG KONG
BRONZE WORLDMEDAL, SINGLE
**STREAMLINE
COMMUNICATION LTD.**
HONG KONG

CREATIVE DIRECTOR Lawrence Yu
COPYWRITER Grace Ip
ART DIRECTOR Lawrence Yu
ILLUSTRATOR Doris Lee
OTHER Doris Lee (Typographer)

USA

FINALIST, SINGLE

BUENA VISTA TELEVISION
BURBANK, CA

CLIENT The PJs
CREATIVE DIRECTOR Sal Sardo/
Jimmy Lee
ART DIRECTOR Robert LaDuke

GERMANY

FINALIST, SINGLE

SPRINGER & JACOBY WERBUNG GMBH
HAMBURG

CLIENT Springer & Jacoby Advertising
CREATIVE DIRECTOR Arndt Dallmann/
Guido Heffels
COPYWRITER Patric Butikofer
ART DIRECTOR Patric Butikofer

SPAIN

FINALIST, SINGLE

CP COMUNICACION
MADRID

CLIENT Fundacio Abadia Montserrat, 2025
CREATIVE DIRECTOR Antonio Pacheco
COPYWRITER Antonio Pacheco
ART DIRECTOR Borja Orozco
PHOTOGRAPHER Still Life/Madrid

CORPORATE IMAGE

USA
GOLD WORLDMEDAL, SINGLE
AGENCY.COM
NEW YORK, NY
CLIENT British Airways
CREATIVE DIRECTOR
C.Needham/L.Stanevich/
C.Briggs
COPYWRITER E.Niemack
ART DIRECTOR J.Esquivel/
P. Laughlin/S. Stein/
Drudamico
DESIGNER/DESIGN T. Moran/
J. Gutierrez/C. Briggs
OTHER Aaron Sugarman
(President)

USA
FINALIST, SINGLE
AUSTIN KNIGHT INC.
CHICAGO, IL
CLIENT US West University Relations
CREATIVE DIRECTOR Bryan Sethre
COPYWRITER Dan Gershenson
ART DIRECTOR Tony Kernagis

ART NOT AVAILABLE

USA
FINALIST, SINGLE
FLAIR COMMUNICATIONS AGENCY
CHICAGO, IL
CLIENT Brown & Williamson/Tobacco
CREATIVE DIRECTOR Stan Hardwick
COPYWRITER Mary Bunker
PHOTOGRAPHER Bart Harris & Elite Studios/Chicago
DESIGNER/DESIGN Digital Vision/Chicago

FINALIST, SINGLE
2 DIMENSIONS
TORONTO, ONTARIO
CLIENT   Two Dimensions
CREATIVE DIRECTOR   Kam Wai Yu
COPYWRITER   James McKinnon
ART DIRECTOR   Yodo Lam
DESIGNER/DESIGN   Anh Nguyen
(Web Designer)

BRAND BUILDING / PROMOTION

USA

FINALIST, SINGLE
AGENCY.COM
NEW YORK, NY
CLIENT   Brasilian National Team Sponsored By NIKE
CREATIVE DIRECTOR   Deanne Draeger/Andrew Leiteh
COPYWRITER   Tim Doherty
ART DIRECTOR   Tim Carrier/PJ Loughran
DESIGNER/DESIGN   Tim Carner/Heidi Stephens/Min Chang
OTHER   Chad Ruble (Account Executive)

USA

FINALIST, SINGLE
INTERACTIVE8 INC.
NEW YORK, NY
CLIENT   A&E Television Networks
CREATIVE DIRECTOR   Doug Rice/Howard Coale
ART DIRECTOR   Tom Misner
DESIGNER/DESIGN   Howard Coale
OTHER   M. Vohr/T. Brancato/
J. Chang (Production Managers)

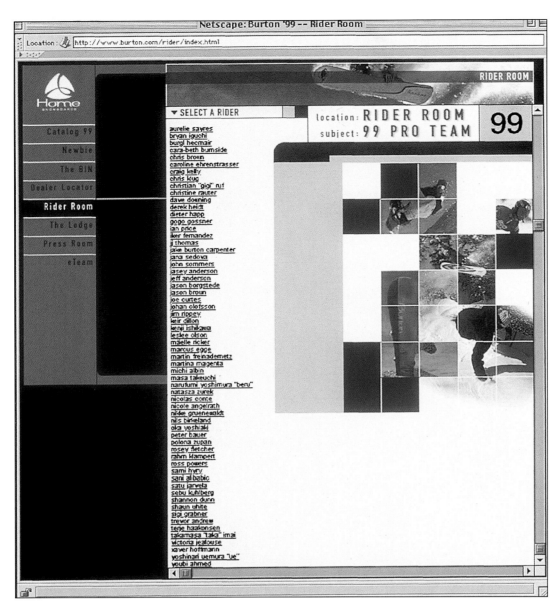

USA

GOLD WORLDMEDAL, SINGLE
RESOURCE MARKETING
COLUMBUS, OH

CLIENT   Burton Snowboards
COPYWRITER   Brian Reed
ART DIRECTOR   Dennis Bajec
ILLUSTRATOR   James Towning
DESIGNER/DESIGN   Todd Yuzwa

USA

FINALIST, SINGLE
**MARQUARDT & ROCHE/
MEDITZ & HACKETT**
STAMFORD, CT

CLIENT   FUJI Medical Systems USA
CREATIVE DIRECTOR   Gerry O'Hara/
Thomas Hackett
COPYWRITER   Lisa Meditz
ART DIRECTOR   David Wood
OTHER   Randy Nagel/
Danielle Vincent

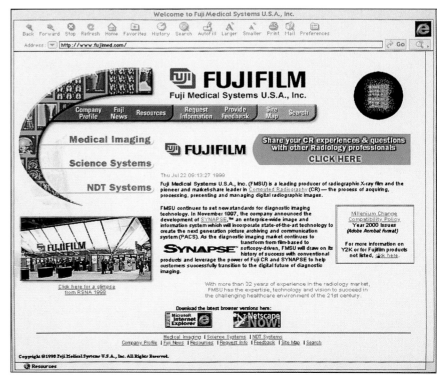

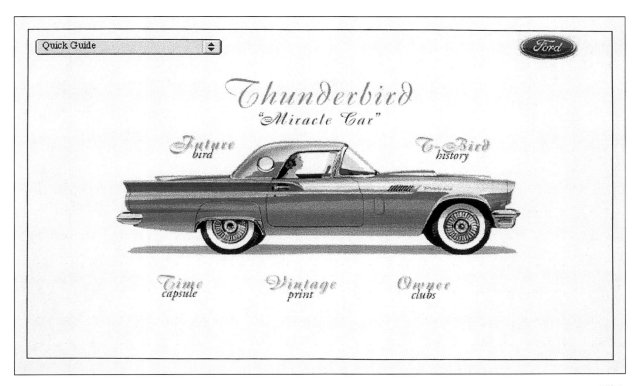

USA
SILVER WORLDMEDAL, SINGLE
J. WALTER THOMPSON
DETROIT, MI
CLIENT   Ford Thunderbird
CREATIVE DIRECTOR   Bruce Rooke/
Rob Donnell
COPYWRITER   Carol Roth
ART DIRECTOR   Carole Adam
DESIGNER/DESIGN   M. Cicerone
(Multi-Media Designer)

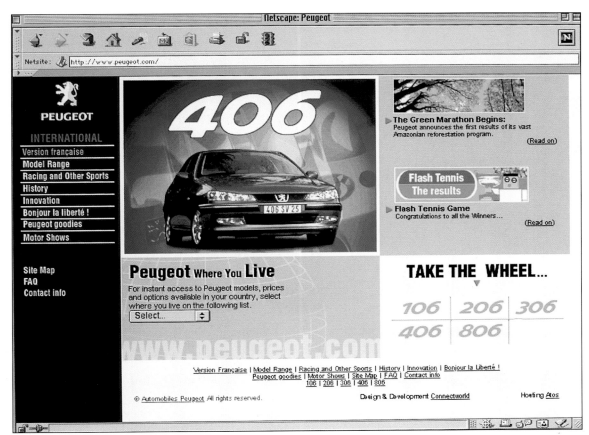

FRANCE
BRONZE WORLDMEDAL, SINGLE
CONNECTWORLD
PARIS
CLIENT   Peugeot Automobiles
CREATIVE DIRECTOR
Laurent Thomas-Gerard
COPYWRITER   Randall Koral
ART DIRECTOR   Thomas Aubrun
DESIGNER/DESIGN   Connectworld

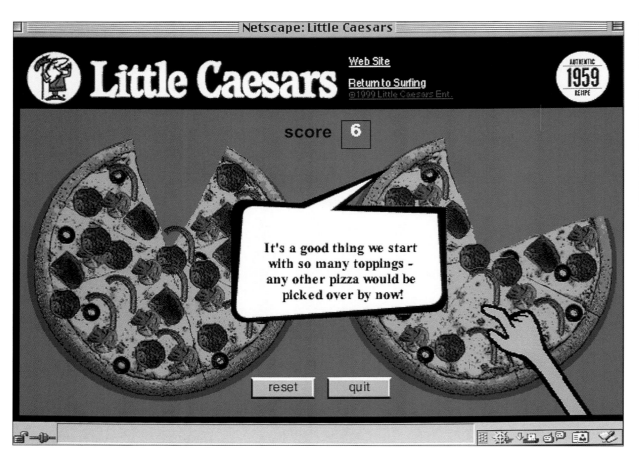

USA
SILVER WORLDMEDAL, SINGLE
BOZELL WORLDWIDE
SOUTHFIELD, MI
CLIENT Little Caesars Pizza
CREATIVE DIRECTOR
Gary Topolewski/
Mark Simon/
Husam Ajluni
COPYWRITER John Gregory
ART DIRECTOR Peter Arndt/
Geoffrey Gates
ILLUSTRATOR
Dragonfly Studios/
Tom Helland

USA
FINALIST, SINGLE
BOZELL WORLDWIDE
SOUTHFIELD, MI
CLIENT Grand Cherokee
CREATIVE DIRECTOR Gary Topolewski/Bill Morden/Husam Ajluni
COPYWRITER John Gregory
ART DIRECTOR Peter Arndt/Scott Lange
PHOTOGRAPHER Brad Stanley/Royal Oak
ILLUSTRATOR Dragonfly Studios

CANADA
FINALIST, SINGLE
SOUND SOURCE NETWORKS
TORONTO, ONTARIO
CLIENT Sound Source Networks
CREATIVE DIRECTOR Andrew Elvish
COPYWRITER Bob Weir
ART DIRECTOR Rob Lee

FINALIST, CAMPAIGN
LG AD INC.
SEOUL

CLIENT LG Flatron /LG Electronics
CREATIVE DIRECTOR Min-Soo Kim
COPYWRITER Tei-Won Hwang
ART DIRECTOR Kwan-Ho Jung/
Chul-Hyun Kim
ILLUSTRATOR Ki-Joon Kim
DESIGNER/DESIGN MES/Seoul

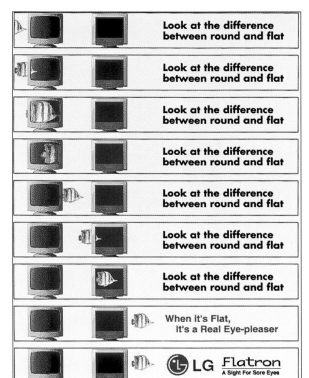

USA

FINALIST, SINGLE
TBWA/CHIAT/DAY
SAN FRANCISCO, CA

CLIENT Levi's (R) Hard Jeans (R)
CREATIVE DIRECTOR L. Clow/P. Angelos/
R. Smiley/M. Borosky
COPYWRITER Craig Namba
ART DIRECTOR Rob Smiley/Guthrie Dolan
DESIGNER/DESIGN CKS Partners/San Francisco

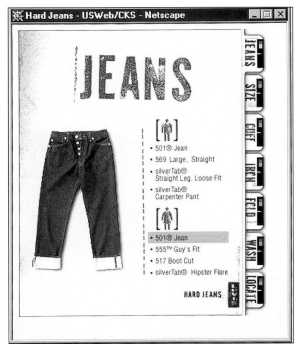

SELF PROMOTION

USA

FINALIST, SINGLE
ARCHRIVAL
LINCOLN, NE

CLIENT Digital Design
ILLUSTRATOR Charles Hull

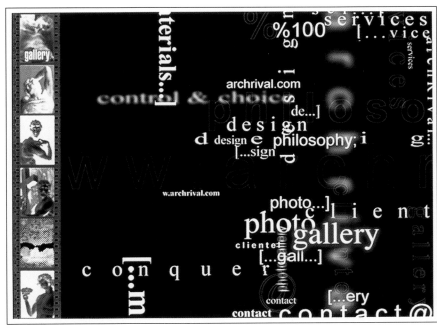

BRONZE WORLDMEDAL, SINGLE
DKB & PARTNERS, INC.
MORRISTOWN, NJ
CREATIVE DIRECTOR Leticia Martin
COPYWRITER Leticia Martin
ART DIRECTOR Dreux Sawyer

SERVICE ADVERTISING

USA

FINALIST, SINGLE
HEALTHTECH DIGITAL
NEW YORK, NY
CLIENT Acne-DTC
COPYWRITER Mario Coccia
DESIGNER/DESIGN SimStar Digital Media/
Princeton, NJ

USA

FINALIST, SINGLE
WORLD WILDLIFE FUND
WASHINGTON, DC
DESIGNER/DESIGN
New Media Publishing, Inc.

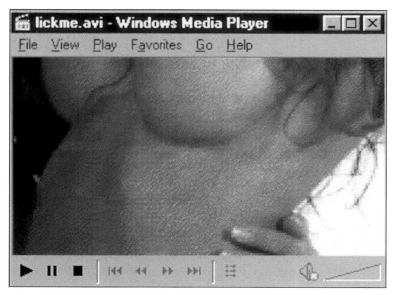

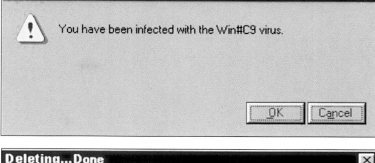

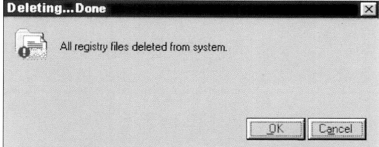

SOUTH AFRICA

SILVER WORLDMEDAL, SINGLE
OGILVY & MATHER RIGHTFORD SEARLE-TRIPP & MAKIN
GAUTENG
CLIENT   Aids & HIV information
CREATIVE DIRECTOR   Brett Wild
COPYWRITER   George Low
ART DIRECTOR   Sergio Lacueva/ Alana Alston

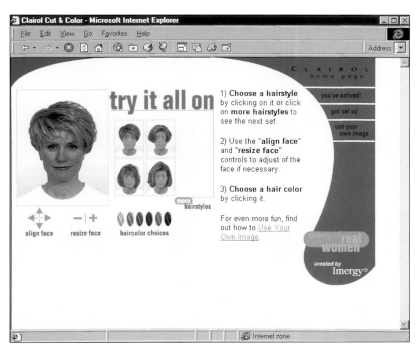

USA

BRONZE WORLDMEDAL, SINGLE
IMERGY
NEW YORK, NY
CLIENT   Clairol Try It All On Website
CREATIVE DIRECTOR   Debra Schwartz
COPYWRITER   Flora Perskie
ART DIRECTOR   Patricia Di Pasquale

BANNERS

USA

GOLD WORLDMEDAL, CAMPAIGN

INTERACTIVE8 INC.

NEW YORK, NY

CLIENT   M&M/Mars
COPYWRITER   Jonathan Lewis/Martin Torres
ART DIRECTOR   David Lewis/Jonathan Lewis/Martin Torres
DESIGNER/DESIGN   Martha Gradisher/David Lewis
OTHER   Stephanie Chin (Production Manager)

HOME PAGE

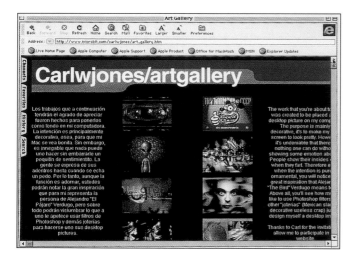

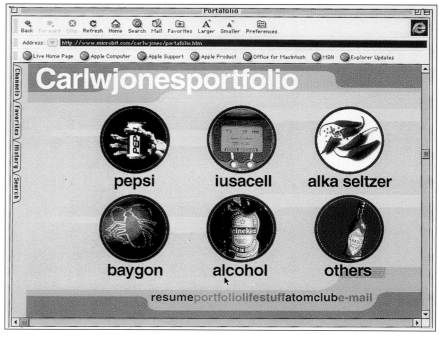

MEXICO

FINALIST, SINGLE

BBDO/MEXICO

MEXICO CITY

CREATIVE DIRECTOR   Carl Jones
ART DIRECTOR   Carl Jones
DESIGNER/DESIGN   Octavio Romero/
Raul Vaugier (Web Designer)

GERMANY

BRONZE WORLDMEDAL, SINGLE

TRURNIT & PARTNER VERLAG GMBH
OTTOBRUNN

CLIENT   Bewag Aktiengesellschaft
CREATIVE DIRECTOR   Andre Link
COPYWRITER   Irene Wambach
ART DIRECTOR   Katarina Marevic
DESIGNER/DESIGN   Hessedesign/Dusseldorf

USA

FINALIST, SINGLE

NICOSIA CREATIVE EXPRESSO LTD. (NICE LTD.)
NEW YORK, NY

CLIENT   Nicosia Creative Expresso, Ltd.
CREATIVE DIRECTOR   Davide Nicosia/Mike Sheehan
COPYWRITER   Richard Lynch
DESIGNER/DESIGN   Nice Ltd./New York
OTHER   Eric Walczak (Multimedia Designer/Programmer)

USA

GOLD WORLDMEDAL, SINGLE
McCANN-ERICKSON
TROY, MI

CLIENT   Buick Motor Division
COPYWRITER   Al Malouin
ART DIRECTOR   Ted Hoot
DESIGNER/DESIGN   Bowne Internet Systems

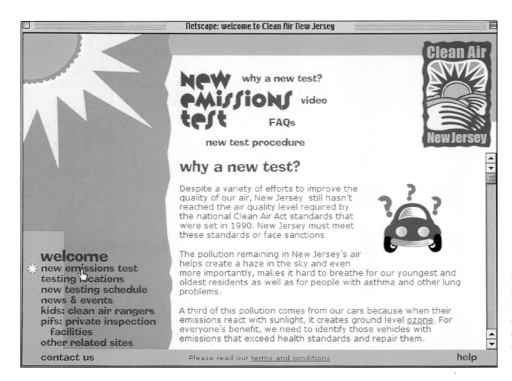

USA

FINALIST, SINGLE
DKB & PARTNERS, INC.
MORRISTOWN, NJ

CLIENT   Parsons Group
CREATIVE DIRECTOR   Leticia Martin
COPYWRITER   Jo Stapleton
ART DIRECTOR   Dreux Sawyer

GERMANY

SILVER WORLDMEDAL, SINGLE

N.A.S.A.2.0

HAMBURG HH

CREATIVE DIRECTOR John Eberstein
COPYWRITER Guido Edowzok
ART DIRECTOR Oliver Hinrichs
ILLUSTRATOR Oliver Hinrichs

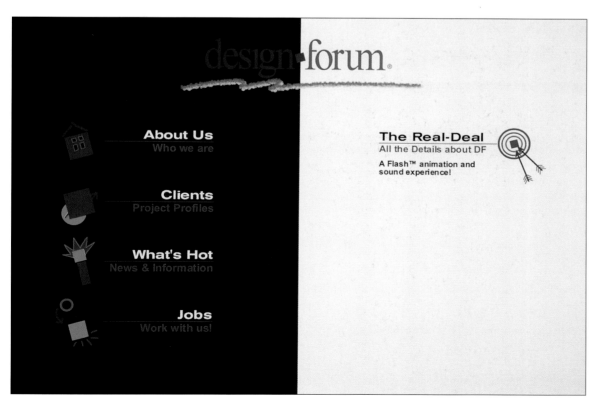

USA

BRONZE WORLDMEDAL, SINGLE

DESIGN FORUM

DAYTON, OH

OTHER Design Forum Creative Team

The New York Festivals

The World's Best Work

DESIGN: PACKAGE DESIGN, COMPANY LITERATURE, CORPORATE IDENTITY

DESIGN

GRAND AWARD

BEST DESIGN

USA

GRAND AWARD BEST DESIGN

ARNOLD COMMUNICATIONS INC.

BOSTON, MA

CLIENT Volkswagen Of America
CREATIVE DIRECTOR Alan Pafenbach/Lance Jensen
CREATIVE DIRECTOR Lance Jensen
COPYWRITER Lance Jensen
OTHER Ron Lawner (Chief Creative Officer)

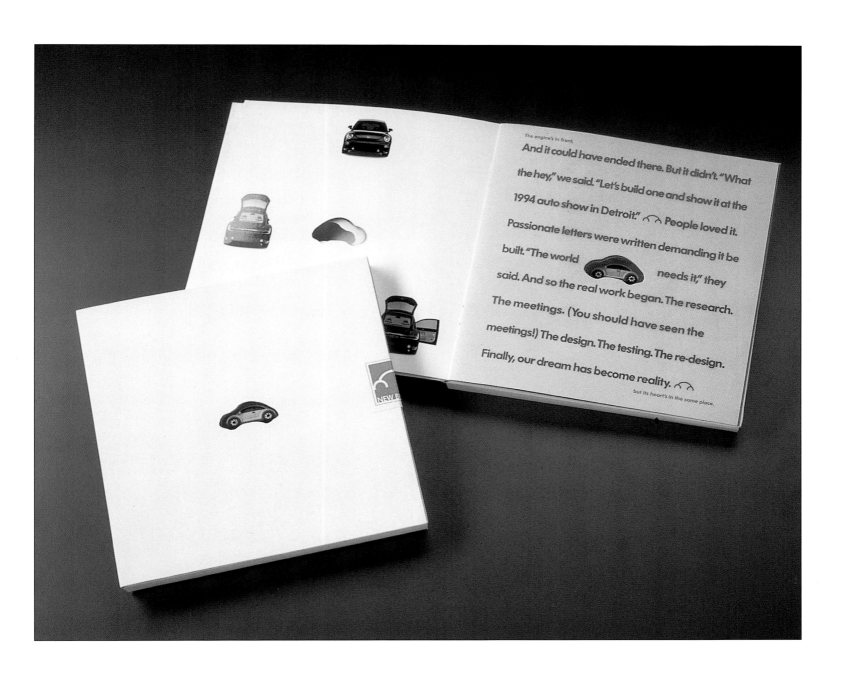

The engine's in front.

And it could have ended there. But it didn't. "What the hey," we said. "Let's build one and show it at the 1994 auto show in Detroit." People loved it. Passionate letters were written demanding it be built. "The world needs it," they said. And so the real work began. The research. The meetings. (You should have seen the meetings!) The design. The testing. The re-design. Finally, our dream has become reality.

but its heart's in the same place.

APPAREL / FASHION ACCESSORIES

SPAIN

BRONZE WORLDMEDAL, SINGLE

ABM SERVEIS DE COMUNICACIO
BARCELONA

CLIENT Grupo Industrial Marti
CREATIVE DIRECTOR Jaume Anglada
ART DIRECTOR Jaume Anglada
DESIGNER/DESIGN Jaume Guasch

USA

FINALIST, SINGLE

TBWA/CHIAT/DAY
SAN FRANCISCO, CA

CLIENT Levi's® Workwear®
CREATIVE DIRECTOR Lee Clow/Rob Smiley/
Peter Angelos
PHOTOGRAPHER Jock McDonald
DESIGNER/DESIGN R. Romney/A. Willard/
D. Marzorati

AUTOMOTIVE PRODUCTS

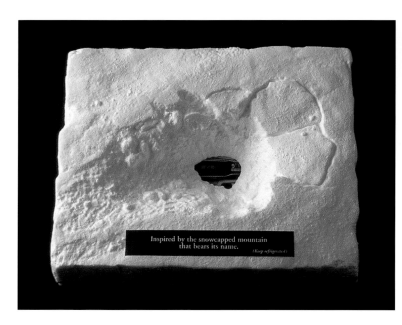

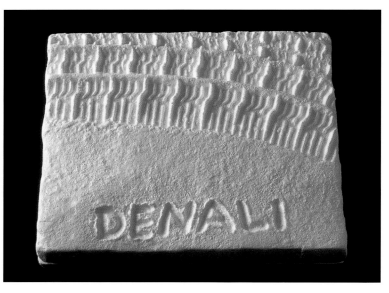

USA

FINALIST, SINGLE

McCANN RELATIONSHIP MARKETING
NEW YORK, NY

CLIENT GMC Yukon Denali
CREATIVE DIRECTOR Richard Eber
COPYWRITER Gary Scheiner/John Steinhardt
ART DIRECTOR Herb Passberger/Lisa Pfitzner
DESIGNER/DESIGN Tom Newberry
OTHER W. Patterson (Management Sup.)/R. Kaufamn (Production)

USA

GOLD WORLDMEDAL, SINGLE

KLIM DESIGN, INC.

AVON, CT

CLIENT Gran Centenario Gran Reserva
CREATIVE DIRECTOR Matt Klim
ART DIRECTOR Matt Klim
PHOTOGRAPHER Greg Klim/Boston

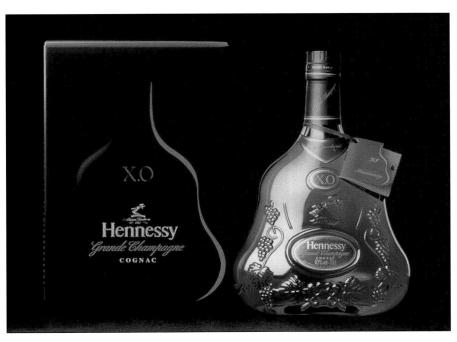

U K

FINALIST, SINGLE

DESIGN BRIDGE LTD

LONDON

CREATIVE DIRECTOR Graham Shearsby
ILLUSTRATOR Antonia Hayward
OTHER S. Kimble/B. Goodenough/S. Le Camus

UK

SILVER WORLDMEDAL, SINGLE
DESIGN BRIDGE LTD
LONDON

CLIENT BASS
CREATIVE DIRECTOR Tim Perkins/Dave Helps
OTHER Steve Elliott/Jill Marshall

AUSTRALIA

BRONZE WORLDMEDAL, SINGLE
**LKS BRANDING CONSULTANTS &
DESIGNERS**
NORTH SYDNEY

CLIENT 34 S From Southcorp Wines
CREATIVE DIRECTOR Mike Staniford
ART DIRECTOR Nichola Dearn
PHOTOGRAPHER Gerald Colley/Sydney
DESIGNER/DESIGN Mike Staniford/
Nichola Dearn

ENGLAND

FINALIST, SINGLE
BLACKBURN'S LTD.
LONDON

CREATIVE DIRECTOR John Blackburn
ART DIRECTOR John Blackburn
ILLUSTRATOR Sarah Roberts/London
DESIGNER/DESIGN Sarah Roberts (Designer)
DESIGNER/DESIGN Matt Thompson/
Sarah Roberts

SWEDEN

FINALIST, SINGLE

FALTMAN & MALMEN
STOCKHOLM

CLIENT Part Nan Angelen,
Bruichladdich
ART DIRECTOR Anders Eliasson
OTHER B. Tidelius (Copy)/
M. Ekberger (Account Executive)/
F. Mikelsson (DP)

USA

FINALIST, SINGLE

KLIM DESIGN, INC.
AVON, CT

CLIENT Jose Cuervo Anejo
CREATIVE DIRECTOR Matt Klim
ART DIRECTOR Matt Klim
PHOTOGRAPHER Greg Klim/
Boston

USA

FINALIST, SINGLE

VAN NOY GROUP
TORRANCE, CA

CLIENT Kahlua
CREATIVE DIRECTOR Jim van Noy
ART DIRECTOR Bill Murawski/Amanda Park
PHOTOGRAPHER Lefteris Padavos
ILLUSTRATOR Michel Dinges
DESIGNER/DESIGN Van Noy Group

U K

GOLD WORLDMEDAL, CAMPAIGN
LEWIS MOBERLY
LONDON

CLIENT Waitrose Juices
ART DIRECTOR Mary Lewis
PHOTOGRAPHER Juliette Piddington
OTHER Ann Marshall/Daniela Nunzi

AUSTRIA
FINALIST, CAMPAIGN
BURO X DESIGN
VIENNA
CLIENT Siggis Drinks
ADVERTISING AGENCY Wirz Burnett/Vienna
ART DIRECTOR Andreas Miedaner
ILLUSTRATOR Florian Ribisch/Vienna

NEW ZEALAND

SILVER WORLDMEDAL, CAMPAIGN

DASHWOOD DESIGN

AUCKLAND

CLIENT Frucor Beverages/"V"
CREATIVE DIRECTOR Paul Dashwood
ART DIRECTOR Lisa Lipscombe
PHOTOGRAPHER SPID
ILLUSTRATOR Scott Kennedy/
Henrick Drescher
OTHER Simon Moen

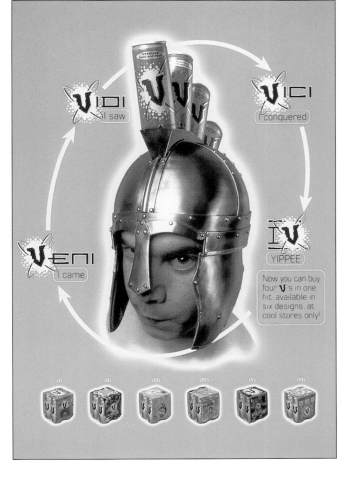

ENGLAND

BRONZE WORLDMEDAL, CAMPAIGN

BLACKBURN'S LTD.

LONDON

CLIENT Allied Domecq Spirits & Wine
CREATIVE DIRECTOR John Blackburn
ILLUSTRATOR David Draper/London
DESIGNER/DESIGN Belinda Duggan

ENGLAND

FINALIST, SINGLE
THE FORMATION
LONDON

CLIENT Pret A Manger Ltd
CREATIVE DIRECTOR Adrian Kilby
ART DIRECTOR Adrian Kilby
PHOTOGRAPHER John Sims/London

CANADA

FINALIST, CAMPAIGN
KARACTERS DESIGN GROUP
VANCOUVER, BC

CLIENT Clearly Candian Super Oxygenated Water
CREATIVE DIRECTOR Maria Kennedy
ART DIRECTOR Matthew Clark
OTHER T. Belcher (Production Artist)/
J.Ziros (Package Producer)/S. Tinglin (Project Mngr.)

ISRAEL

FINALIST, CAMPAIGN
**WISSOTZKY TEA
(ISRAEL) LTD**
TEL-AVIV

ART DIRECTOR
Dana Rozen
DESIGNER/DESIGN
Studio Adler
GRAPHICS COMPANY
Studio Adler

SWEDEN

FINALIST, SINGLE
KORBERG & CO.
GOTHENBURG

CLIENT Rozzo Espresso
ART DIRECTOR Pelle Korberg
OTHER Annika Moberg

U K

GOLD WORLDMEDAL, CAMPAIGN

DESIGN BRIDGE LTD

LONDON

CLIENT Elida Faberge

CREATIVE DIRECTOR

Graham Shearsby

ART DIRECTOR Neil Hirst

OTHER A. Hayward/
S. Le Camus/N. Sherlock

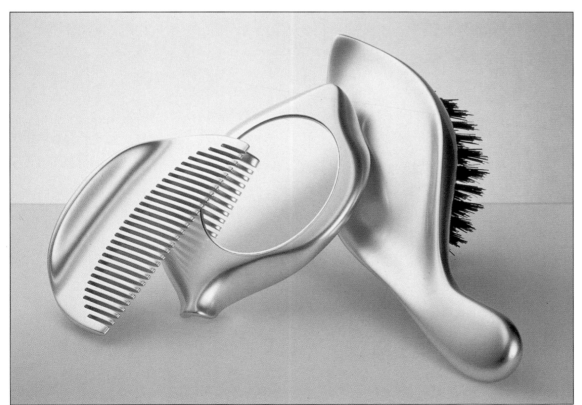

JAPAN

SILVER WORLDMEDAL, CAMPAIGN

SHISEIDO CO., LTD.

TOKYO

CLIENT Fleur Excellent

CREATIVE DIRECTOR Shunsako Sugiura

ART DIRECTOR Shunsako Sugiura

DESIGNER/DESIGN A. Caminings/
C. Keba/A. Jinnai

JAPAN

BRONZE WORLDMEDAL, CAMPAIGN
KOSE CORPORATION
TOKYO

CLIENT Cosme Decorte
ART DIRECTOR Chihiro Hayashi
OTHER Hitoshi Watanabe
OTHER Keiko Ito

JAPAN

FINALIST, CAMPAIGN
KOSE CORPORATION
TOKYO

CREATIVE DIRECTOR Fujio Hanawa
ART DIRECTOR Yoshimi Iguthi
OTHER Kazuha Yonetoku/Tomomi Hiroki

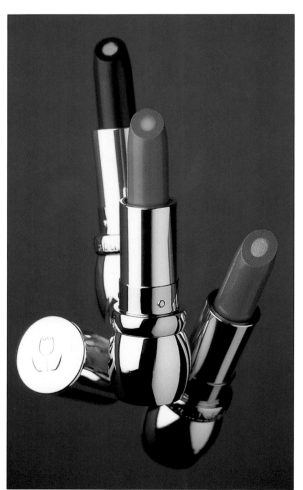

JAPAN

FINALIST, CAMPAIGN
KOSE CORPORATION
TOKYO

ART DIRECTOR Tenji Motoda
OTHER Junichiro Kaneko

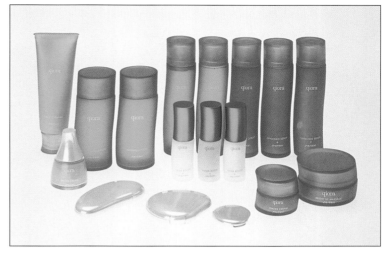

JAPAN

FINALIST, CAMPAIGN

SHISEIDO CO., LTD.

TOKYO

CLIENT D'Ici La
CREATIVE DIRECTOR Tetsuo Togasawa
ART DIRECTOR Tetsuo Togasawa
DESIGNER/DESIGN Chieko Yotsuda

JAPAN

FINALIST, CAMPAIGN

SHISEIDO CO., LTD.

TOKYO

CLIENT Giora
CREATIVE DIRECTOR Shyuichi Ikeda
ART DIRECTOR Shyuichi Keda
DESIGNER/DESIGN Aoshikudo/K. Hirano/
I. Matsumoto/T. Kikuchi/J. Ikegaya

FOODS / SNACKS / CONFECTIONERIES

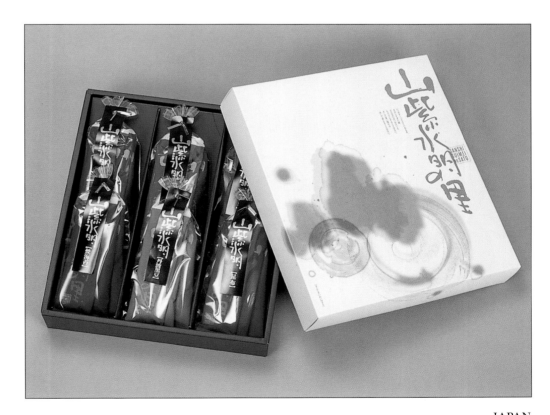

CANADA

FINALIST, SINGLE

CUNDARI

NORTH YORK, ONTARIO

CLIENT What's Cookin' Louie?
CREATIVE DIRECTOR Rob Worling/
Michel Lang
ART DIRECTOR Sylvia Latina
ILLUSTRATOR Sue Todd/Toronto

JAPAN

SILVER WORLDMEDAL, SINGLE

YOSUKE HARA DESIGN ROOM

TOKYO

CLIENT Tamura
CREATIVE DIRECTOR Akira Kazama
COPYWRITER Yosuke Hara
ART DIRECTOR Yosuke Hara
ILLUSTRATOR Tomoko Kikuchi/Tokyo
GRAPHICS COMPANY Yosuke Hara (Design Room)

JAPAN

SILVER WORLDMEDAL, SINGLE

MOROZOFF

KOBE

CLIENT Morozoff
(Chocolate Shop In Kobe
Kitano Meister Garden)

CREATIVE DIRECTOR
Shin'ichiro Komatsu

ART DIRECTOR
Shin'ichiro Komatsu

ILLUSTRATOR
Hiromi Karatu/Osaka

DESIGNER/DESIGN
Design Office New Man/
Osaka

GRAPHICS COMPANY
Sintani Limited/Osaka

SWEDEN

BRONZE WORLDMEDAL, SINGLE

NORDIN & CO

STOCKHOLM

CLIENT Cerealia Pasta Kungsoren AB
ART DIRECTOR Katrin Gullstrom
ILLUSTRATOR Katrin Gullstrom/Stockholm
OTHER Leena Berglof

JAPAN

GOLD WORLDMEDAL, CAMPAIGN
MOROZOFF LIMITED
KOBE CITY

CLIENT   Morozoff Christmas Book
ART DIRECTOR   Atsushi Takahashi
ILLUSTRATOR   Hisako Nakayama
DESIGNER/DESIGN   Mariko Yamashita/
Kenji Yoshida

CANADA

FINALIST, SINGLE
CUNDARI
NORTH YORK, ONTARIO

CLIENT   What's Cookin' Louie?
CREATIVE DIRECTOR   Rob Worling/Michel Lang
ART DIRECTOR   Sylvia Latina
ILLUSTRATOR   Lisa Ringnalda/
Jeff Panek (Toronto)

SPAIN

FINALIST, CAMPAIGN

AMMIRATI PURIS LINTAS
BARCELONA

CLIENT   Nestle Grands Chocolats
CREATIVE DIRECTOR   Anouk Suner
ART DIRECTOR   Cristina Roviro
ILLUSTRATOR   Josep Ramon Domingo

CANADA

FINALIST, CAMPAIGN

MAROVINO DESIGN GROUP
TORONTO, ONTARIO

CLIENT   E.D. Smith Deluxe Jams
CREATIVE DIRECTOR   John Marovino
ART DIRECTOR   Phil Slous
PHOTOGRAPHER   Ron Tanaka

JAPAN

FINALIST, CAMPAIGN

MOROZOFF LIMITED
KOBE CITY

CLIENT   Morozoff White Day Sweets
ART DIRECTOR   Atsushi Takahashi
DESIGNER/DESIGN   Mariko Yamashita/
Kenji Yoshida

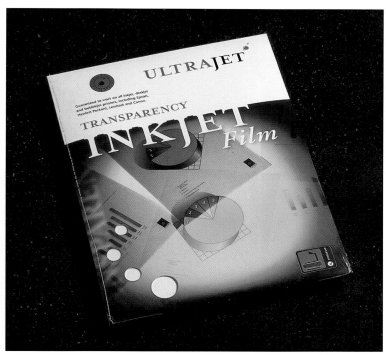

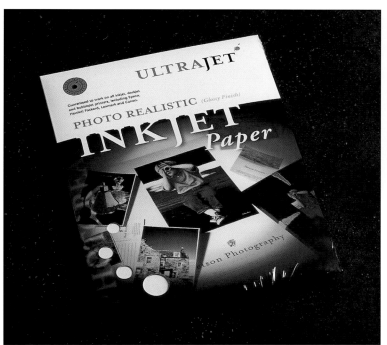

SOUTH AFRICA

FINALIST, CAMPAIGN
IMAGINATION DESIGN CORPORATION
RIVONIA

CLIENT Ultrajet
CREATIVE DIRECTOR Heather Gomes-Selsick/
Lee Selsick
ART DIRECTOR Paul Henriques (Designer)

PUBLISHING

USA

FINALIST, CAMPAIGN
BLUE MOON PRODUCTIONS
MINNEAPOLIS, MN

CLIENT Minnesota Soybean
Growers Association
CREATIVE DIRECTOR Will Hommeyer
ART DIRECTOR Will Hommeyer
ILLUSTRATOR Carol Hinz/Minneapolis
DESIGNER/DESIGN Circus Design/
Minneapolis

USA

SILVER WORLDMEDAL, SINGLE
HOME BOX OFFICE
NEW YORK, NY

CREATIVE DIRECTOR Gary Dueno
DESIGNER/DESIGN HBO /in house

USA

BRONZE WORLDMEDAL, SINGLE
PLOWSHARE GROUP
STAMFORD, CT
CLIENT World WildLife Fund
CREATIVE DIRECTOR John La Rock
ART DIRECTOR Tony Kremka
GRAPHICS COMPANY Marina Merzel/PlowShare)
OTHER Jeff Boal-Fernando (Account Ececutive)

ART NOT AVAILABLE

USA

FINALIST, CAMPAIGN
RAPP COLLINS WORLDWIDE-DALLAS
IRVING, TX

CLIENT Sony Playstation
CREATIVE DIRECTOR Frank Laudo/Khris Niblett
COPYWRITER Brittany McGinnis
ART DIRECTOR Frank Laudo
DESIGNER/DESIGN Chris Capron

JAPAN

GOLD WORLDMEDAL, CAMPAIGN

DENTSU, INC.

TOKYO

CLIENT Mitsubishi VCR
CREATIVE DIRECTOR Akio Shizume
ART DIRECTOR Daisuke Sano/
Masatoshi Kagawa
ILLUSTRATOR Tetsuya Kitada

RETAIL: OWN BRAND PRODUCTS

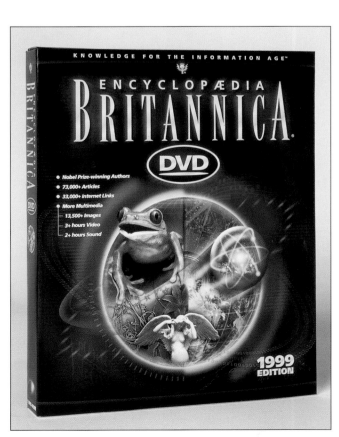

USA

BRONZE WORLDMEDAL, SINGLE

ENCYCLOPAEDIA BRITANNICA

CHICAGO, IL

CREATIVE DIRECTOR Sam Knight, Tim Girvin Design, Inc.
COPYWRITER Ned Simonson
ART DIRECTOR Bob Ciano
ILLUSTRATOR Sam Knighy/Tim Girvin Design, Inc./Seattle
DESIGNER/DESIGN Tim Girvin Design, Inc./Seattle, WA

ENGLAND

SILVER WORLDMEDAL

VINEYARD DESIGN LIMITED
LONDON

CLIENT   J. Sainsbury Plc
CREATIVE DIRECTOR   Nigel Bullivant
ART DIRECTOR   Helen Howat

USA

BRONZE WORLDMEDAL, CAMPAIGN

ICON GRAPHICS INC.
ROCHESTER, NY

CLIENT
Eastman Kodak Company
CREATIVE DIRECTOR
Icon Graphics, Inc.
ART DIRECTOR
Icon Graphics, Inc.

BRONZE WORLDMEDAL, SINGLE
GYNTHER & COMPANY A/S
AARHUS C
CLIENT Ben Mobile Phone System
CREATIVE DIRECTOR Jan Gynther
ART DIRECTOR Rune Johansen

USA
FINALIST, SINGLE
ARISTA/NASHVILLE
NASHVILLE, TN
CLIENT Arista/Nashville
CREATIVE Director Maude Gilman-Clapham
ART DIRECTOR Maude Gilman-Clapham
DESIGNER/DESIGN Maude Gilman-Clapham
(Graphics Designer)

SWEDEN
FINALIST, SINGLE
BRANDO OGILVY DESIGN
STOCKHOLM
CLIENT Skal 2000
ART DIRECTOR
Lotta Akerlund Palmback

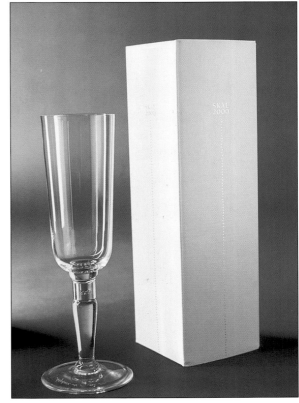

ANNUAL REPORT

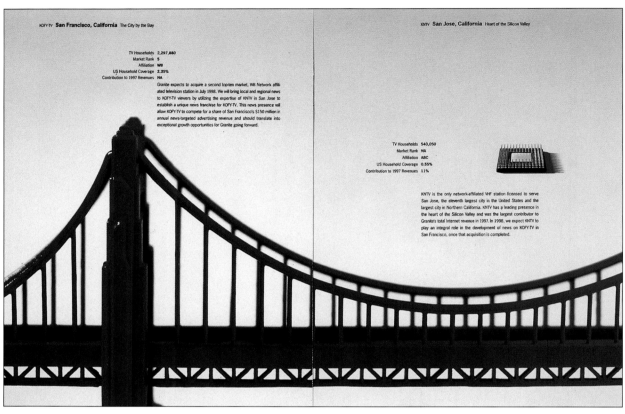

KOFY-TV **San Francisco, California** The City by the Bay

TV Households	2,297,880
Market Rank	5
Affiliation	WB
US Household Coverage	2.35%
Contribution to 1997 Revenues	NA

Granite expects to acquire a second top-ten market, WB Network affiliated television station in July 1998. We will bring local and regional news to KOFY-TV viewers by utilizing the expertise of KNTV in San Jose to establish a unique news franchise for KOFY-TV. This news presence will allow KOFY-TV to compete for a share of San Francisco's $150 million in annual news-targeted advertising revenue and should translate into exceptional growth opportunities for Granite going forward.

KNTV **San Jose, California** Heart of the Silicon Valley

TV Households	540,050
Market Rank	NA
Affiliation	ABC
US Household Coverage	0.55%
Contribution to 1997 Revenues	11%

KNTV is the only network-affiliated VHF station licensed to serve San Jose, the eleventh largest city in the United States and the largest city in Northern California. KNTV has a leading presence in the heart of the Silicon Valley and was the largest contributor to Granite's total Internet revenue in 1997. In 1998, we expect KNTV to play an integral role in the development of news on KOFY-TV in San Francisco, once that acquisition is completed.

Granite Broadcasting Corporation Annual Report 1997

USA

GOLD WORLDMEDAL, SINGLE

GRANITE BROADCASTING
NEW YORK, NY

CLIENT
Granite Broadcasting

CREATIVE DIRECTOR
Victor Rivera

ART DIRECTOR
Anna Tan

PHOTOGRAPHER
William Vasquez/NYC

SINGAPORE

FINALIST, SINGLE

EPIGRAM PTE. LTD.
SINGAPORE

CLIENT   Board Annual Report 1997-1998
CREATIVE DIRECTOR   Edmund Wee
ART DIRECTOR   Paul van der Veer
PHOTOGRAPHER   Michael Bradfield/Singapore

USA

SILVER WORLDMEDAL, SINGLE
CAHAN & ASSOCIATES
SAN FRANCISCO, CA

CLIENT   Vivus, Inc.
CREATIVE DIRECTOR   Bill Cahan
ILLUSTRATOR   Kevin Roberson
DESIGNER/DESIGN   Kevin Roberson

SOUTH AFRICA

FINALIST, SINGLE
CROSS COLOURS
JOHANNESBURG

CLIENT   Nando's
CREATIVE DIRECTOR   Joanina Pastoll
ART DIRECTOR   Joanina Pastoll
PHOTOGRAPHER   David Pastoll
ILLUSTRATOR   Joanina Pastoll/Janine Rech

children's
television
workshop

CTW

Annual Report 1998

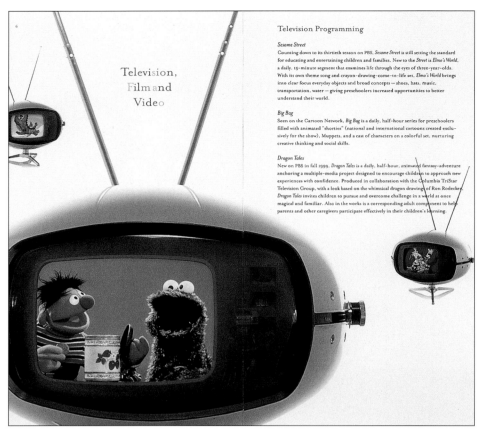

Television,
Film and
Video

Television Programming

Sesame Street

Counting down to its thirtieth season on PBS, *Sesame Street* is still setting the standard for educating and entertaining children and families. New to the *Street* is *Elmo's World*, a daily, 15-minute segment that examines life through the eyes of three-year-olds. With its own theme song and crayon-drawing-come-to-life set, *Elmo's World* brings into clear focus everyday objects and broad concepts — shoes, hats, music, transportation, water — giving preschoolers increased opportunities to better understand their world.

Big Bag

Seen on the Cartoon Network, *Big Bag* is a daily, half-hour series for preschoolers filled with animated "shorties" (national and international cartoons created exclusively for the show), Muppets, and a cast of characters on a colorful set, nurturing creative thinking and social skills.

Dragon Tales

New on PBS in fall 1999, *Dragon Tales* is a daily, half-hour, animated fantasy-adventure anchoring a multiple-media project designed to encourage children to approach new experiences with confidence. Produced in collaboration with the Columbia TriStar Television Group, with a look based on the whimsical dragon drawings of Ron Rodecker, *Dragon Tales* invites children to pursue and overcome challenge in a world at once magical and familiar. Also in the works is a corresponding adult component to help parents and other caregivers participate effectively in their children's learning.

USA

BRONZE WORLDMEDAL, SINGLE

CHILDREN'S TELEVISION WORKSHOP
NEW YORK, NY

CLIENT   Children's Television Workshop
CREATIVE DIRECTOR   David Kohler
ART DIRECTOR   Anna Tan
PHOTOGRAPHER   Jody Dole/Dan Bigelow/
David Katzenstein

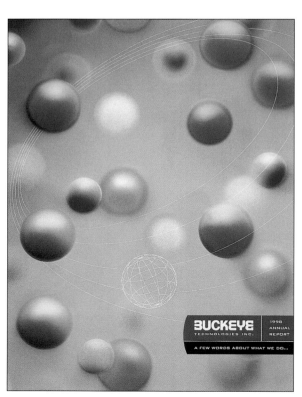

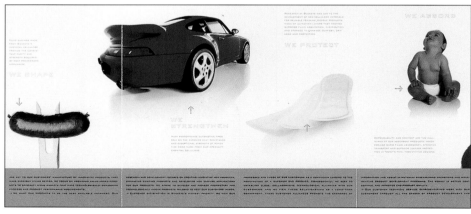

USA

FINALIST, SINGLE

BUCKEYETECHNOLOGIES INC.
NEW YORK, NY

CLIENT   Buckley Technologies
CREATIVE DIRECTOR   Victor Rivera
ART DIRECTOR   Richard Colbourne
PHOTOGRAPHER   Alex Hayden/NYC

COR THERAPEUTICS, INC.

1997 Annual Report

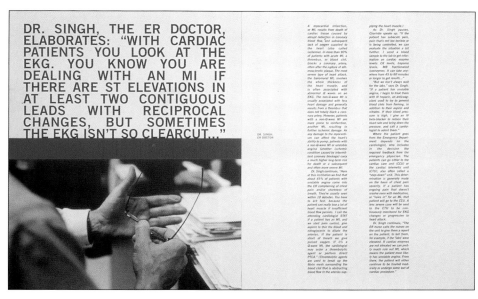

DR. SINGH, THE ER DOCTOR, ELABORATES: "WITH CARDIAC PATIENTS YOU LOOK AT THE EKG. YOU KNOW YOU ARE DEALING WITH AN MI IF THERE ARE ST ELEVATIONS IN AT LEAST TWO CONTIGUOUS LEADS WITH RECIPROCAL CHANGES, BUT SOMETIMES THE EKG ISN'T SO CLEARCUT..."

USA

FINALIST, SINGLE

CAHAN & ASSOCIATES
SAN FRANCISCO, CA

CLIENT   COR Therapeutics
CREATIVE DIRECTOR   Bill Cahan
PHOTOGRAPHER   William Mercer McLeod
DESIGNER/DESIGN   Michael Braley

Behind the many faces of Asia; the many achievements of Prudential.

HONG KONG

FINALIST, SINGLE

EURO RSCG PARTNERSHIP
HONG KONG

CLIENT
Prudential Corporation Asia
CREATIVE DIRECTOR   Nick Gordon/
Tania Viskovich
COPYWRITER   Nick Gordon
ART DIRECTOR   Tania Viskovich
PHOTOGRAPHER   Liu/Hong Kong

Some of the most demanding people aren't interested in insurance at all.

We're expanding so fast it's a wonder we're not out of breath.

USA

FINALIST, SINGLE
JOHN HANCOCK MUTUAL LIFE INS. CO.
BOSTON, MA

CREATIVE DIRECTOR Richard Bevilacqua/
Susan Chavez
ART DIRECTOR Nancy Cowen
PHOTOGRAPHER Bob Frechette/Boston
OTHER Steve Turgeon/Bob Moir (Writing)

SLOVENIA

FINALIST, SINGLE
KOMPAS DESIGN
LJUBLJANA, SI

ART DIRECTOR Zare Kerin/Ljubljana
PHOTOGRAPHER Janez Puksic/Ljubljana

BRAZIL

FINALIST, SINGLE
PUBLIVENDAS COMUNICACAO LTDA.
SALVADOR/BAHIA

CLIENT Print Annual Report
CREATIVE DIRECTOR Antonio Luiz Nilo
PHOTOGRAPHER Elcio Carrico/Almir Bindilatt/Salvador
ILLUSTRATOR Jorge Barreto/Salvador
GRAPHICS COMPANY Grafos, Intergraf/Salvador
OTHER Claudio Oliveira (Production Manager)

UAE

FINALIST, SINGLE
SAATCHI & SAATCHI
DUBAI

CLIENT MashreqBank
CREATIVE DIRECTOR Kurt Blanckenburg
ART DIRECTOR Habib Patel
PHOTOGRAPHER Tejal Putni/Dubai

PRODUCT BOOKLET / BROCHURE / PAMPHLET

USA

GOLD WORLDMEDAL, SINGLE
ARNOLD COMMUNICATIONS INC.
BOSTON, MA

CLIENT Volkswagen Of America
CREATIVE DIRECTOR
Alan Pafenbach/ Lance Jensen
CREATIVE DIRECTOR Lance Jensen
COPYWRITER Lance Jensen
OTHER Ron Lawner
(Chief Creative Officer)

SEE GRAND AWARD PAGE 307

USA

FINALIST, SINGLE
CADMUS COM
RICHMOND, VA

CLIENT Demaco Block
CREATIVE DIRECTOR Ed Paxton
ART DIRECTOR Susan M. Walsh
PHOTOGRAPHER Susan Bryant, Clarksville/
Kip Dawkins, Richmond
OTHER Karen Smith (Producer)

USA

SILVER WORLDMEDAL, SINGLE
LESLIE EVANS DESIGN ASSOCIATES
PORTLAND, ME

CLIENT Georgia Pacific Corporation
CREATIVE DIRECTOR Leslie Evans
COPYWRITER Liz Peavey/Steve Treat
ART DIRECTOR Leslie Evans
ILLUSTRATOR J.Fisher/Veneux-Les-Sablons, France/
M.Sweet, Portland , Maine/C.Clayton, Los Angeles, CA/
J.E. Meagher, Reading, MA/P.Corrigan, Portland
DESIGNER/DESIGN C. Bryant/L. Evans/T.O. Cummings

ENGLAND

FINALIST, SINGLE
ELMWOOD
LEEDS

CLIENT Perspex
CREATIVE DIRECTOR James Backhurst
ART DIRECTOR Julian Hoyes
PHOTOGRAPHER Jonathan Oakes/Manchester

CANADA

FINALIST, SINGLE
SAINT-JACQUES VALLEE YOUNG & RUBICAM
MONTREAL/QUEBEC

CLIENT Cornwall coated cover
CREATIVE DIRECTOR Daniel Larocque
ART DIRECTOR Pascal Hierholz
PHOTOGRAPHER Caroline Jarvis

BRONZE WORLDMEDAL, SINGLE
TBWA/CHIAT/DAY
SAN FRANCISCO, CA
CLIENT Levi's Brand
CREATIVE DIRECTOR Lee Clow/Peter Angelos/Rob Smiley
ART DIRECTOR Rob Smiley/Mega Williams
DESIGNER/DESIGN Mega Williams

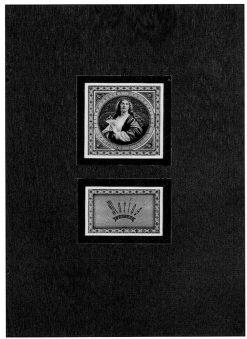

AUSTRIA

FINALIST, SINGLE
McCANN ERICKSON GMBH
VIENNA

CLIENT Menu For Mexican Restaurant
CREATIVE DIRECTOR Max Jurasch
COPYWRITER Helge Haberzettl
ART DIRECTOR Max Jurasch
ILLUSTRATOR Max Jurasch

ENGLAND

FINALIST, SINGLE
TANGO DESIGN
LONDON

CLIENT Nike Europe
CREATIVE DIRECTOR Peter Rae
ART DIRECTOR Glenn Harisson, Robert D'Andria
PHOTOGRAPHER Tim Simmons/London

SERVICE BOOKLET / BROCHURE / PAMPHLET

ENGLAND

FINALIST, SINGLE
CONRAN DESIGN GROUP
LONDON

CREATIVE DIRECTOR David Worthington
ART DIRECTOR Alan Watt/Clare Nation
PHOTOGRAPHER D.Gilbert/C.Ridley/S.McCale/
G.Trevor/M.Williams/B.J.Holmes

ENGLAND

FINALIST, SINGLE
PEMBERTON & WHITEFOORD
LONDON

CLIENT James Murphy Photography Pack
CREATIVE DIRECTOR Simon Pemberton/
Adrian Whitefoord
ART DIRECTOR Simon Pemberton
PHOTOGRAPHER James Murphy/London

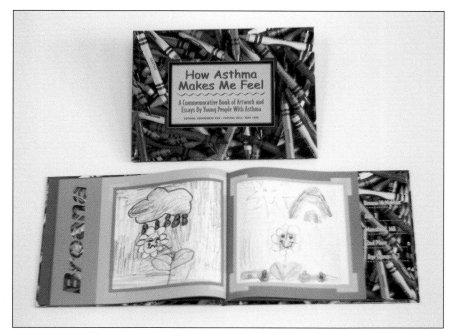

USA

FINALIST, SINGLE
**SUMMIT HEALTHCARE
COMMUNICATIONS**
SUMMIT, NJ

CLIENT Sepracor Inc.
CREATIVE DIRECTOR Ken Messinger
ART DIRECTOR Ken Messinger

ENGLAND

SILVER WORLDMEDAL, SINGLE
INTERBRAND NEWELL AND SORRELL
LONDON
CLIENT Cable & Wireless
CREATIVE DIRECTOR Simon Wright
DESIGNER/DESIGN J. Hubbard/S.Bellamy/
M.Smith/R.Andrews/Z.Scutts/J.Hubbard

GREECE

FINALIST, SINGLE
RED DESIGN CONSULTANTS
ATHENS

CLIENT Metaxa International
CREATIVE DIRECTOR Rodanthi Senduka
ART DIRECTOR Rodanthi Senduka/Mark Oeser
PHOTOGRAPHER R. Senduka, Studio Target/Athens
ILLUSTRATOR Anna-Maria Potamitis/Athens

USA

BRONZE WORLDMEDAL, SINGLE
**HORNALL ANDERSON
DESIGN WORKS**
SEATTLE, WA
CLIENT U.S. Cigar
ART DIRECTOR Jack Anderson/
Larry Anderson
PHOTOGRAPHER David Emmite
ILLUSTRATOR John Fretz/
Jack Unruh/Bill Halinann
DESIGNER/DESIGN
M.Hermes/M.Calkins/
M. Brugman/L.Anderson

FINLAND

FINALIST, SINGLE
BRAND SELLERS DDB
HELSINKI
CLIENT Finlandia Vodka
CREATIVE DIRECTOR Pekka Hamberg
ART DIRECTOR Aslak Bredenberg
PHOTOGRAPHER Kira Gluschkoff/
Mario Tokkari/Helsinki

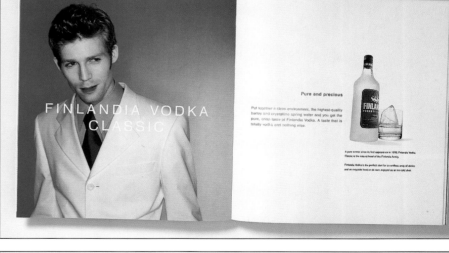

**Die Erde, das Rad, die Kugel, der Mond:
Gutes Design beruht auf einfachen Formen.**

Ein gutes Auto orientiert sich an einfachen Prin-
zipien. Der Audi TT ist für alle, die ihre Träume
Wirklichkeit werden lassen wollen. Die mutig
auf ihre Intuition hören und die Grenzen des
Alltags jeden Tag neu überwinden wollen. Die
ein Auto fahren möchten, das Auto und Fahrer
wieder näher zusammenbringt – und die einfach
Lust aufs Fahren haben. Vor allem aber ist der
Audi TT ein Sportwagen, der dem Autofahren
das zurückgibt, was uns heute oft fehlt: Freiheit.

GERMANY
GOLD WORLDMEDAL, SINGLE
JVM WERBEAGENTUR GMBH
HAMBURG
CLIENT   Audi TT Coupe

GERMANY
FINALIST, SINGLE
**CLAUS KOCH CORPORATE
COMMUNICATIONS**
DUESSELDORF

CLIENT   CKCC
CREATIVE DIRECTOR   Claus Koch/
Josephine Prokop
ART DIRECTOR   Josephine Prokop/
Jochen Theurer

USA

SILVER WORLDMEDAL, SINGLE
ROSS ROY COMMUNICATIONS
BLOOMFIELD HILLS, MI
CLIENT DaimlerChrysler/Dodge
CREATIVE DIRECTOR Kent Woodman/Jojn J. Keenan
COPYWRITER Dennis Staszek/Bob Pearson
ART DIRECTOR Sara Spillum/Doug Renton
PHOTOGRAPHER Jim Secreto
OTHER Kathy MacManus (Account Manager)

USA

BRONZE WORLDMEDAL, SINGLE
TODD JOHNSON PRODUCTIONS
CULVER CITY, CA
CLIENT Harley-Davidson Motorcycles

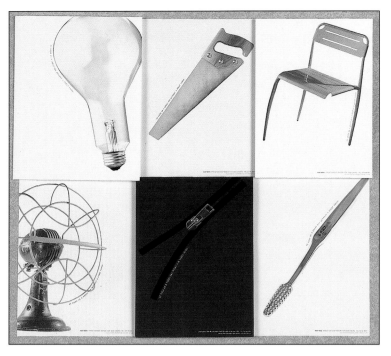

CHINA

FINALIST, SINGLE
GALLERY LTD
HONG KONG

CLIENT Sylvia & Cheuk Hung
CREATIVE DIRECTOR Benny Cheng
COPYWRITER Kelvin Parker
ART DIRECTOR Benny Cheng/Giles Tse
PHOTOGRAPHER Ricky Chan/Hong Kong
ILLUSTRATOR Giles Tse
GRAPHICS COMPANY Gallery Ltd./Hong Kong
OTHER Michelle Tsui (Print Production)

USA

FINALIST, SINGLE
ROSS ROY COMMUNICATIONS
BLOOMFIELD HILLS, MI

CLIENT Plymouth
CREATIVE DIRECTOR John J. Keenan/Stella Kappos
COPYWRITER Kyle Given III
ART DIRECTOR Sue McKay/Karen Frey
PHOTOGRAPHER Ken Stidwell
OTHER B. Sperber (Print Productions Manager)

GERMANY

FINALIST, SINGLE
WUSCHNER UND ROHWER WERBEAGENTUR
MUNCHEN

CLIENT New Balance Classic Footwear
CREATIVE DIRECTOR E. Frnekler/J. Balz/S.Sehlmann
ART DIRECTOR Stefan Hempel
PHOTOGRAPHER Stefanos Notopoulos, Stuttgart
ILLUSTRATOR Makrus Gruber

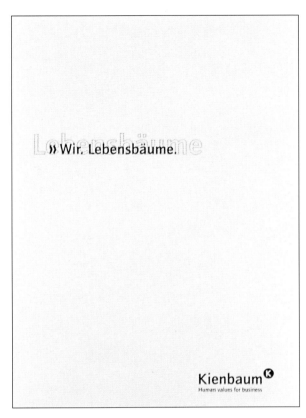

GERMANY

FINALIST, SINGLE

CLAUS KOCH CORPORATE COMMUNICATIONS
DUESSELDORF

CLIENT Krenbaum Consultants International
CREATIVE DIRECTOR Claus Koch
ART DIRECTOR Birgit Geisler/Claus Koch
PHOTOGRAPHER Marcus Pietrek

NON-PROFIT ORGANIZATION

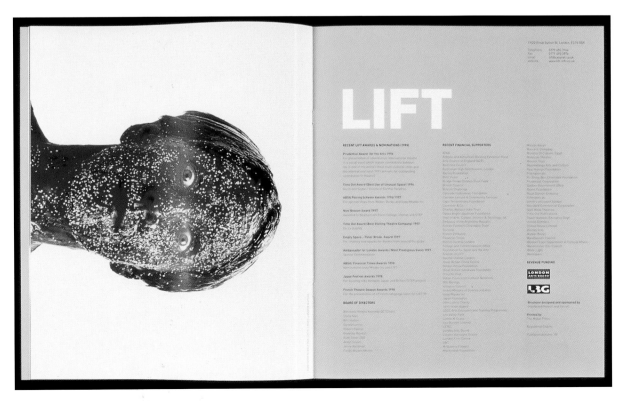

ENGLAND

FINALIST, SINGLE

**INTERBRAND NEWELL
AND SORRELL**
LONDON

CLIENT LIFT
CREATIVE DIRECTOR
Frances Newell
COPYWRITER
Anne Torreggiani
DESIGNER/DESIGN
Justina Sanchis

ENGLAND
GOLD WORLDMEDAL, SINGLE
INTERBRAND NEWELL AND SORRELL
LONDON
CLIENT RSA
CREATIVE DIRECTOR Frances Newell
ART DIRECTOR Frances Newell
DESIGNER/DESIGN Zoe Scutts

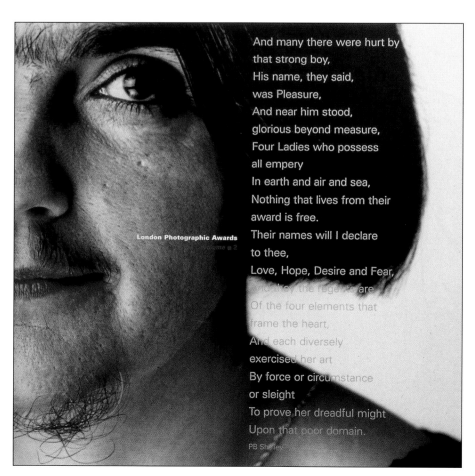

ENGLAND
SILVER WORLDMEDAL, SINGLE
E-FACT. LIMITED
LONDON
CLIENT London Photographic Awards
ART DIRECTOR Natalie Woolcock
OTHER Kevin O'Connor

GREECE

BRONZE WORLDMEDAL, SINGLE

McCANN-ERICKSON ATHENS

ATHENS

CLIENT Levi Strauss
CREATIVE DIRECTOR Yiannis Apergis
COPYWRITER Dimitra Zakinthinou
ART DIRECTOR Panos Mouzakitis
ILLUSTRATOR Theologis Marios

USA

FINALIST, SINGLE

ARCHRIVAL

LINCOLN, NE

CLIENT Digital Design
CREATIVE DIRECTOR Clint! Runge
ART DIRECTOR Charles Hull

GREECE

FINALIST, SINGLE

McCANN-ERICKSON ATHENS

ATHENS

CLIENT White Tab Levi Strauss

SPECIAL EVENT

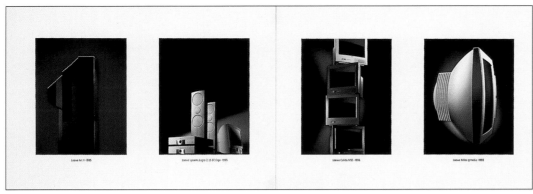

GERMANY

FINALIST, SINGLE

LEONHARDT & KERN WERBUNG GMBH

STUTTGART

CLIENT   Loewe Opta GmbH
CREATIVE DIRECTOR   Dr. Detlef Kulessa
ART DIRECTOR   Joachim Silber
PHOTOGRAPHER   Ernesto Martens/
G. Pfannmuller

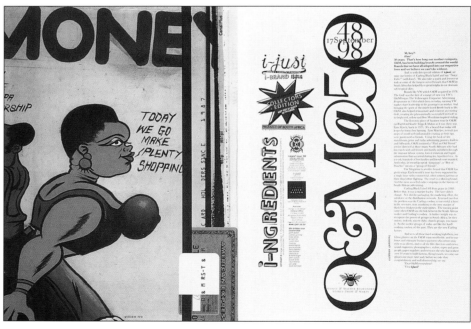

SOUTH AFRICA

FINALIST, SINGLE

ORANGE JUICE DESIGN

DURBAN

CREATIVE DIRECTOR   Garth Walker
PHOTOGRAPHER   I-jusi Creative Team
ILLUSTRATOR   I-jusi Creative Team

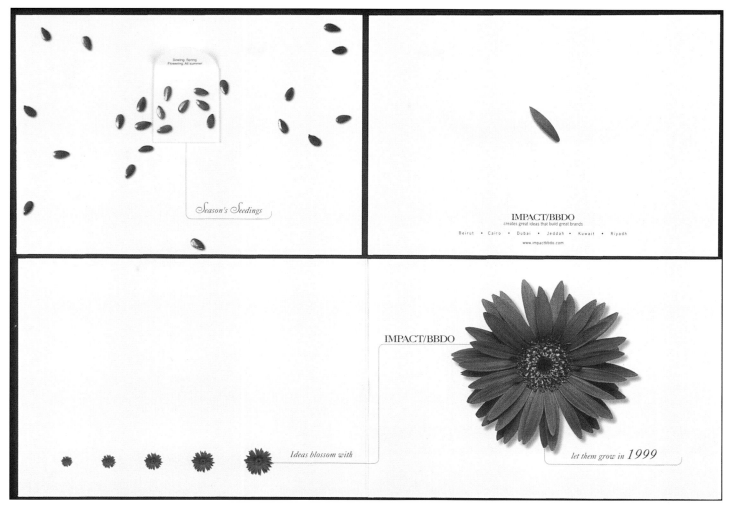

UNITED ARAB EMIRATES
GOLD WORLDMEDAL, SINGLE
IMPACT/BBDO
DUBAI
CREATIVE DIRECTOR Paul Fayad
ART DIRECTOR Paul Fayad
OTHER Douglas Palau

CHINA
SILVER WORLDMEDAL, SINGLE
GALLERY LTD
HONG KONG SAR

CLIENT Sylvia & Cheuk Hung
COPYWRITER Benny Cheng/
Kelvin Parker
ART DIRECTOR Benny Cheng/
Raymond Fu
ILLUSTRATOR Raymond Fu/Hong Kong
GRAPHICS COMPANY Gallery Ltd/
Hong Kong
OTHER Michelle Tsui
(Print Production)

To celebrate Jane Waring's Thirtieth Birthday on Saturday 28 November at The Royal Chase Hotel from 8pm onwards

ENGLAND

BRONZE WORLDMEDAL, SINGLE
PEMBERTON & WHITEFOORD
LONDON

CREATIVE DIRECTOR Simon Pemberton

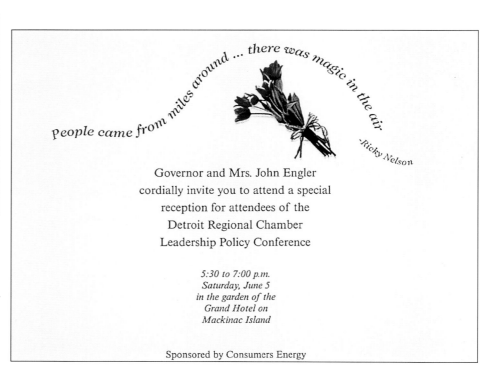

THE SCOTIABANK CAMPAIGN LAUNCH PARTY.

BBDO INVITES YOU to take a peek at our bank account. On Thursday, October 22nd, we'll be celebrating the launch of the new Scotiabank advertising campaign. Please join us at the Milano Billiard Lounge and Bistro, 325 King Street West. Cocktails will be served at 5:30 pm, with dinner starting at 7:30 pm. To RSVP, call Amanda Dring at (416) 972-5739. And yes, the drinks are free.

CANADA

FINALIST, SINGLE
BBDO CANADA
TORONTO, ONTARIO

CLIENT Launch Party
CREATIVE DIRECTOR Michael McLaughlin/Jack Neary
COPYWRITER Zak Mroueh
ART DIRECTOR David Houghton
PHOTOGRAPHER Terry Collier

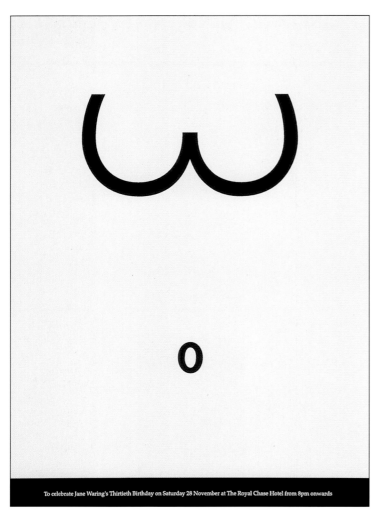

I went to a garden party to reminisce with my old friends ... A chance to share old memories and play our songs again

USA

FINALIST, SINGLE
CONSUMERS ENERGY
JACKSON, MS

CREATIVE DIRECTOR Ron Mason
ART DIRECTOR Brian Preuss
PHOTOGRAPHER Tom Brayne/Kalamazoo,
OTHER Nancy Baldwin (Writer)

People came from miles around ... there was magic in the air
—Ricky Nelson

Governor and Mrs. John Engler
cordially invite you to attend a special
reception for attendees of the
Detroit Regional Chamber
Leadership Policy Conference

*5:30 to 7:00 p.m.
Saturday, June 5
in the garden of the
Grand Hotel on
Mackinac Island*

Sponsored by Consumers Energy

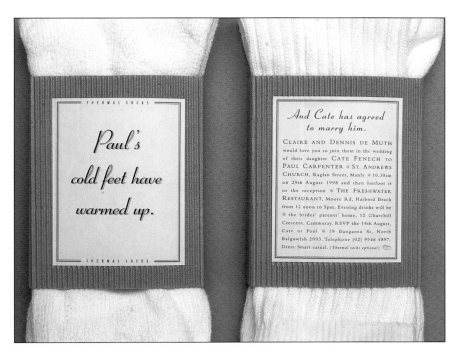

AUSTRALIA

FINALIST, SINGLE
DDB NEEDHAM
NORTH SYDNEY
CLIENT Paul Carpenter & Cate Carpenter
CREATIVE DIRECTOR Garry Horner
COPYWRITER Paul Carpenter
ART DIRECTOR Paul Carpenter

SPAIN

FINALIST, SINGLE
ESC COMUNICACION
MADRID
CLIENT Camper/Shoes
CREATIVE DIRECTOR Quico Vidal (camper)
ART DIRECTOR Pep Carrio /Sonia Sanchez
DESIGNER/DESIGN Pep Carrio /Sonia Sanchez/Madrid

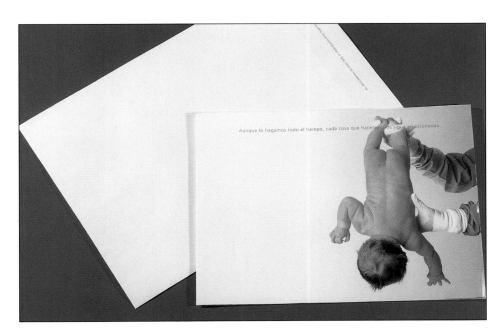

ARGENTINA

FINALIST, SINGLE
DE LUCA PUBLICIDAD
BUENOS AIRES
CREATIVE DIRECTOR Omar Di Nardo
ART DIRECTOR Eduardo Arnau
PHOTOGRAPHER Juan castagnola/Buenos Aires
GRAPHICS COMPANY Gramma S.A./Buenos

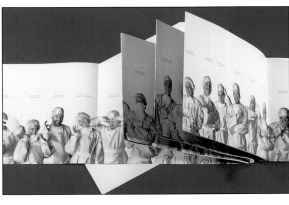

USA

FINALIST, SINGLE
HORNALL ANDERSON DESIGN WORKS
SEATTLE, WA

CLIENT Mahlum
ART DIRECTOR Jack Anderson
ILLUSTRATOR Todd Apjones (Calligrapher)
DESIGNER/DESIGN J. Anderson/H. Favour/
B. Branson-Meyer/M. Hermes

ENGLAND

FINALIST, SINGLE
NE6 DESIGN CONSULTANTS
NEWCASTLE UPON TYNE

CREATIVE DIRECTOR Alan Whitefield
DESIGNER/DESIGN Gavin Uren/
Alan Whitefield

GERMANY

FINALIST, SINGLE
OGILVYONE WORLDWIDE
FRANKFURT

CLIENT Ogilvy & Mather's 50th Birthday
CREATIVE DIRECTOR Folker Wrage
ART DIRECTOR Irena Pawelczyk
ART DIRECTOR Oliver Honnicke

USA
FINALIST, SINGLE
LA AGENCIA DE ORCI & ASOCIADOS
LOS ANGELES, CA

CLIENT   La Agencia de Orci
CREATIVE DIRECTOR   Cristina Plotkin
ART DIRECTOR   Jeannette Brignoni
DESIGNER/DESIGN   Tanesi/Mexico City, Mexico

UAE
FINALIST, SINGLE
OSTERADS
DUBAI

CLIENT   Royal Mirage
CREATIVE DIRECTOR   Mike Platts
ART DIRECTOR   Craig Falconer

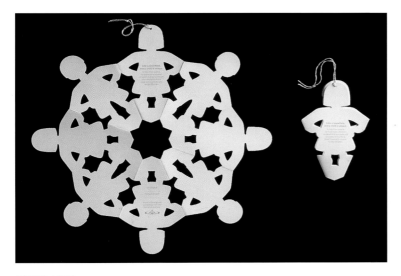

ENGLAND
FINALIST, SINGLE
PEARLFISHER
LONDON

CREATIVE DIRECTOR   Johnathan Ford

GERMANY
FINALIST, SINGLE
SPRINGER & JACOBY WERBUNG GMBH
HAMBURG

CREATIVE DIRECTOR   Rafaela Schmidt/ Stefan Schmidt
COPYWRITER   Alex Jaggy
ART DIRECTOR   Christina Petrich
PHOTOGRAPHER   Christina Petrich

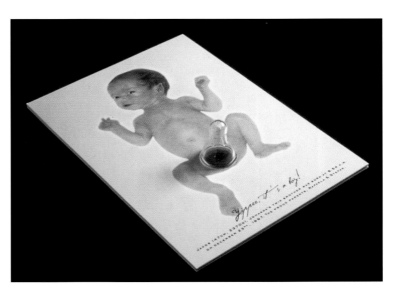

UAE

FINALIST, SINGLE
SAATCHI & SAATCHI
DUBAI

CLIENT   The One
CREATIVE DIRECTOR   Kurt Blanckenberg
ART DIRECTOR   Louise Miller

USA

FINALIST, SINGLE
SIDES & ASSOCIATES
LAFAYETTE, LA

CLIENT   SECON
CREATIVE DIRECTOR   Larry Sides
ART DIRECTOR   Will Bailey

HONG KONG

FINALIST, SINGLE
STREAMLINE COMMUNICATION LTD.
HONG KONG

CREATIVE DIRECTOR   Lawrence Yu
COPYWRITER   Lawrence Yu
ART DIRECTOR   Lawrence Yu
PHOTOGRAPHER   Stephen Ip/Hong Kong

USA

FINALIST, CAMPAIGN
FLAIR COMMUNICATIONS AGENCY
CHICAGO, IL

CLIENT   Brown & Williamson/Tobacco
CREATIVE DIRECTOR   Stan Hardwick
ART DIRECTOR   Don Williams

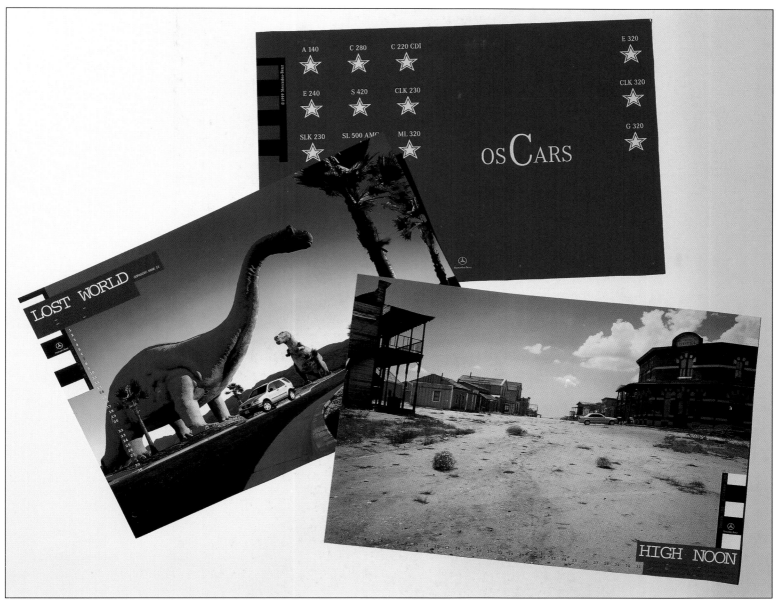

GERMANY

GOLD WORLDMEDAL, SINGLE
DIETMAR HENNEKA
STUTTGART

CLIENT DaimlerChrysler AG
ART DIRECTOR Urs Schwerzmann
GRAPHICS COMPANY Recom GmbH/
Diaservice GmbH

USA

FINALIST, SINGLE

ARNOLD COMMUNICATIONS INC.
BOSTON, MA

CLIENT Volkswagen
CREATIVE DIRECTOR Lance Jensen/Alan Pafenbach
COPYWRITER Lance Jensen/Dana Satterwhite
OTHER Ron Lawner (Chief Creative Officer)

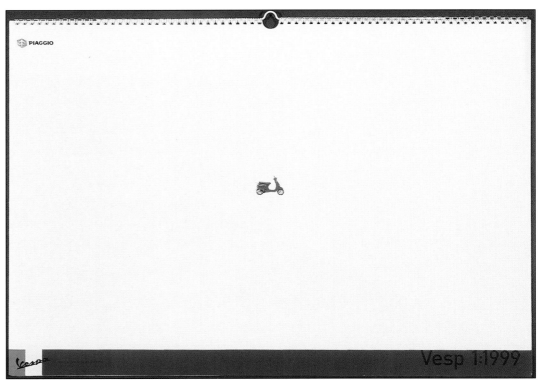

ITALY

SILVER WORLDMEDAL, SINGLE
BBDO ITALY
MILANO

CLIENT Vespa/Piaggio
COPYWRITER Lorenzo Petrantoni
ART DIRECTOR Lorenzo Petrantoni

GERMANY

FINALIST, SINGLE
**D-OFFICE COMMUNICATION DEVELOPMENT
GMBH**
MUNCHEN

CLIENT Adidas International
CREATIVE DIRECTOR Andreas Dohring
ART DIRECTOR Karl Bates/Jurger Salerbaches

JAPAN

BRONZE WORLDMEDAL, SINGLE
C'CO., LTD.
TOKYO

CLIENT   Honda Clio Kyoritsu
Advertising Agency
HYPER/Tokyo
CREATIVE DIRECTOR
Kozo Koshimizu
COPYWRITER   Kozo Koshimizu
ART DIRECTOR   Setsue Shimizu
PHOTOGRAPHER   Setsue Shimizu/
Tokyo
ILLUSTRATOR   Setsue Shimizu/
CG ART, Tokyo

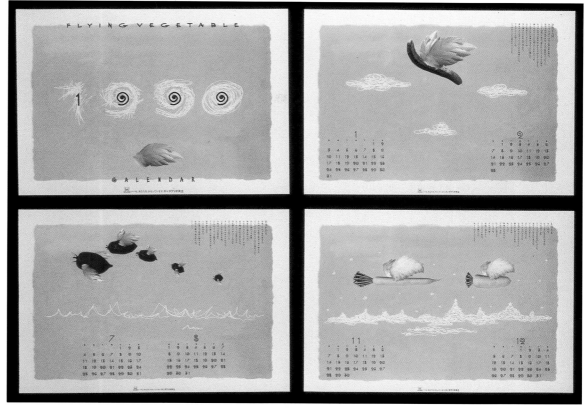

SPAIN

FINALIST, SINGLE
ENRIC AGUILERA ASOCIADOS
BARCELONA

CLIENT   Errecerre International Productions Co.
CREATIVE DIRECTOR   Enric Aguilera
ART DIRECTOR   Enric Aguilera
PHOTOGRAPHER   Enric Aguilera
GRAPHICS COMPANY   Enric Aguilera/Barcelona

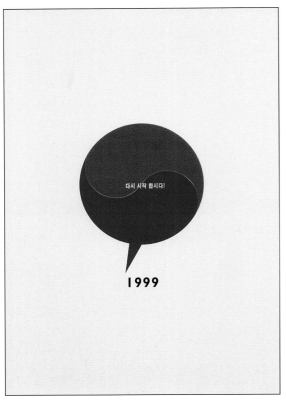

The T'aeguk Image of Korea

KOREA

SILVER WORLDMEDAL, CAMPAIGN

CHEIL COMMUNICATIONS
SEOUL

CLIENT   Ministry of Culture & Tourism
CREATIVE DIRECTOR   Sang Min Nam
COPYWRITER   Hong Tak Kim
ART DIRECTOR   Ji Wang Hong/Moon Soo Kang/Kyung Sun Lee
PHOTOGRAPHER   Sang Mo Koo

BAHRAIN

FINALIST, SINGLE

GULF ADVERTISING
MANAMA

CLIENT   1999 Batelco Wall Calendar/1999
Batelco Postcard Calendar
COPYWRITER   Donald Aranha
ART DIRECTOR   Bill Ditchfield
PHOTOGRAPHER   Tony Nelson
ILLUSTRATOR   6 Bahrain Artists

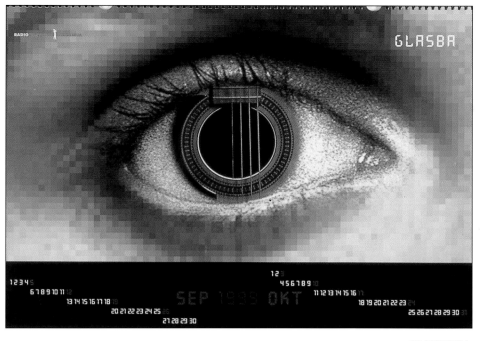

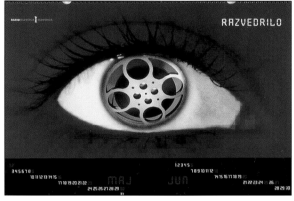

SLOVENIA

FINALIST, SINGLE
KOMPAS DESIGN
LJUBLJANA, SI
ART DIRECTOR Zare Kerin/
Ljubljana
PHOTOGRAPHER Janez Puksic/
Ljubljana

SCOTLAND

FINALIST, SINGLE
RANDAK DESIGN CONSULTANTS
GLASGOW
CREATIVE DIRECTOR Charles Randak
ART DIRECTOR Lin H. Gibbon

LOGO-CORPORATE

U K

SILVER WORLDMEDAL, SINGLE
LEWIS MOBERLY
LONDON

CLIENT   Finca Flichman
ART DIRECTOR   Joanne Smith

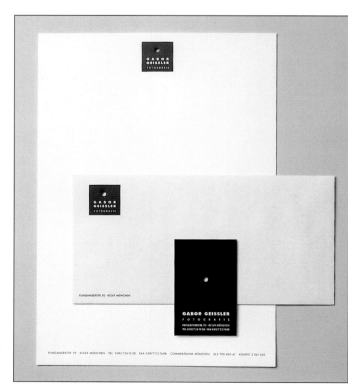

GERMANY

BRONZE WORLDMEDAL, SINGLE
**WUSCHNER UND ROHWER
WERBEAGENTUR**
MUNCHEN

CLIENT   Gabor Geissler Photographer
CREATIVE DIRECTOR   Ekki Frenkler/Sven
Sehlmann/Joachim Balz
ART DIRECTOR   Ekki Frenkler

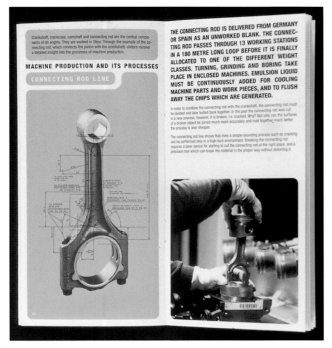

AUSTRIA
FINALIST, SINGLE
BURO X DESIGN
VIENNA
CLIENT   BMW
CREATIVE DIRECTOR   Andreas Miedaner
ART DIRECTOR   Gunter Eder

ENGLAND
FINALIST, SINGLE
DALZIEL AND POW
LONDON
CLIENT   S.F. Cody's Emporium
CREATIVE DIRECTOR   David Dalziel
ART DIRECTOR   Meredith Duke

USA
FINALIST, SINGLE
MICHAEL MEYERS & ASSOCIATES
CHICAGO, IL
CLIENT Boys Hope Girls Hope of Illinois

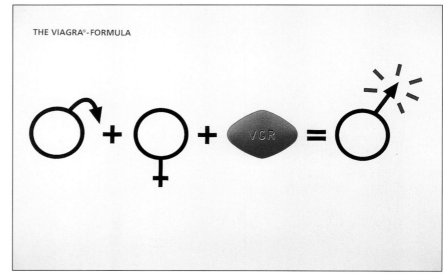

THE VIAGRA®-FORMULA

GERMANY
FINALIST, SINGLE
SCHMITTGALL WERBEAGENTUR GMBH
STUTTGART
CLIENT Viagra
CREATIVE DIRECTOR Bernd Schmittgall
ART DIRECTOR Bert Neumann

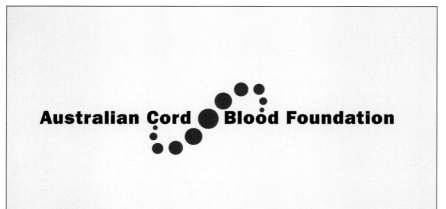

AUSTRALIA
FINALIST, SINGLE
SUDLER & HENNESSEY
NORTH SYDNEY
CLIENT Australian cord blood foundation
CREATIVE DIRECTOR Robert Lallamant
ART DIRECTOR Robert Lallamant

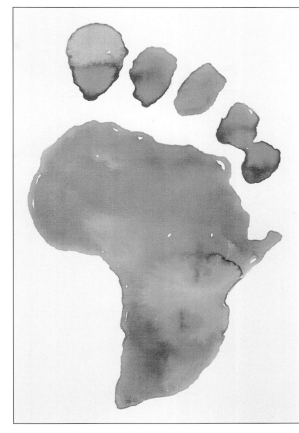

AUSTRALIA
FINALIST, SINGLE
STORM IMAGE DESIGN
MELBOURNE, VICTORIA
CLIENT All Male Retail Store
CREATIVE DIRECTOR David Ansett/Dean Butler
ART DIRECTOR Dean Butler
ART DIRECTOR David Ansett
ILLUSTRATOR David Ansett/Dean Butler

ART NOT AVAILABLE

SOUTH AFRICA
FINALIST, SINGLE
SAATCHI & SAATCHI
CAPE TOWN
CLIENT Afrika Tourism
CREATIVE DIRECTOR Eric Frank
ART DIRECTOR Eric Frank
ILLUSTRATOR Eric Frank/Cape Town

GERMANY
FINALIST, SINGLE
SYNDICATE BRAND & CORPORATE DESIGN
HAMBURG
CLIENT Jet
CREATIVE DIRECTOR Marcus Greinke
ART DIRECTOR Audrey Oberdiek

LETTERHEAD/STATIONERY

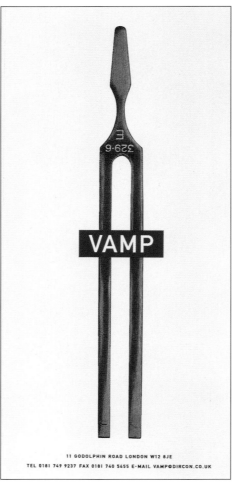

ENGLAND

BRONZE WORLDMEDAL, SINGLE

TANGO DESIGN
LONDON

CLIENT Vamp
CREATIVE DIRECTOR Peter Rae
ART DIRECTOR Roberto D'Andria
PHOTOGRAPHER Polly Eiles/London

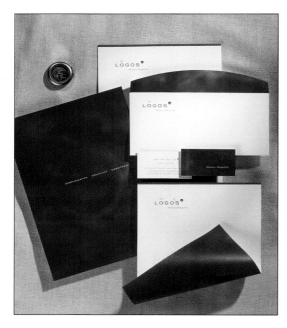

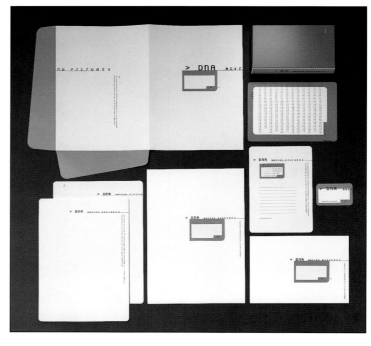

CANADA

FINALIST, SINGLE

LOGOS IDENTITY BY DESIGN LIMITED
TORONTO, ONTARIO

CLIENT Logos Identity by Design Limited
CREATIVE DIRECTOR Brain Smith
ART DIRECTOR Sunny Chan
ILLUSTRATOR Sunny Chan/Toronto

DENMARK

FINALIST, CAMPAIGN

DDB NEEDHAM DENMARK
COPENHAGEN

CLIENT DNA Moving Pictures
CREATIVE DIRECTOR Poul Mikkelsen
ART DIRECTOR Sanne Frank

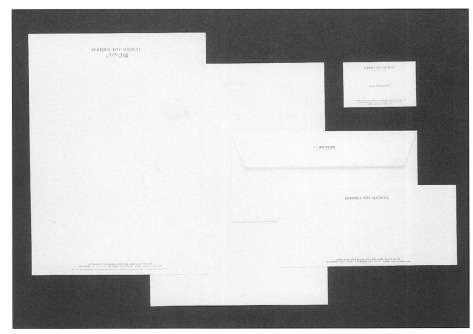

ENGLAND

FINALIST, CAMPAIGN

THE FORMATION

LONDON

CLIENT Serious Toy Societe
CREATIVE DIRECTOR Adrian Kilby
ART DIRECTOR Adrian Kilby
ILLUSTRATOR Chris Jepson
OTHER Cambridge University Press (Print)

CORPORATE IMAGE BROCHURE

USA

FINALIST, SINGLE

ADDISON

NEW YORK, NY

CLIENT Splash
CREATIVE DIRECTOR Victor Rivera
ART DIRECTOR David Kohler
PHOTOGRAPHER Jody Dole/William Vasquez
ILLUSTRATOR Chris Yun, Hot Jazz

GERMANY

GOLD WORLDMEDAL, SINGLE

**REMPEN & PARTNER
WERBEAGENTUR GMBH**
MUNICH

CLIENT
Cross Marketing Production
CREATIVE DIRECTOR Frank Lubke
COPYWRITER Silke Schluter
ART DIRECTOR Sabine Sauber
PHOTOGRAPHER Jens Heilmann/
Munich

GERMANY

BRONZE WORLDMEDAL, SINGLE

**FOR SALE WERBEAGENTUR
GMBH**
MUNICH

CLIENT
Media Markt Saturn Holding
CREATIVE DIRECTOR Kai Fehse
ART DIRECTOR Grit Fiedler

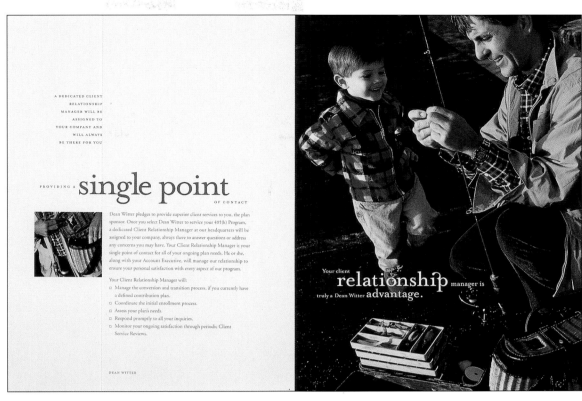

USA

SILVER WORLDMEDAL, SINGLE
MORGAN STANLEY/DEAN WITTER
NEW YORK, NY

CREATIVE DIRECTOR   Victor Rivera
ART DIRECTOR   Cindy Goldstein

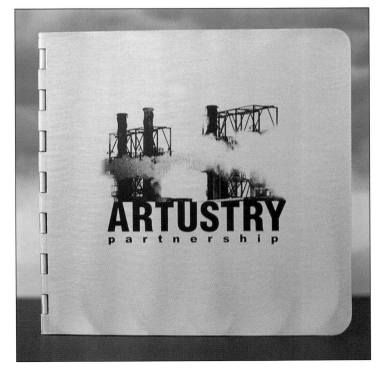

USA

FINALIST, SINGLE
ARTUSTRY PARTNERSHIP
NEW YORK, NY

CREATIVE DIRECTOR   Bob Giraldi
COPYWRITER   David Sklaver
ART DIRECTOR   Rachel Allgood
PHOTOGRAPHER   William Drury/NY

ENGLAND

FINALIST, SINGLE

INTERBRAND NEWELL AND SORRELL
LONDON

CLIENT PricewaterhouseCoopers
CREATIVE DIRECTOR Marksteen Adamson
ART DIRECTOR Marksteen Adamson
PHOTOGRAPHER Robert Maxwell/Sam Jones/Hannes Schmid/
Igor Emmerich/Nigel Parry/Marksteen Adamson/
David Bailey/Michael O'Neil
OTHER Jane Stanyon (Designer)/Sarah Cromwell/
Marksteen Adamson (Designer)

GREECE

FINALIST, SINGLE

McCANN-ERICKSON ATHENS
ATHENS

CLIENT British School At Athens
CREATIVE DIRECTOR
Gerrassimos Neofytos
ART DIRECTOR Grania Kelway
OTHER Andreas Fountoukos
(Agency Producer)

CRAFT CATEGORIES

ENGLAND
GOLD WORLDMEDAL, SINGLE
INTERBRAND NEWELL AND SORRELL
London
CLIENT Pricewaterhouse Coopers
CREATIVE DIRECTOR Marksteen Adamson
ART DIRECTOR Marksteen Adamson
PHOTOGRAPHER M. Adamson/D.Bailey/I.Emmerich/
S.Jones/M.O'Neil/H.Schmid/N.Parry/R.Maxwell
DESIGNER/DESIGN S.Cromwell/M.Adamson/J.Stanyon

GERMANY
SILVER WORLDMEDAL, SINGLE
DIETMAR HENNEKA
STUTTGART

CLIENT DaimlerChrysler AG
ART DIRECTOR Urs Schwerzmann/Stuttgart
GRAPHICS COMPANY Recom GmbHDiaservice GmbH

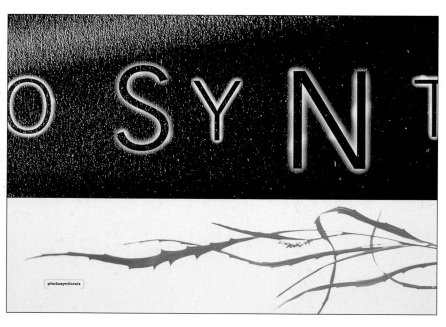

SCOTLAND
FINALIST, SINGLE
MOUNTAIN CDC
GLASGOW

CREATIVE DIRECTOR Andy Bowman
PHOTOGRAPHER The Picture House/Glasgow

ENGLAND

BRONZE WORLDMEDAL, CAMPAIGN
E-FACT. LIMITED
LONDON
CLIENT Mercedes-Benz/S-Class
ART DIRECTOR Ruth Holden
PHOTOGRAPHER Dietmar Henneka/
Stuttgard

DIE NEUE S-KLASSE

Mercedes-Benz

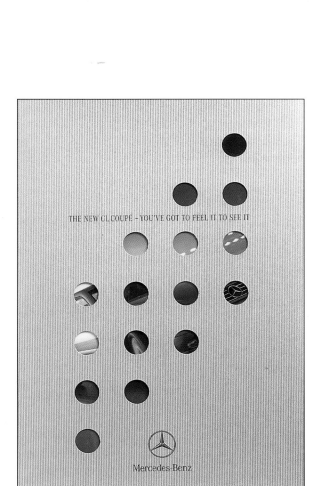

ENGLAND

FINALIST, CAMPAIGN
E-FACT. LIMITED
LONDON

CLIENT The CL-Coupe from Mercedes-Benz
ART DIRECTOR Iain Ross/Ben Carratu
PHOTOGRAPHER Willie von Recklinghausen
OTHER Anna van Ommen (copy)

U K

FINALIST, CAMPAIGN
LEWIS MOBERLY
LONDON
CLIENT Waitrose Limited
ART DIRECTOR Mary Lewis
PHOTOGRAPHER Juliette Piddington
OTHER Daniela Nunzi/Ann Marshall

SEE PAGE 312

BEST WRITING

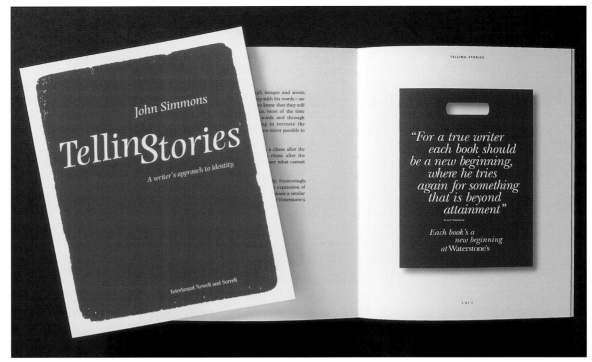

ENGLAND

FINALIST, SINGLE
INTERBRAND NEWELL AND SORRELL
LONDON

CLIENT Telling stories
CREATIVE DIRECTOR Frances Newell
OTHER John Simmons (Writer)

BEST ART DIRECTION

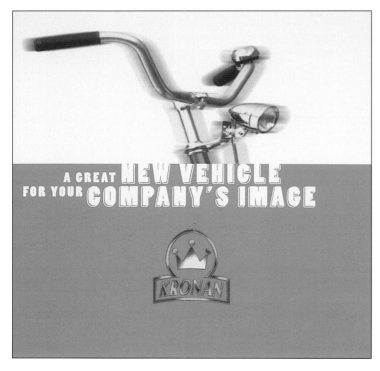

THE NETHERLANDS

FINALIST, SINGLE
ANDERSON & LEMKE
AMSTERDAM

CLIENT Kronan Cykel
CREATIVE DIRECTOR Tore Claesson
ART DIRECTOR Jan Dirk Snel
PHOTOGRAPHER Hans Pieterse/Amsterdam

YUGOSLAVIA

FINALIST, SINGLE
S TEAM BATES SAATCHI & SAATCHI BALKAN
BELGRADE/SERBIA

CLIENT New moment magazine/new moment
CREATIVE DIRECTOR Dragan Sakan
ART DIRECTOR Slavimir Stojanovic
PHOTOGRAPHER Vladimir Baclija/Belgrade

BRAZIL
SILVER WORLDMEDAL, SINGLE
A 10 DESIGN
SAO PAULO
CLIENT   Melman/Margarete Takeda
CREATIVE DIRECTOR   Renata
ART DIRECTOR   Marie-Elise Carrara
PHOTOGRAPHER   Rodrigo Petrela/
Thomas Baccaro
OTHER   Neno Formiga (Producer)

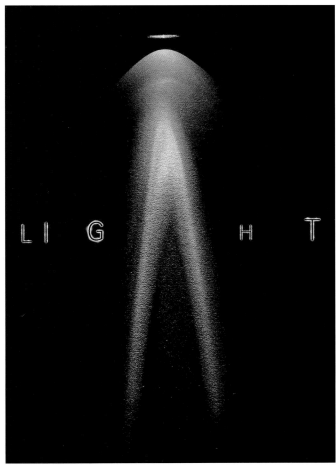

SCOTLAND
BRONZE WORLDMEDAL, SINGLE
MOUNTAIN CDC
GLASGOW
CLIENT   The Picture House
CREATIVE DIRECTOR   Andy Bowman
PHOTOGRAPHER   The Picture House/
Glasgow

USA
FINALIST, SINGLE
SELTZER KAUFMANN MARKETING
BLOOMFIELD HILLS, MI
CREATIVE DIRECTOR   Renee Voit
ART DIRECTOR   Renee Voit
DESIGNER/DESIGN   SKM, Inc./
Bloomfield

INDEX

ARTISTS, ILLUSTRATORS, PHOTOGRAPHERS & ANIMATORS

CLIENTS

CREATIVE DIRECTORS